Political Econc
United States

Joel W. Johnson

 Routledge
Taylor & Francis Group

NEW YORK AND LONDON

First published 2019
by Routledge
52 Vanderbilt Avenue, New York, NY 10017

and by Routledge
2 Park Square, Milton Park, Abingdon, Oxon, OX14 4RN

Routledge is an imprint of the Taylor & Francis Group, an informa business

© 2019 Taylor & Francis

Library of Congress Cataloging-in-Publication Data
A catalog record for this title has been requested

ISBN: 9781138490758 (hbk)
ISBN: 9781138490772 (pbk)
ISBN: 9781351034623 (ebk)

Typeset in Sabon
by Deanta Global Publishing Services, Chennai, India

To my parents

Contents

Political Economy of the United States

How have the policies of recent administrations shaped today's economy? To what extent has federal policy contributed to growth in income inequality? Why have the parties become so polarized and how has polarization influenced economic policy? This book provides an introduction to the contemporary political economy of the United States. It examines the politics of economic policymaking, the influence of federal policies and programs on the economy, and the co-evolution of politics and the economy over the past five decades. Along the way, it explains the causes and consequences of many contemporary phenomena, such as the government's deficits and debt and the ideological polarization of the parties.

The book is divided into two parts. The first half explains how America's political economy "works." It explains what the federal government does, why it does what it does, and how its policies influence the economy. The second half explains "how we got here" with a review of major political and economic developments since the 1970s, all the way up to the early years of the Trump Administration. This weaving together of theory and history provides both the tools and the context so that readers can properly understand the nation's current-day politics and policy debates.

Joel W. Johnson is Associate Professor of Political Science at Colorado State University–Pueblo, where he has taught since 2010. He received his doctorate in Political Science from the University of California, San Diego in 2009. His research focuses on political institutions and political economy in developed and developing democracies. His work has been published in *The Oxford Handbook on Electoral Systems* and journals such as *Comparative Political Studies*, *Electoral Studies*, and *The Journal of Politics in Latin America*.

Figures

Tables

Boxes

Acknowledgments

I am grateful to the many people who helped bring this project to fruition. First, I would like to thank my colleagues at Colorado State University–Pueblo, especially those in my college and academic department who provided the resources and freedom to work on this book. In particular, I thank my fellow political scientists Gayle Berardi, Colette Carter, and Steven Liebel, who gave me constant support and good cheer while I worked on this project. I am also indebted to Grant Weller, Matt Harris, William Folkestad, Rick Kreminski, Lori Blase, and Alysse McKanna, each of whom assisted me in one form or another. The university's support in the form of a sabbatical during the spring semester of 2017 is also much appreciated. Without that time to focus exclusively on writing and research, this book might never have been completed.

Students in my American National Politics courses at CSU–Pueblo read and reacted to early drafts of several chapters in this volume. I appreciate their participation in that trial phase, and their questions helped me think about how I wanted to design and write this book.

Further afield, I wish to thank all of my former political science professors, whose lessons and guidance I have routinely revisited throughout the course of this project. They continue to teach me, long after I have left their classrooms.

Three anonymous reviewers provided extensive feedback and helpful criticisms on draft portions of this book. I greatly appreciate their suggestions. I also thank my editor at Routledge, Jennifer Knerr, for her enthusiasm for the project and her expert guidance through the editing and production process.

I am extremely grateful to my parents and siblings for support and encouragement throughout my life. My mother Brenda and my father David deserve special thanks. They always encouraged my passions and pursuits, and they taught me much about tolerance, patience, and compassion. I have dedicated this book to them.

Finally, I thank my wife, Whitney Duncan, for all of her love and support. While I worked on this book, she somehow juggled her own academic projects and near full-time care of our young daughters – the lights of our lives. She also helped me think through this book project, and she occasionally lent her remarkable editing skills to smooth out the rough edges in my writing. She greatly enriched this book, as she does every part of my life.

1 Democratic Political Economy in the United States

The federal government's influence on the nation's economy is tremendous. Hundreds of federal agencies regulate nearly every sector of the economy, including food, finance, pharmaceuticals, and transportation. Meanwhile, the government's tax and monetary policies influence the housing market, retirement savings, business investments, and, more generally, borrowing and saving throughout the economy. At the same time, government departments spend billions on everything from agricultural subsidies and food stamps to infrastructure and technology, and they spend considerably more on items like health care and national defense. Medicare, alone, spends over $500 billion a year – a sum that is on a par with the annual income of Pennsylvania – to provide health care for more than fifty million senior citizens nationwide.[1] On national defense, the government spends at least $600 billion a year, of which about $100 billion is paid to private companies for new procurements. Perhaps the only thing that is more staggering is the government's payroll. The federal government is the nation's largest employer. It employs more than one million employees in the armed forces, and it employs many millions more in government agencies or as independent contractors.[2] Undeniably, the government of the United States has a profound influence on the economy in which we work and live.

Even so, that influence can be easy to underestimate – or at least take for granted. Consumers rarely think about how government agencies improve the safety of products and services when they shop at the grocery store, fly on an airplane, or keep their money in a bank. And they may be unaware of how the interest rates that they pay to banks for home loans, auto loans, and education loans are affected by federal policies. Similarly, probably few of the millions of people who receive health insurance through their employers understand that those benefits owe much to the government's tax code. And how many citizens know that the market price of sugar is elevated due to government protections of sugar farmers?

This type of list could go on and on, and so it would seem difficult to overestimate the government's influence. Yet, that is also common. For example, voters seem to overestimate the government's ability to stop the drug trade or control the price of gasoline. And the public routinely credits or blames the president for the state of the economy, including its rate of growth or level of unemployment, despite the fact that presidents are very limited in their ability to manipulate the entire "macro" economy.

On that matter, at least, politics deserves some of the blame. Presidents are always trying to claim credit when the economy is growing, and their critics are always trying to blame them when it is not. In 2016, both were happening simultaneously – as presidential candidate Donald Trump was promising to improve the economy and to create "tons of new jobs," outgoing President Barack Obama was busy claiming credit for what economic growth had occurred since the financial crisis of 2008. In the 1990s, when the economy's growth rate was impressive, President Bill Clinton was not shy about claiming credit; and he had won his first presidential campaign in 1992 in large part because the economy was still weak from a recession in 1990, giving punch to his campaign's famous "it's the economy, stupid" charge against President George H. W. Bush.[3] The pattern was similar in the 1980s. In the 1980 election, Ronald Reagan blamed President Jimmy Carter for the poor economy.[4] Four years later, in his bid for reelection, President Reagan was claiming credit for the economic rebound that began in 1983.

Such claims are indeed good politics. However, they are false – or, at least, greatly exaggerated. The US economy is enormous, market-driven, and globally interconnected; it is influenced by many things besides changes in federal policy, including technological advances, market expectations, energy prices, and international events. Moreover, the rhetoric about presidents tends to ignore the fact that the most significant changes in economic policy are those that come from Congress, the branch that designs the government's budget, tax system, and social programs. Also, short-term swings in the economy tend to have less to do with budgets and regulations than with the Federal Reserve, the central bank of the United States. Indeed, each turn in the "business cycle"[5] from 1980 to 2000 – including the 1979 recession that helped Reagan to power, the 1983 rebound that helped Reagan win his reelection, the 1990 recession that hurt Bush I's reelection, and the sustained economic boom that occurred on Clinton's watch in the 1990s – was closely related to Federal Reserve policies.

These observations illustrate that it can be challenging to ascertain the degree to which the government – or a single government institution, like the presidency – shapes the economy. But they do not diminish the government's importance. And they underscore that economic policies have political and economic implications. The winners and losers of policy choices are not just political camps, like liberals and conservatives or Democrats and Republicans. More fundamentally, tax policies, economic regulations, and budgetary decisions pit consumers against producers, taxpayers against special interests, poor against rich, importers against exporters, and different communities against each other.

Economic conflicts are resolved in the political system, where policies are shaped by party politics, legislative processes, and the push and pull of different interest groups and the votes and money behind them. From an economic point of view, the results are seldom pretty. The tax code has become so littered with provisions and narrow tax breaks that its length is a matter of estimation.[6] Budgets are often passed with ample doses of pork projects (i.e., projects that bring tax dollars to a representative's district) and special-interest giveaways, and they often contain large deficits, which add to the government's large debt burden.

But such is politics. The US Constitution is not designed to make government simple. It is designed to produce policies that enjoy support from many constituencies and interests across a vast nation. The policymaking process requires that reforms be shepherded through two legislative chambers and around potential roadblocks from the president and the judiciary. And members of Congress, who face routine reelection contests, face competitive pressure from within and outside their parties. The policies that they make reflect the democracy in which they are a part.

About This Book

This book studies the contemporary *political economy* of the United States. The first half of the book focuses on what the federal government does, how its policies influence the economy, and why it chooses the economic policies that it does. The second half of the book analyzes how politics and the economy have co-evolved and shaped each other over the past several decades, and they explain phenomena such as the polarization of the parties, the growth in government debt, and the increase in income inequality. Overall, the book aims to provide both analytical and historical perspective on the political economy of the United States.

The subject matter of political economy is wide-ranging. In fact, it is much wider than what the previous paragraphs suggest. Writ large, political economy explores all sorts of comparative and historical questions, such as why some governments are better than others at protecting private property rights, or whether democracy or dictatorship is more conducive to economic growth. On that level of analysis, political economy also contrasts different systems of economic thought, from laissez-faire capitalism to Marxism and everything in between.

This book does not analyze those topics. It focuses on politics and policy within the contemporary United States, a constitutional democracy with a (regulated) market economy. Yet, the scope remains broad, and it covers a range of topics in political economy, including both "political economics" and "economic politics." The former is concerned with matters of economic policy and economic outcomes. Among other things, it studies topics such as the politics of macroeconomic policy, the politics of regulatory policy, and the politics of taxation and redistribution. A more-narrow analysis might focus on the politics of a Social Security reform or the politics of price supports for sugar farmers.

By contrast, "economic politics" uses economic theories and methods to analyze political phenomena. For democratic systems like the United States, such analyses consider things like party platforms, voter behavior, and congressional organization and procedure. In many cases, the economic models are used to understand economic policies, like regulations or redistributive taxation (i.e., the transfer of wealth among citizens via taxation and social programs). However, some economic models of politics are more general and not focused on economic policy, per se.

The academic field of political economy differs from the fields of public finance and public economics, both of which focus on policy analysis instead of politics. Public finance studies government taxation and expenditures and the economic consequences of both. Public economics is the modern incarnation of welfare economics, and it analyzes how government policies affect the economy, including economic efficiency and overall welfare. Both public finance and public economics are inherently *normative*, as they try to estimate the "best" or "optimal" policies. By contrast, political economy has a *positive* focus; it studies facts and explanations instead of what is desirable. To be sure, fields like political economy, public finance, and public economics overlap and inform each other; and this book draws from each of them. It also draws from other traditions in political science and from historical accounts. However, this book is focused primarily on issues of political economy, and its approach is positive.

As noted already, this book has two parts. The second half of the book is historically focused, whereas the first half provides more of a theoretical and empirical foundation. The table of contents provides a full map of what is included in each chapter. But here is a brief overview. First, the remainder of this chapter discusses aspects of policy and politics that are worth highlighting at the outset. Then, Chapter 2 provides a survey of the government's social programs, tax policies, and regulatory policies. Chapter 3 studies the government's influence on the macroeconomy over the short run and long run, and it includes sections on stabilization policies, the Federal Reserve, and political macroeconomics. Chapter 4 focuses on politics, and it surveys several theories of economic policymaking. The second half of the book begins with Chapter 5, which traces political and economic developments from the 1960s through the 1980s and includes a detailed review of Reagan-era policies. Chapter 6 studies politics and policymaking in the Bill Clinton and George W. Bush years, and Chapter 7 covers the financial crisis of 2008 and the Obama years. Chapter 8 documents how politics and policies changed as a result of the 2016 election and Trump's first year and a half in office, and Chapter 9 offers a conclusion and some thoughts about oft-proposed reforms to the political system.

Public Policies

This book attends to a variety of federal policies and programs, including everything from small "earmarks" in the budget to the massive health care programs. Some policies and programs have an unmistakable influence on the economy. Others, like small pork projects, grants, and subsidies, have a negligible effect. Yet, we consider them because they are an important part of politics and policymaking.

It is important to maintain a sense of perspective on different policies, and it is important to recognize that there are all kinds of policies that we do not consider that may have notable economic consequences. For example, policies that are meant to influence access to abortion providers have economic consequences – they affect the market for abortion services. Likewise, foreign aid, civil rights protections, drug policies, and all sorts of other regulations and programs cost tax dollars, employ people, and otherwise influence the economy. If this book ignores such policies, it is because it focuses on "economic" policies.

Economic policy is a loose term that refers to the government's most economically significant policies, like monetary policies (which influence the money supply), fiscal policies (which pertain to levels of taxation, spending, and debt), tax policies (which affect what and whom are taxed), financial regulations, and trade policies. This book also considers various other types of policies that are economically "notable." For example, environmental regulations, the defense budget, and major social programs like the health care programs are large and consequential enough to fit under a broader definition of economic policy.

Distribution

Policies and programs have *distributional* consequences – they have winners and losers and affect the distribution of wealth in society. That point is rather obvious with respect to tax rates, agricultural subsidies, and social programs like food stamps. Indeed, taxes and transfers are inherently *redistributive* – they transfer resources from some households to others. Less obvious is that government policies also affect the *pre*-tax-and-transfer distribution of wealth, which is often called *market inequality*. For example, pre-tax incomes are affected by minimum wage regulations, overtime pay requirements, and laws that govern labor unions and labor-management relations. Thus, a worker's pay is not solely a function of her productivity or education, and it is erroneous to think that government policies intervene with a division of wealth that is "natural" and unaffected by government.

Even public goods have distributive consequences. A *public good* is a good that is collectively provided, available to all, and cannot be denied to particular individuals. Classic examples include national defense, clean air, and freeways. They benefit everyone, and it is impossible for the government to target the benefits to some people, leaving their neighbors without the good. (By contrast, a social program that alleviates poverty is not a "public good" because it provides direct benefits only to those citizens who meet eligibility requirements.) Although it is beside the point, public goods do create winners and losers. For example, regulations to reduce air pollution from power plants damage the coal industry and benefit businesses that produce clean energy. Likewise, to build a freeway the government must pick a particular firm to do the construction, and it often must invoke its power of "eminent domain" to confiscate privately owned land (with compensation). And, with national defense, there are distributional questions about how much to give employees in both pay and benefits, what defense equipment to purchase and in what quantities, and how many military bases will exist nationwide and where they will be placed.

Policymaking is conflictual because policies have distributional consequences. Also, political conflict occurs because people have different opinions about public priorities. For example, regardless of how defense expenditures are distributed, people disagree about how much of the nation's wealth should be spent on national defense.

General Interests vs. Special Interests

This book often draws a distinction between policies that advance a broad, general interest or a narrow, special interest. Policies and programs that clearly do the former include unemployment insurance, a tax cut for middle-income households, and consumer protections. By contrast, a narrow, special-interest policy might be funds for a small town's library, subsidies for beet farmers, or a tax break that applies to just a small number of firms.

Many policies have both general-interest and special-interest elements to them, and people will argue about which aspect is more prominent. For example, subsidies for renewable energy companies may be touted by advocates as an attempt to advance clean air (a public good), or they may be derided by critics as a special-interest policy that expends a public resource (tax dollars). Likewise, a military procurement may be said to advance the nation's defense capabilities, or it may be deemed an unnecessary giveaway to a defense contractor. Another example: a member of Congress may defend a grant to a university for contributing to academic innovations and public knowledge, whereas others see the grant as pork.

The distinction between general-interest policies and special-interest policies is sharper when we consider large, expensive programs. For example, the food stamp program is nothing like an earmark for a university because it has millions of direct beneficiaries and it was established by sweeping legislation, not just a single line in a budget bill. Indeed, the politics of general-interest policies and special-interest policies are dissimilar. A small earmark for a university will attract no attention from the press, the public, or from members of Congress other than she who adds it to a budget bill. Also, the earmark is probably related to the political activities of the university, including lobbying efforts and campaign contributions. By contrast, changes to the food stamp program or to income tax rates affect millions of citizens, and they have notable effects on government finances. An attempt to reform the food stamp program or income taxes will prompt a partisan battle, and it will feature in the news and national political campaigns. Also, passage will require compromise in Congress and a major effort to steer the proposal through the legislative process.

When this book refers to something as a special-interest policy it will ignore arguments about its second-order effects and potential benefits for a broad public. A congresswoman may be correct that a university grant will eventually benefit the public, but we will refer to it as a special-interest policy because the direct beneficiaries are very few. If we were to do otherwise, and describe it by its potential second-order consequences, then any small earmark might be as consequential as the defense budget or a major tax cut – who knows? That type of thinking is obviously problematic and false.

This book will also describe policies or legislation as being either "programmatic" or "particularistic," a distinction that closely mirrors the contrast between general-interest and special-interest policies. Programmatic policies are linked to a party's general agenda, program, or platform, and they typically advance some general interest. By contrast, particularistic policies provide narrowly targeted benefits, either to specific congressional districts, special interests, or narrow voter groups.

Complexity

Federal programs and policies owe some of their complexity to the compromises and deals that are required to unite hundreds of House and Senate members – and the many interests that they may represent. Federal policies also owe some of their complexity to other features of America's political system, like federalism or the separation of legislative and executive powers. Federalism – the division of government into a national (federal) government and autonomous, state-level governments – presents special challenges because federal policies and programs often must work across and in concert with fifty different state governments, each of which has its own policies and programs.

Simple necessity is another reason for complex federal laws and programs. To illustrate, consider one piece of legislation – the drug benefit program that Republicans added to Medicare in 2003. To establish the program the government needed to clarify a large number of issues, including how seniors could enroll, during what time periods they could enroll, what fees could be associated with late enrollment, under what conditions plans could be terminated by either the beneficiary or their insurance company, what drugs the insurance plans would have to cover, how disputes between consumers and insurance companies would be handled, the procedures that insurance companies would have to follow to demonstrate that they were not charging excessive "out-of-pocket" costs to consumers, what subsidies would be available for the plans, and how subsidies to consumers would be administered.[7] In large part because Congress sought to answer such questions, the law, called the Medicare Prescription Drug, Improvement, and Modernization Act of 2003 (Medicare Modernization Act, or MMA, for short), ran 416 pages long. However, that was just the beginning. The MMA's pages did not deal with the finer policy details, which Congress left to the agency that would oversee the program, the Center for Medicare and Medicaid Services (CMS), a unit within the Department of Health and Human Services (HHS). By the time CMS was finished writing the rules to implement the MMA, the procedures that defined the drug benefit program were so extensive that they filled thousands of small-print pages in the *Federal Register*, the government's daily journal of new regulations. (The pages included more than just rules. They also include public comments, estimates, and rationales. Agencies are required to undertake those steps before they settle on regulations.)

No member of Congress can attend to all of the details of any significant piece of legislation, especially because each is compelled to pay attention to many other things, including foreign and domestic politics, issues in their home district and state, and other goings-on in Congress, from congressional investigations to budget negotiations. Moreover, the government is so big and complex that elected officials cannot understand very many programs or policies in much detail, especially if they are relatively new to the federal government. To understand policy and draft legislation, members of Congress rely on various sources of help, including aides, party organizations, think tanks, policy experts, and lobbyists. (Lobbyists seek to influence policies in ways that benefit their clients, who include many types of interests, from corporations, trade associations, and universities, to state, local, and foreign governments. To influence policy, it is helpful to have access to lawmakers. And so, to establish trust and relationships with members of Congress, lobbyists help them with all manner of tasks. They provide useful and technical information about politics and policy. They draft legislation to be introduced in congressional committees.[8] They help build coalitions of lawmakers in both chambers to support pieces of legislation. And they hold campaign fundraisers.[9])

Whereas members of Congress seek policymaking help from aides, think tanks, and lobbyists, the president can rely on a much larger army of advisors and experts. Some work within the Executive Office of the President (EOP), which includes a set of White House institutions that serve the president alone – they are not part of the executive branch of the government, which the president administers according to the laws and budgets that are established by Congress. Key economic advisors in the EOP include economists in the Council of Economic Advisers (CEA), policy analysts in the National Economic Council (NEC), and budget officers in the Office of Management and Budget (OMB). The president also consults the government agencies that are within the executive branch, especially the cabinet secretaries who manage executive branch agencies and serve under the president's command.

Naturally, the set of advisors that the president consults varies with the type of policy under consideration, and even rather simple policy ideas can touch a large number of issues that justify a large number of advisors. For example, if the president were considering whether to support a $1 increase in the gas tax, he would rely on the combined analysis of the White House's economics offices (NEC, CEA, and OMB) and all of the executive branch departments that have a stake in the gas tax, including Treasury, Commerce, Transportation, Agriculture, Interior, Energy, and the Environmental Protection Agency (EPA).[10] All of those agencies would assist the president because the proposal would affect the government's budget, the environment, imports and exports, oil producers, and a wide range of other businesses. Again, even simple policies may have complex economic consequences.

Politics

We have already made some observations about the *politics* of policies, including a contrast between special-interest politics and general-interest politics. But there are several other such observations that are worth making at this point, before the next two chapters give more attention to policies and their consequences.

The Purposes of the Political System

As a first point, note that although government is meant to provide public goods like national defense and law and order, it is a mistake to think that that is its only purpose, for it is also a forum to reconcile competing ideas and agendas, including those that derive from naked self-interest. Put another way, political and economic conflict exists in society; it is resolved through the political system; and groups that succeed in elections or in influencing policymakers are able to steer public policies in the direction of their liking.

Americans sometimes forget these points when they think about their government's purpose. Instead, they often focus on two very notable features of US Constitution. One is the separation of executive, legislative, and judicial powers and the "checks and balances" that prevent any single branch from acting unchecked. The second is the set of limits on government power, especially those that appear in the Bill of Rights, where the First Amendment protects free speech, free press, and the free exercise of religion, and other amendments protect individuals from arbitrary and unjustified government power.[11]

Those two ideas were revolutionary, and they were later copied into many other countries' constitutions. However, their significance should not obscure the fact that the federal government was created in order to make laws and to govern. The Constitution gives Congress the powers to tax, regulate commerce, spend money, and assume debts. And, in addition to those "enumerated" powers, the Constitution gives Congress the power "to make all laws which shall be necessary and proper for carrying into execution" its enumerated powers.[12] Although Congress can be checked by a presidential veto or by the Supreme Court, its authority is sweeping.

Of course, the Constitution established that members of the House of Representatives would be popularly elected.[13] Like free speech, free exercise of religion, and other individual liberties enshrined in the Constitution, democratic elections are an expression of respect for individuals and the idea that they should have some say in who governs them. And of all the limits on government power that appear in the Constitution, elections may be the most significant because they allow voters to replace elected officials for any reason whatsoever.

Yet, the existence of elections also underscores the fact that people disagree about what constitutes "good" public policy, and elections give people license to compete peacefully for control of government. Put another way, democracy is not a system to manufacture agreement about economic policies, and it is not a system that produces the "best" public policies. It is a system in which elections – rather than monarchical rule or military might – determine who gets to control government and make public policy.

James Madison, the principal architect of the US Constitution, was well aware of the fact that people would pursue their economic interests in the political arena. He famously remarked in *Federalist #10* that such "factionalism" cannot be removed from society, and so our task is to design a system of government that is unlikely to allow some factions to run roughshod over others. *Federalist #10* was most preoccupied with the possibility of a "majority faction" of poor voters using government to advance their interests at the expense of a smaller, richer, propertied class. Madison argued that the system of government established by the Constitution would stymie such attempts. Contemporary observers have a range of opinions on the matter. Many conservatives think that the poor have been too successful at taxing the rich to pay for social programs, whereas many liberals think that the rich have been too successful at blocking programs that would counter poverty and expand socioeconomic opportunities. At the same time, many Americans from across the ideological spectrum think that the political system works too much to the benefit of corporate and special interests at the expense of taxpayers and consumers. In other words, concerns about the distributional consequences of public policies are as alive today as they were when the United States was founded.

Politics and Policymaking

It is in Congress – the main policymaking arena of the federal government – that the nation's diverse interests, values, and coalitions collide. In Congress, deals are struck, priorities are determined, and winners and losers are made.

Congress is not the only policymaking institution in the federal government. Hundreds of government agencies routinely make policy as they change regulations, administer programs, and shift priorities. Some agencies are structured to be independent from the elected branches – i.e., Congress and the president – so they can make policy with less worry about blowback from disaffected groups and the elected officials that rally to their cause. But most agencies are located in the executive branch, where policies can be influenced by the chief executive (the president) or his appointees. And because there are so many executive branch programs and agencies the president's power over economic policy is breathtaking in its scope.

Still, Congress's power is much greater. All agencies (including independent ones) must operate within the laws and bounds that have been established by Congress, and Congress can amend or curtail those powers at any time. To understand the essential elements of federal economic policies, we must study Congress and the legislative process.

Congress's most basic and significant feature is that each member represents a small slice of a very diverse country. Together, Congress represents rural and urban America, small states and large states, and everyone from Alaska to Anaheim and Mississippi to Manhattan. Also, each of Congress's 535 members (435 in the House, 100 in the Senate) aims to serve not just his or her district but also the nation as a whole via national policy. Their constituents demand as much.

Deals and compromises are an inevitable part of lawmaking – both within each chamber and in the negotiations for the two chambers to pass identical bills. Within the legislature, the most profound "deal" is not about public policy but rather organization and agenda-setting. Formally, all members of Congress are equal. But to get anything done there must be agenda-setting and leadership. Otherwise, the legislature might never be able to pass a budget or law on account of endless tinkering and coalition-building, and its only accomplishment might be the distribution of pork to congressional districts (because that is something that all members want). To make the legislature work, members of Congress establish rules, organization, and hierarchy. Most significantly, they form legislative parties, and the party with the majority sets rules for the chamber.

Put another way, legislators form standing coalitions called parties so that they can get some sort of unified agenda accomplished, and the primary reason for that is to fulfill a demand from voters. Voters want Congress to do more than just target monies for local pork projects. They also want changes in labor rules, the income tax, environmental rules, and Medicare, and the existence of parties allows Congress to deliver. Also, politicians' party affiliations allow voters to easily differentiate among candidates for office. Voters can simply look to a politician's party affiliation – Republican or Democrat – to quickly ascertain which group and which policies the politician will support in Congress. In the absence of parties, voters would have great difficulty understanding each candidate's issue positions and record in Congress. Without parties, democracy would be hopelessly chaotic, complex, and ineffectual.[14]

Party building in the legislature is far from effortless, and each party has very salient internal divisions. Within each party, policy goals and priorities are contested, and deals are struck. Still, the formation of parties in Congress – and the fact that each group works to advance its common agenda at the exclusion of the other's – means that parties are important in the policymaking system.

To underscore that point, consider a hypothetical midterm election in which the president's party loses twenty House seats and five Senate seats to the opposing party and, as a result, its majority in each chamber. Even though the partisan composition of each chamber changes by only 5 percent, the policymaking dynamic in Washington, DC would be completely upended. The reason, of course, is that the majorities flip, and *divided government* replaces *unified government*. With that simple change, the president's agenda becomes dead-on-arrival in Congress. Instead, the new majority party will work to advance its own agenda, and it will send legislation to the president that he dislikes. The president will respond by exercising his veto power, which he almost never does during unified government. And because the majority party in Congress does not have the requisite two-thirds of members to override the president's veto,[15] the policymaking system may be stuck on account of partisan *gridlock* – little or no legislation can be enacted because proposals cannot receive the requisite approval from the House, Senate, and president.

In contemporary American politics, partisan conflict is highly pitched. The two parties prefer starkly different social and economic policies – they are ideologically polarized. They are also rather evenly matched at the national level, so they are constantly engaged in "party warfare" in order to improve their prospects in the next election. Consequently, the policymaking system is quite gridlocked. In fact, there is significant gridlock even during unified government, on account of "filibuster" power in the Senate. The self-imposed rules of the Senate allow any senator to *filibuster* – or permanently delay, and thus permanently obstruct – legislation, unless a supermajority of three-fifths of the Senate (60 of 100 senators) votes for *cloture*, which ends the filibuster. Because it is very rare for the Senate majority to have sixty or more members, the minority party can stop the Senate – and a unified government – from advancing its agenda. For this reason, unified governments often flirt with the idea of changing Senate rules and lowering the cloture requirement. Such a change would allow the Senate to function more like the House, where the majority party can essentially block the minority party from exercising any influence in the policymaking process.

An important exception to the filibuster-induced gridlock is worth noting. Under a special process called *budget reconciliation*, filibusters are prohibited, and thus the Senate majority can advance legislation without having to accommodate the minority party. Congress created the budget reconciliation process to consider budget, tax, or debt issues in an expedited, unencumbered fashion. The process is important because its use over the past several decades has been responsible for the most consequential and partisan economic reforms, including the Democrats' health care reform in 2010 and the Republicans' tax cuts of 2001, 2003, and 2017.

Although partisan conflict overshadows all other conflicts in the modern Congress, intra-party conflict is no less important or common. Furthermore, members of Congress are highly attentive to voters, groups, and businesses in their districts. In fact, when representatives face a decision about whether to support their district or their party, they almost always choose the former.

Interest group and campaign finance pressures provide another dimension to the politics of legislative action. Corporations and business groups spend fortunes on lobbying efforts to influence policy.[16] According to the Center for Responsive Politics (2016), a government watchdog group, corporate lobbying expenditures exceed $2 billion annually, which is more than $4 million per member of Congress. Not surprisingly, the biggest lobbyists are industries that are subject to many government regulations. In 2013, the top three sectors by lobbying expenditures were pharmaceuticals/ health ($226 million), insurance ($153 million), and oil and gas ($146 million). Also high on CRP's list were electric utilities (ranked #5), investment banks (#8), and air transport (#14). As for individual companies, the biggest spenders – all of whom spent in excess of $15 million on lobbying in 2013 – included the health insurer Blue Cross/Blue Shield, the defense contractor Northrup Grumman, Comcast, General Electric, AT&T, Google, and Boeing. Business associations also lobby heavily, and they exist for nearly every trade, industry, and profession. Associations that are notable for their size and influence include the Chamber of Commerce, the National Association of Manufacturers, and PhRMA, an organization of drug and pharmaceutical companies. Other associations notable for their influence include the AFL-CIO (a union group) and AARP (a group for seniors and retirees).

These same groups also loom large in the world of campaign finance. Candidates for federal office need large sums of money to finance their campaign activities and advertisements. A candidate running in a competitive House district can expect her major-party opponent to spend at least $1.5 million on his campaign, and possibly several times more; so, she should be prepared to finance an equally robust and sophisticated campaign. The stakes are higher in senate races, and the districts are bigger, too. Senate candidates routinely spend in the tens of millions, and the sums get especially large in states where the parties are evenly matched. Candidates in competitive districts often attract lots of campaign donations simply because their races are key battlegrounds that determine which party wins control of Congress. However, those candidates still must spend most of their time attending fundraising events and dialing for dollars. And most of what they raise comes from business.

The corporate tilt of political finance affects policy, but we must be careful to keep things in perspective. Toward that end, note the following. First, politicians' demand for campaign finance causes them to pay special attention to their donors, and the heavy flow of corporate money in politics generates some policy successes for industry at the expense of broad voter groups, like taxpayers and consumers.

Second, that outcome is less common or severe when there is significant counter-pressure from voters or parties. In fact, members of Congress place the concerns of their voters ahead of those of campaign contributors and corporate lobbyists whenever there is a clear and potentially significant political conflict between the two. That last part is important because many policies are too parochial or insignificant to generate a reaction from the public. Also, virtually every policy that is good for some business or industry is also good for the local economies where they are employers. So, service to a corporate donor can also be service to one's district. Therefore, interest group success in the policymaking process may often have less to do with money than with representation.

Finally, and similarly, interest groups with voter power can easily outmatch interest groups that only have money. For example, the National Rifle Association (NRA) is one of the most powerful interest groups in the nation not because of its money, but because of its large, politically active membership. Many members of the NRA are single-issue voters, and they will vote against any politician in the NRA's crosshairs. It is they – and not the NRA's campaign finance operation – that really commands lawmakers' attention.

At its core, Congress is an electorally focused institution. Members do relentless fundraising so that they can finance their reelection campaigns. They build legislative parties so that they can fulfill voters' demands. And when faced with a choice between their districts and donors, parties, or "good" policy, they most often choose the former. Of course, it is self-serving for politicians to do that, because it is how they get reelected. But that is precisely how democracy is supposed to work.

Ideologies and Parties

It is useful to step back from the world of voters and interest groups and consider this central question of governance: how should the government allocate resources and prioritize different collective goals? To make the matter more concrete, consider an issue like the government's debt burden, which is currently $21 trillion. Then let us ask: would it be worthwhile to cut military spending by, say, $200 billion a year in order to decrease the debt? Or would the costs – which may include both current and future defense technologies and capabilities – exceed the benefit of a smaller debt? The question is difficult to answer because it is difficult to calculate the various costs and benefits of the proposal. Only if the nation were experiencing an acute crisis related to war or debt would the best path be easy to determine.

The question only gets more difficult when we consider alternative actions. For example, would cuts to Medicaid, a health care program for low-income households, be more or less costly than defense cuts? Which would be the better way to reduce the debt? To begin to answer those questions, we must answer other challenging questions. Would cuts to basic family medicine and preventative care lead to more high-cost emergency room visits? Would a reduction in health coverage reduce worker productivity and thus the economy's output?

And then what about taxes? Should they be considered as a means to reduce the debt? If so, which taxes should be increased? Those on corporate income? On investment income? On wage income? If the answer is the last, should low-income, middle-income, or high-income wage earners face proportionally equal increases in their wage income taxes? Or would it be more beneficial for a tax increase to hit the rich disproportionately, in turn making the income tax system more progressive?[17] Or is the income tax already too progressive?

The obvious point here is that it is very difficult to determine budgetary priorities via some sort of cost–benefit analysis. Alternatively, then, we might approach such questions by simply considering how policies have changed over time. For example, it could be argued that Medicaid and Medicare benefits should be trimmed because the programs' costs have increased so dramatically over time. Or it could be argued that income tax rates on rich households should be increased because they have declined substantially over the past several decades. Of course, the problem with this type of approach is that it does not provide any real guidance about which policies make the most sense for today's economy and society.

Now, put aside how policy analysts might approach these questions and consider how voters and politicians actually approach them. They do not determine their policy preferences and priorities through some sort of cost–benefit analysis; nor do most of them understand how policies have changed over time. Instead, their political opinions are driven mostly by *self-interest, political ideology,* or *partisanship.* Self-interest leads farmers to support government subsidies for agriculture, seniors to support Medicare, health care providers to support higher compensation for their Medicare and Medicaid services, businesses to support looser regulations, defense contractors to support defense spending, and high-income citizens to support a less-progressive tax schedule.

Political ideologies like *liberalism* and *conservativism* guide views more generally. In theory, ideologies are supposed to "promote consistency among political attitudes by connecting them to something greater, a more general principle or set of principles."[18] In practice, neither liberalism nor conservativism is a precise, coherent philosophy, and the attitudes that they reflect may originate more from coalitional politics than any underlying principle. For example, modern-day conservatives tend to support things like legal restrictions on abortion and a larger military – neither of which fits comfortably with their opposition to "big government."[19]

That said, liberalism and conservativism are more coherent when it comes to economic policies like taxation, regulation, and social programs. On such issues, liberals tend to support government policies that counter socioeconomic disparities, and they support progressive taxes to afford economic security and opportunity for all. By contrast, conservatives generally view the government's social programs and economic regulations as meddlesome and counterproductive; they prefer flatter taxes, and their vision for government is focused less on the attenuation of economic disparities than on the maintenance of law and order and national defense. (This ideological divide is mirrored in other societies and democracies. Everywhere, the political "left" wants "more government" so as to counteract socioeconomic disparities, whereas the "right" wants more free market capitalism, with fewer government regulations and tax-and-transfer programs.)

Partisanship is closely related to ideology, as most Democrats are liberal, and most Republicans are conservative. However, each party contains diverse interests that work together only with considerable friction in pursuit of electoral victories and policy influence. Indeed, one cannot understand national politics without understanding the politics that is internal to each party. Similarly, party platforms morph over time in ways that reflect politics, not philosophies. A dramatic illustration was Republicans' views on the 2010 Affordable Care Act, better known as Obamacare. The main element of the reform – the creation of exchanges with an individual mandate and subsidies (see Chapter 2) – was originally a conservative proposal, and it had been backed by many Republican politicians. However, when Obama and congressional Democrats pushed for those provisions many of those same Republicans came out against the reform, having calculated that opposition was a better political posture vis-à-vis the Democrats. Their voters followed suit, and the entire Republican Party was quickly in firm opposition to a proposal that had originally been one of their own.[20]

As already implied, the analyses that parties and ideologues use to defend their positions – although often quite compelling and sophisticated – are not borne of some sort of unbiased analysis. Instead, partisans and ideologues embrace and advance arguments that they find persuasive. Naturally, those tend to be arguments that gibe with their ideological and partisan perspectives – a point on which we expand below.

However, a more fundamental point is that ideologies and parties are useful – indispensable, even. Ideologies help people navigate complexity and chart a course for government, and they allow political competition to be about something larger than self-interest and local issues. Also, the existence of parties with meaningful reputations – e.g., Democrats want to address socioeconomic inequalities, Republicans want less "big government" – greatly simplifies voting because it allows voters to cast informed votes with very little information about individual candidates. Voters only need to know a candidate's party affiliation to know how he will approach many policy issues.

Political parties also enhance governance by allowing voters to hold politicians *collectively* accountable. Because members of Congress organize themselves into party caucuses, voters are able to reject a Republican or Democratic majority and select a different course for government – if they are so inclined. That would scarcely be possible if congressional parties did not exist. Also, as noted above, general-interest legislation would be extremely difficult to enact in the absence of congressional parties on account of the disorganized diversity of interests and opinions, the lack of agenda control, and the possibility of endless tinkering and coalition-building in the legislative process.

Turning these points around, we may ask: why do parties exist? There are three main reasons. One is that members of Congress would be unable to get anything done without forming standing coalitions that aim to pursue some sort of common agenda. So, they build parties in the legislature. A second reason is that party *organizations* are electorally useful: they fundraise, groom candidates, share electoral techniques, and mobilize voters. And the third reason is that party *reputations* are electorally useful – they help voters. So, politicians and activists cultivate a party "brand," like "pro-worker" or "anti-government."

Why Only Two Parties?

Many Americans complain about the two-party system and would like to see more parties in the mix. That could happen someday, and there have been periods of American history with prominent third parties. But there is a simple reason why people tend to coalesce into just two camps: groups that ally together into a large coalition have the potential to win control of government and enact a policy agenda, and they will be much more successful at those goals than groups that remain fragmented and disunited. However, with cooperation comes internal conflict and compromise. Indeed, both of America's two big parties are racked with internal divisions, and the two-party system they comprise is not an ossified structure that blocks the absorption of new viewpoints and agendas. Its contours and battle lines are fluid.

The strategic forces that sustain the two-party system can be observed in each district-level election. America's legislative electoral system selects a single member of Congress per district by plurality rule, which encourages voters to coalesce behind only two candidates because (a) the two most popular candidates have the best chance of securing a plurality of votes and (b) votes for any less-popular candidate can be thought of as "wasted" votes that could have been used to swing the race between the top two candidates. In fact, those are the reasons why many would-be supporters of the right-of-center Libertarian Party or left-of-center Green Party vote to help Republicans defeat Democrats or vice versa. In effect, they help cement the electoral dominance of the two big parties, and they do so for the same reason that everyone else does: by constructing a broad coalition, groups can put policymaking power in friendly hands.

The same considerations explain why the nationwide Tea Party movement of 2010 did not launch a political party to field its own general election candidates (see Chapter 7). If it had done so, conservative voters in conservative-leaning congressional districts might have split their support between Tea Party candidates and Republican candidates and inadvertently handed electoral victories to Democrats.[21] Instead, Tea Partyers stayed within the Republican fold, and they sought to win Republican primary elections and to shape the Republican Party's agenda. Their efforts were successful, and so new fissures appeared within the Republican Party. And in both respects, history was repeated. At several moments in American history, new political currents have transformed the nation's politics not by shattering the party system but by influencing one party or the other.

Most countries that have more than two parties in their legislature use some type of proportional representation (PR), an electoral system that elects more than one legislator per district and awards seats to parties according to their share of the vote. PR systems allow smaller parties to win some seats, so voters do not feel compelled to coalesce into large, plurality-winning groups. Also, because PR-elected legislatures have within them more than two party groupings, they rarely have what the US House and Senate always have: a majority party. That motivates a multiparty coalition – a group of parties that strikes a deal to jointly control the legislative agenda until the next election. Some people think that interparty collaboration in government is desirable and that multipartism is better than bipartism. We cannot consider that debate here, but we shall note that two-party legislatures are superior to multiparty legislatures in one sense: collective accountability is stronger when there are single-party majorities because voters know exactly which party deserves blame or credit for governing missteps and successes.[22]

Partisan Identities and Partisanship

The fact that the major parties are heterogeneous, internally divided coalitions may seem at odds with certain aspects of party politics, such as the durability of voters' attachments to parties. Why is it that so few people ever change their party affiliations? We might think that it is because today's parties are so ideologically polarized, and that does have something to do with it. However, voters' party loyalties were strong and durable before the parties became polarized over the past few decades.[23] And, indeed, the main answer lies not in the parties' issue positions and the ideological gap between them. It lies instead in the social roots of partisan identities.[24]

What this suggests is that voters who identify as Republican or Democrat do not regularly reevaluate their partisanship based on new information or events. Instead, they have a firm social identity and belief system that is similar in both nature and origin to a religious identity. Catholics, Protestants, Jews, and Muslims do not choose their faith after a comparative study of religious traditions. They become who they are via socialization, and in that way they absorb a particular belief system. Partisanship is similar. People often get their party loyalties and political views from their families and communities, and their party affiliations become a part of their identities and a source of their views on politics and policy.

Significantly, this point also hints at why the party system became so polarized. As later chapters explain, the main driver of polarization was that the partisan divide came to reflect a deep socio-cultural divide in the electorate. In other words, the parties did not become polarized because voters veered into opposing groups based on their separate analyses of the issues. Instead, the parties became more socially distinct and segregated, and ideological polarization followed.

The process by which partisans absorb their party's issue positions is aided and abetted by humans' psychological tendencies regarding information processing and analysis. In particular, when people "reason" they tend to dismiss or discount information that does not sit well with their prior beliefs – not out of a conscious attempt to sustain their opinions but because the information actually seems incorrect, trivial, or misrepresentative. For the same reason, people tend to quickly and uncritically embrace beliefs and ideas that support their pre-existing attitudes. To put it another way, people interpret information and events through their own perceptual screens, and those screens reinforce their political views.

These tendencies explain why policy debates can be so intractable. And they are the reason why people may hold erroneous, partisan-tinged beliefs about undisputable facts, of which illustrations are aplenty. Here are two that are reported in a 2002 study by the political scientist Larry Bartels: "in a 1988 survey a majority of respondents who described themselves as strong Democrats said that inflation had 'gotten worse' over the eight years of the Reagan administration," when in fact it had fallen by 70 percent; and "a majority of Republicans in a 1996 survey said that the federal budget deficit had increased" during Clinton's first term, when in fact it had fallen by 90 percent.[25]

These types of mistakes are examples of what psychologists call *motivated reasoning*, which is broadly defined as a person conforming his beliefs to some sort of interest or goal.[26] The behavior is commonplace and subconscious, and it illustrates that political reasoning is more like justification than neutral analysis. "Most of the time," write Christopher Achen and Larry Bartels, "voters adopt issue positions, adjust their candidate perceptions, and invent facts to rationalize decisions they have already made."[27] Jonathan Haidt put it more succinctly: "intuitions come first, strategic reasoning second."[28] But, again, the behavior is not necessarily deliberate or conscious. People simply advance arguments that make sense to them, and the arguments that make sense are those that mesh with their political views.

Significantly, partisanship and partisan-motivated reasoning do not stem from a poor understanding of politics or government. In fact, the opposite is closer to the truth. Citizens with very low levels of knowledge about politics and government tend not to care about politics, and thus few of them care about there being a good fit between facts and their political opinions. By contrast, voters who are more knowledgeable about public affairs are more likely to have ideological viewpoints and partisan leanings, and thus their political reasoning is much more likely to be "motivated."

The Uninformed Electorate

Notwithstanding their biases, partisan voters tend to be relatively well-informed about the basic workings of government. The electorate as a whole is not, however. Polls routinely illustrate that the public is quite ignorant about the federal government and its influence on the economy. Some recent examples include:[29]

- Only a quarter (25 percent) of Americans know that a US Senator's term is six years, and only a slightly larger percentage (30 percent) know that members of the House of Representatives serve two-year terms.[30]
- A near majority (49 percent) of Americans does not know (or cannot remember) that the name for the first ten amendments to the US Constitution is the Bill of Rights.
- The statistically average American thinks that the federal government spends 28 percent of its budget on foreign aid – which is 28 times larger than the actual figure.[31]
- A near majority (43 percent) of Americans cannot provide a description of an economic recession when a satisfactory answer would consist of nothing more than "economic slowdown" or "rising unemployment."
- A near majority of Americans (48 percent) cannot note a likely economic consequence of a US tax on foreign goods. Acceptable answers

include "the US would buy less from foreign countries", the tax would "improve the balance of trade", and "other countries would retaliate."
- A majority of Americans (54 percent) does not know the purpose of the Federal Reserve.[32]

The primary reason why the public is so uninformed about political economy is straightforward: most people have little need to know such things. It does not help one to advance her career or improve her household finances by knowing miscellaneous facts about government and public policy. Of course, homeowners are likely to benefit from knowing about the tax deduction for mortgage interest, and seniors would do well to know something about the various Medicare programs, and business managers must make sure that they comply with various tax and regulatory requirements. But none of those people – and indeed very few people at all – really need to know more than a few things about government in order to navigate the policies and programs that require or merit their attention.

Economists and political scientists often note that voters' ignorance about government and public policy is instrumentally *rational*. If voters are instrumental, and thus use their vote to obtain the best political and economic outcomes in the future, then it is rational for them to study politics, government, and public policy in order to maximize the "payoff" of their vote – *except* for the fact that each voter's political voice is miniscule, with only a tiny probability that it makes the difference in an election. That means that the *expected* payoff of any such effort is essentially nil, and the effort is irrational. Indeed, unless a voter believes that an election will be extremely close, and her vote may make or break a tie, it is not even rational to spend the time to vote, much less to study government and public policy.[33] Things are different in other spheres of life. For example, most people conduct serious research when they are in the market for a car or a house. The reason is obvious – their decisions about which items to buy and which loan terms to assume are, with 100 percent certainty, materially consequential for them.

The public's ignorance about government matters in multiple respects. For one, it contributes to negativity in campaigns, because uninformed voters (in particular) are swayed by negative ads.[34] The public's ignorance also increases the chance that it will support ill-conceived public policies or politicians who promise much more than they can deliver.[35] From the perspective of this book, it would be interesting to know how policies and the economy would differ if voters were more knowledgeable. Would politicians focus less on the short run and pay more attention to what helps the economy over the long run? Would tax rates and social programs be different?

However, such questions are too hypothetical for this volume. Besides, it is far from clear how a more-informed electorate would come into being. Nor is it clear what types of information about government would be most important. Would it be better for citizens to understand the legislative process or to understand the government's tax policies? Which better serves our democracy: if citizens can catalog Article I of the Constitution (which specifies the powers of Congress) or if they can trace the historical growth of regulatory agencies and welfare programs? Should citizens prioritize studying the history of the Constitutional Convention of 1787 or the partisan "realignment" of the South after the 1960s, when Southern states switched from solidly Democratic to solidly Republican? There are no obvious answers to these questions. The following pages will address topics that are relevant for understanding contemporary political economy, but there is much more about American government and history that we might like citizens to know.

Conclusion

This chapter made several general and introductory points about policies and politics in the United States – too many to review in this concluding section. However, two main points deserve reiteration. First, the nation's politics and economy are closely intertwined. Each affects the other in several ways, and we must understand those relationships in order to understand the shape and workings of each. Second, economic policies are inescapably political. That is because disagreement about priorities and distribution are inescapable, and it is because the Constitution vests policymaking power in Congress, whose hundreds of members represent a vast and varied nation. The economic policies that it produces are compromises between various interests and ideas, and they are always strongly rooted in electoral incentives. In particular, majority parties work to accumulate legislative accomplishments on which they can campaign, and individual legislators court reelection by contributing to their party's collective efforts and championing the interests and public sentiments of their constituents.

Notes

1 In 2014, Medicare enrollment was 54 million persons and government spending (net of premiums and other income items) was approximately $512 billion (Kaiser Family Foundation, 2014).
2 Light (2002) estimates that about 17 million jobs are either within the federal government or in institutions that contract with it.
3 The slogan appeared on a sign in Clinton's campaign headquarters. It read: "Change vs. more of the same. The economy, stupid. Don't forget health care" (Kelly, 1992).
4 Reagan's most memorable charge came in one of the presidential debates: "Ask yourself," he said to viewers, "Are you better off now than you were four years ago? Is it easier for you to go and buy things in the stores than it was four years ago?"
5 The *business cycle* is the term economists use for the period of time over which the economy shifts from expansion to recession and back. The cycle does not have precise intervals – periods of recession and expansion can vary in their length of time. For an economy to grow over the long run, its periods of recession need to

be less frequent and/or pronounced than its periods of expansion. Because periodic recessions accompany even the best-functioning economies, the business cycle appears to be inevitable.

6 One estimate puts its length at 2,600 pages; other estimates are higher. See Grossman, 2014.

7 The program that was created is not easy for consumers to navigate. See Ridgeway, 2008.

8 Both chambers of Congress have "standing committees" that "mark up" or draft legislation. The committees have different jurisdictions, and they largely control the types of legislative proposals that pertain to their issue areas. Important House committees include the Committee on Agriculture, the Financial Services Committee, the Committee on Ways and Means (tax policy), the Committee on the Budget (budget guidelines), and the Committee on Appropriations, which specifies expenditures by program.

9 Lobbyists' efforts do *not* produce a steady stream of favorable results (Baumgartner et al., 2009). However, if and when they do succeed in influencing policy, clients' "return on investment" may be considerable. Consider just one example: a 2004 tax holiday for corporate foreign income that was held in foreign tax havens. Although we cannot say that the policy was strictly due to lobbying effort, those who lobbied for the policy benefited greatly. Alexander, Mazza, and Scholz (2009) found that 93 firms accounted for 70% of the foreign income that was repatriated during the tax holiday, and that those firms received $62.5 billion in tax savings. Those firms spent some $282.7 million on lobbying in relation to the 2004 law, which was equivalent to a 220:1 return on investment.

10 This example is from Keith Hennessey, who served as George W. Bush's Director of the NEC from 2007 to 2009. Hennessey (2010) notes that "[On] a straightforward question like a gas tax increase for which the substantive analysis is easy, there would probably be three meetings: one of mid-level White House and Agency staff chaired by the NEC Deputy or the NEC Special who handles energy issues, a *principals meeting* of Cabinet-level officials and senior White House advisors chaired by the NEC Director, and then a meeting with the President. I'd guess that maybe 200–300 man hours (of very senior people) would precede a 45-minute decision meeting with the President" (emphasis in original). His explanation also noted that the NEC would chair the meetings; the CEA would explain the economics of a gas tax increase, including the effects on fuel consumption and imports; that Treasury would focus on issues of "tax policy, design, and administration issues"; that OMB would "be happy that the deficit would be lower ... [and it would] explain how gas taxes interact with the Highway Trust Fund."

11 The US Constitution was the first constitution to include either of these features, but the ideas themselves came from Enlightenment thinkers such as the Englishman John Locke and the Frenchman Baron de Montesquieu.

12 This is the so-called "necessary and proper" or "elastic" clause.

13 Originally, members of the Senate were appointed by state governments. The 17th Amendment (1913) changed the Constitution to make them popularly elected.

14 Schattschneider (1942, p. 1) famously put the point this way: "political parties created democracy and ... modern democracy is unthinkable save in terms of parties."

15 Per the Constitution, an override occurs upon a two-thirds vote of voting members in *both* chambers. Overrides are rare because two-thirds is a high threshold, and because a president who anticipated a successful override may decide to spare himself that embarrassment and let Congress's proposal become law.

16 Labor unions and other non-business groups also lobby and make campaign contributions to members of Congress; but their expenditures are dwarfed by corporate money.

17 A *progressive* income tax has tax rates that increase with income, so that higher-income households pay a higher rate than lower-income households. It contrasts with a flat tax, in which all incomes are taxed at the same percent.

18 Kernell et al., 2018, p. 404.

19 Libertarians argue that they are more consistent because they favor "small government" on both economic issues and social issues.

20 Klein, 2012.

21 Exactly that type of problem occurred for the left in the 2000 presidential election. The election proved to be razor-thin in Florida, but it would have been won by Democrat Al Gore instead of Republican George W. Bush if more Green Party sympathizers had voted for Gore. Green Party sympathizers seemed to apply the lesson in subsequent elections: no Green presidential candidate has polled anything close to the 2.9% that Ralph Nader won in 2000.

22 On legislative electoral systems, their consequences, and their tradeoffs, see Cox 1997; 2006.

23 Campbell et al., 1960.

24 Green, Palmquist, and Schickler, 2002.

25 These quotes are of from the journalist Jonathan Chait (2010), who summarizes' Bartels' 2002 study.

26 Here is another definition, offered by Dan Kahan, professor of law and psychology at Yale, and reported by Klein (2012): motivated reasoning is "when a person is conforming their assessments of information to some interest or goal that is independent of accuracy." Klein adds that the interest or goal may be "winning the next election, or even just winning an argument."

27 Achen and Bartels, 2006.

28 Haidt, 2012, p. 59.

29 Unless noted otherwise, these examples are from Delli Carpini and Keeter, 1991, p. 592. The list could go on. See Delli Carpini, 1999.

30 Delli Carpini and Keeter, 1997.

31 The survey question was open-ended: respondents could pick any number between 0% and 100%. And they could respond "Don't Know." Yet, 50% of respondents guessed that foreign aid constituted 20% or more of the budget (Kaiser Family Foundation, 2013).

32 Walstad and Larsen, 1993.

33 In a typical presidential election 55% to 60% of eligible voters exercise their right to vote. In a typical midterm election, in which the House and one-third of the Senate is up for reelection, about 40% of eligible voters vote.

34 See West, 2013. Negative ads also contribute to citizen disengagement and disgust with politics (Ansolabehere and Iyengar, 1995); though Wattenberg and Brians (1999) argue otherwise.

35 Low levels of information do not necessarily prevent voters from voting in accordance with their preferences or interests (McKelvey and Ordeshook, 1986; Popkin, 1994; Lupia and McCubbins, 1998).

References

Achen, Christopher H., and Larry M. Bartels. (2006). It feels like we're thinking: The rationalizing voter and electoral democracy. Annual Meeting of the American Political Science Association, Philadelphia, PA.

Alexander, Raquel, Stephen W. Mazza, and Susan Scholz. (2009). Measuring rates of return on lobbying expenditures: An empirical case study of tax breaks for multinational corporations. *Journal of Law and Politics*, 25, 401–458.

Ansolabehere, Stephen, and Shanto Iyengar. (1995). *Going negative: How political advertising shrinks and polarizes the electorate.* New York, NY: The Free Press.

Bartels, Larry M. (2002). Beyond the running tally: Partisan bias in political perceptions. *Political Behavior*, 24(2), 117–150.

Baumgartner, Frank R., Jeffrey M. Berry, Marie Hojnacki, Beth L. Leech, and David C. Kimball. (2009). *Lobbying and policy change: Who wins, who loses, and why.* Chicago, IL: University of Chicago Press.

Campbell, Angus, Philip E. Converse, Warren E. Miller, and Donald E. Stokes. (1960). *The American voter.* New York, NY: John Wiley & Sons.

Center for Responsive Politics. (2016). Retrieved from: www.opensecrets.org/lobby/ (accessed March 28, 2017).

Chait, Jonathan. (2010, August 26). How Republicans learn that Obama is Muslim. *The New Republic.*

Cox, Gary W. (1997). *Making votes count.* Cambridge, UK: Cambridge University Press.

Cox, Gary W. (2006). Evaluating electoral systems. *Revista de ciencia política* (Santiago), 26(1), 212–215.

Delli Carpini, Michael X. (1999). In search of the information citizen: What Americans know about politics and why it matters. *The Communication Review*, 4, 129–164.

Delli Carpini, Michael X., and Scott Keeter. (1991). Stability and change in the US public's knowledge of politics. *Public Opinion Quarterly*, 55(4), 583–612.

Delli Carpini, Michael X., and Scott Keeter. (1997). *What Americans know about politics and why it matters.* New Haven, CT: Yale University Press.

Green, Donald, Bradley Palmquist, and Eric Schickler. (2002). *Partisan hearts and minds: Political parties and the social identities of voters.* New Haven, CT: Yale University Press.

Grossman, Andrew L. (2014). Is the tax code really 70,000 pages long? *Slate.* Retrieved from: www.slate.com/articles/news_and_politics/politics/2014/04/how_long_is_the_tax_code_it_is_far_shorter_than_70_000_pages.html (accessed May 23, 2018).

Haidt, Jonathan. (2012). *The righteous mind: Why good people are divided by politics and religion.* New York, NY: Vintage.

Hennessey, Keith. (2010, September 22). Roles of the President's White House economic advisors (updated). [Web log comment]. Retrieved from: http://keithhennessey.com/2010/09/22/economic-roles-updated/ (accessed November 14, 2016).

Kaiser Family Foundation. (2013, November 7). 2013 Survey of Americans on the US role in global health. Retrieved from: http://kff.org/global-health-policy/poll-finding/2013-survey-of-americans-on-the-u-s-role-in-global-health/ (accessed June 28, 2018).

Kaiser Family Foundation. (2014). Medicare at a glance. Retrieved from: http://kff.org/medicare/fact-sheet/medicare-at-a-glance-fact-sheet/ (accessed June 28, 2018).

Kelly, Michael. (1992, October 31). Democrat fights perceptions of Bush gain. *The New York Times.*

Kernell, Samuel, Gary C. Jacobson, Thad Kousser, and Lynn Vavreck. (2018). *The logic of American politics* (8th ed.). Washington, DC: CQ Press.

Klein, Ezra. (2012, June 25). Unpopular mandate: Why do politicians reverse their positions? *The New Yorker.*

Light, Paul C. (2002). Fact sheet on the new true size of government. Center for Public Service, Brookings Institution. Retrieved from: www.brookings.edu/~/media/research/files/articles/2003/9/05politics-light/light20030905.pdf (accessed June 28, 2017).

Lupia, Arthur, and Mathew D. McCubbins. (1998). *The democratic dilemma: Can citizens learn what they need to know?* Cambridge, UK: Cambridge University Press.

McKelvey, Richard D., and Peter C. Ordeshook. (1986). Information, electoral equilibria, and the democratic ideal. *The Journal of Politics*, 48(4), 909–937.

Popkin, Samuel L. (1994). *The reasoning voter: Communication and persuasion in presidential campaigns*. Chicago, IL: University of Chicago Press.

Ridgeway, James. (2008, September). Medicare's poison pill. *Mother Jones*. Retrieved from: www.motherjones.com/politics/2008/09/medicares-poison-pill/ (accessed June 28, 2017).

Schattschneider, E. E. (1942). *Party government*. New York, NY: Holt, Reinhart, and Winston.

Walstad, William B., and Max Larsen. (1993). Results from a national survey of American economic literacy. Proceedings of the American Statistical Association. Retrieved from: www.amstat.org/404.aspx?aspxerrorpath=/sections/srms/Proceedings/papers/1993_211.pdf (accessed June 28, 2017).

Wattenberg, Martin P., and Craig Leonard Brians. (1999). Negative campaign advertising: Demobilizer or mobilizer? *American Political Science Review*, 93(4), 891–899.

West, Darrell M. (2013). *Air wars: Television advertising and social media in election campaigns, 1952–2012*. Washington, DC: Sage.

Part I

Economic Policies and Political Economy

2 Taxing, Spending, Regulating

On a 2013 episode of his late-night talk show on ABC, Jimmy Kimmel aired a segment in which random, unsuspecting Los Angeles pedestrians were asked which they preferred: the Affordable Care Act (ACA) or Obamacare. The fun was in the ignorant responses. People reported that they preferred the ACA, not recognizing that it and Obamacare were the same thing. Obamacare was merely the popular nickname for the 2010 law that was fully titled the Patient Protection and Affordable Care Act.

The ACA was a large and complex piece of legislation and, as the responses on Kimmel's show suggested, most people did not understand what it did. The main goal of the law was to reduce the number of households that lacked health insurance. At the time, about 22 percent of adults between the ages of 23 and 64 were uninsured.[1] Most other Americans had insurance either through one of the government's three main health insurance programs – Medicare (for seniors), Medicaid (for low-income households), and the Veterans' Health Administration – or as a fringe benefit from their employers. That employment benefit was also related to federal policy. The government provides a tax break to employers for the employment compensation that they provide in the form of health insurance, rather than wages and salaries. In the absence of that tax break, fewer employers would provide their employees a health insurance benefit.

In general, the individuals who lacked health insurance in the pre-ACA era had jobs that were not good enough to include health benefits but well-paid enough to surpass Medicaid eligibility thresholds. Those individuals and their family members could purchase their own insurance on the "individual market," but that might cost $10,000 or $20,000 a year, which few could afford. And yet, if they did not purchase a plan, they were one accident or unexpected health problem away from financial ruin, given the sky-high costs of emergency room visits, surgeries, cancer treatments, and the like. In the decades prior to the ACA, personal bankruptcies and home foreclosures rose sharply because health emergencies hit households with bills that were far beyond what they could pay. Of course, households that had health insurance from their employer or from one of the government programs were protected from that type of calamity.

The ACA sought to reduce the number of uninsured in several ways. One was a Medicaid expansion. The maximum eligible income was increased so that more households could qualify, and the law specified that the federal government would pay for the cost of that expansion for a number of years, after which states would share the costs (as they do with the rest of Medicaid). A second mechanism was the so-called "employer mandate" – a tax to be levied on businesses with fifty or more employees that did not offer their employees a subsidized insurance plan. The idea was simple: some businesses would choose to offer their employees an insurance plan rather than pay a new tax, and thus coverage would increase.

The third and most significant part of the ACA was a complicated system to expand the individual market. One part of the system was a government regulation that prohibits private insurance companies from discriminating against people with pre-existing health conditions. Prior to the law, insurance companies could deny coverage to people with health issues, and they did so to contain their costs and the premiums they charge their customers. The new rule was destined to make insurance plans more expensive, because insurance companies would have to cover the sick people that they previously refused to cover. That, in turn, would lead more healthy people to take their chances without insurance, which would further increase the costs of insurance, because only sick people would stay in the market. To prevent that "death spiral" from occurring, the law also included an "individual mandate" – a tax on the uninsured. That would motivate people to stay in the individual market, because it was better for them to pay money for health insurance than to pay a tax penalty. Yet, the cost of insurance would remain out of reach for most people. So, the system included a third element: subsidies. The government would help people pay for private health insurance, provided that their incomes were below a certain threshold (400 percent of the poverty line), and in an amount that was inversely proportional to their income. (That is, richer households got smaller subsidies.) The law created this new government benefit as a refundable tax credit, so it would be realized when households completed their tax returns, and it would be administered by the Internal Revenue Service.

This three-pronged system is often called the "three-legged stool" because it requires all three elements to stand. If insurance companies can deny coverage, sick people will remain uninsured. If there is no individual mandate, healthy people will not buy insurance, insurance premiums will skyrocket, and the individual market will collapse. And, still, health insurance is expensive. Without a subsidy, people who are taxed into buying insurance will be unable to afford other living expenses.

Surely, the system is complex, and voters would have better understood the ACA if it had pursued its objective simply by expanding Medicare or Medicaid. However, the system was devised with a purpose in mind: to use the market, rather than the government, as the provider of health insurance.

The idea was to allow consumer choice, to spur competition among insurance companies, and to expand the customer base for private insurance companies.

Obamacare was an unusual piece of legislation in the sense that its main elements were designed to expand a marketplace, but it was not unusual in its use of regulations, taxes, and expenditures. Those are the three main tools of economic policy, and to understand the government's main activities and influence throughout the economy we must study its most significant regulations, expenditures, and tax policies. This chapter provides a brief overview of those activities. More precisely, it provides a brief introduction to the government's budget, revenues, debt, and regulatory agencies. It pays particular attention to programs and policies that are prominent in contemporary partisan debates, like the entitlement programs and the individual income tax.

Although this chapter reviews many of the government's most important economic policies, there are many others that it ignores. For example, it ignores trade policy and monetary policy, both of which are discussed in later chapters. It also ignores things like mortgage underwriting, the government's management of the energy grid, and law enforcement. Those activities, and many others like them, may be very economically consequential even though they are small items in the budget (and thus ignored by this chapter). A good example is federal deposit insurance, which is the government's insurance of customers' deposits in banks and credit unions. As a budget item, the program is tiny. However, it is hugely significant: it strengthens trust in the banking system, reduces the risk of financial crises, supports the extension of credit, and facilitates the economy's growth.

Total Expenditures and Revenues

Before we look at some of the specifics of the budget and tax system, it is useful to get the "big picture." How much does the government spend? How much does it raise in tax revenues? How have those numbers changed over time?

Here are some simple answers to the first two questions: in 2015, the government raised $3.2 trillion and spent $3.7 trillion, which means that it ran a *deficit* of $500 billion. To contextualize such figures, it is useful (and routine) to compare them to the "size" of the nation's economy, the standard measure of which is called *gross domestic product* (GDP) and is the monetary value of all final goods and services produced by the economy during the year. In 2015, US GDP was $17.5 trillion, so federal expenditures were 21 percent of GDP, federal revenues were 18.5 percent of GDP, and the federal deficit was 2.5 percent of GDP.

Figure 2.1 places those figures in historical context. Note three things. First, the budget figures for 2015 were quite normal, at least in the decades since 1980. Over the past forty years, federal *outlays* – as the government's

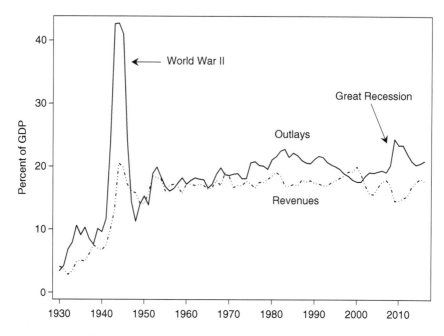

Figure 2.1 Federal government outlays and revenues as a percent of GDP, 1929–2017.

Source: Office of Management and Budget, Historical Tables: Table 1.2.

purchases, payroll expenses, and transfer payments are called – have remained relatively flat and fluctuated between 20 percent and 25 percent of GDP. Meanwhile, revenues have hovered about 3 percent lower, so deficits of 3 percent of GDP have been routine. In fact, the only period over the past fifty years when the government did *not* run a deficit was the late 1990s. From 1998 to 2001, the government collected more money than it spent; it ran a *surplus*.

The second thing to note is that during the Great Recession of 2008–2009 the spending-to-GDP ratio increased and the revenue-to-GDP ratio fell, so the budget deficit increased. Recessions are like that. A *recession* is a decrease in the economy's output, which tends to bring higher unemployment. With fewer incomes and profits to tax, the government's tax revenues fall. At the same time, government spending tends to increase because more people qualify for "safety-net" programs like food stamps and unemployment insurance. And, because that occurs while GDP falls, the spending-to-GDP ratio spikes.

The third thing to note is the government's growth from 1930 to 1980. In the 1930s, spending increased rapidly as the government responded to the Great Depression with more programs and agencies. In the 1940s, spending skyrocketed in order to fund World War II. After the war, spending dropped, but to a higher baseline, which allowed the government to maintain a superpower-sized military. Then, as the economy boomed in the postwar decades, government spending did, too. Various new government initiatives, the most significant being Medicare and Medicaid, caused the spending-to-GDP ratio to increase.

Although government spending leveled off, starting around 1980, it continued to face upward pressure due to fast-rising health care costs. In addition, federal spending on health care ticked up after the ACA's Medicaid expansion in 2010.

Note also that although *federal* spending has stayed rather constant since 1980, *total* government spending – including spending by state and local governments – has increased. That is also partly because of Medicaid, which is partly financed by the states. It is also because of the federal government's "unfunded mandates," which are simply (unfunded) regulatory requirements that the federal government places on state governments. Examples include requirements to protect against employment discrimination, to limit environmental contamination, and to make public facilities accessible to disabled persons.

A final note is that total government spending in the United States is comparable to that in other rich countries. In 2014, total government spending was 38 percent of US GDP. In Japan, the figure was 42 percent. In Germany and the United Kingdom, it was 44 percent, and in France it was 57 percent.[2] Yet, beneath those similarities are important contrasts. Most notably, the United States spends a much larger fraction on defense, whereas peer countries spend a larger proportion of their incomes on transfers and safety-net programs.

Budget Basics

In the government's budget, there are two types of spending: *mandatory* and *discretionary*. The mandatory budget includes most of the *entitlement programs* – i.e., social insurance and welfare programs in which government-financed benefits to individuals are determined by law rather than a budget allocation.[3] Take Medicare as an illustration. It provides a range of health benefits to people over the age of 65. Annual spending on the program is not determined in a budget allocation by Congress but by the benefits and eligibility requirements established by law and the use of those benefits by Medicare recipients. Put another way, no Medicare recipient would be denied program benefits because a predetermined pot of money for the year has run out. Rather, the law *mandates* that the government pays to cover all benefits that are incurred throughout the year, and so the government's total outlays are determined by the use of benefits by enrollees and the prices that the government pays for drugs, operations, and doctors' visits. Congress can change how much money is spent on Medicare and other entitlement programs, but to do that it must change the law that specifies the program's benefits, operations, and eligibility requirements.

By contrast, Congress picks a specific annual budget for all discretionary programs and agencies. Most of the government's activities are funded by the discretionary budget, including all items related to defense, transportation, foreign aid, law enforcement, scientific research, and energy. With total discretion regarding the annual funding of such programs, Congress could, from one year to the next, quadruple the size of one program and eliminate ten others simply by changing their budget allocations. Dramatic changes are rare, however. Congress usually makes more incremental changes in the discretionary budget.

The budget-making process is complex. Congress has developed rules and procedures to choose allocations for thousands of programs while staying within a total budget of its choosing. Yet, Congress frequently strays from its procedures and improvises the budget process, and it often fails to pass a full-year budget and meet its own budget deadlines (like October 1, when the fiscal year is supposed to begin). The main source of budget dysfunction over the past couple of decades has been partisan conflict and gamesmanship.

If the budget process goes according to plan, however, it proceeds as follows. First, in January, the president submits a draft budget to Congress.[4] The draft signals the preferences of the president and the executive branch agencies he oversees, and it includes estimated spending on mandatory programs, estimated revenues, and a detailed discretionary budget. The document is merely a draft; Congress retains the authority to write the budget. Next, the two chambers of Congress pass a budget resolution, which sets overall targets for spending, revenues, and debt, as well some specific budgets for major agencies and programs. Subsequently, the two chambers draft a series of appropriations bills, each of which funds a particular range of government agencies and programs. The appropriations bills specify exact budgets for discretionary programs and agencies, and they may include changes in mandatory programs and tax rates (though they need not).[5] As with all legislation, the two chambers must iron out the differences in their bills to pass identical appropriations bills. After that step, the bills go to the president for approval or veto.

The greatest hurdle to passing a budget (or specific appropriation bill) is divided government. If the two chambers are controlled by different parties, they often struggle to reach a compromise deal. Similarly, if the White House and Congress are controlled by different parties, the two branches may play a game of budget brinkmanship in which the president vetoes the budget in the hope that Congress will cave and pass something more in line with his preferences. The president's leverage remains limited, however, because he can only approve or reject Congress's bills in their entirety. So, when Congress is controlled by the other party, he is liable to accept many things that he dislikes. By contrast, budgets do not stray too far from the president's preferences during periods of unified government.

If the elected branches fail to pass a budget authorization before the prior budget lapses, then a *government shutdown* occurs. Most discretionary programs are prohibited from operating without a current budget authorization, so a funding lapse means that the agency must cease a program's operations and furlough its employees. Some programs, like most units of the Defense Department, can continue to operate for some time during a budget lapse. Mandatory programs can also continue, because their expenditures are governed by standing legislation (though their administration may suffer if some personnel are furloughed because their jobs are classified as appropriations-funded). The most protracted (partial) government shutdowns occurred in 1995 and 2013. The first was due to partisan disagreements between the Congress and the president; the second was due to partisan disagreements between the House and the Senate.

Typically, if Congress is liable to miss a budget deadline, or if it wants to delay budget negotiations to a more politically convenient time (like after an election), it will pass a *continuing resolution*, which specifies that spending should proceed at the previous year's levels for a temporary period of time, sometimes for only a few weeks. If a continuing resolution lapses and there is no replacement, the affected agencies and programs may need to cease operations.

Budget Deficits

Although Congress makes budgetary changes every year, the deficit has two regular aspects to it. First, it is structural. That is, Congress's annual mix of tax-and-spend policies is regularly expected to generate persistent deficits, in each of the next five or ten years into the future (if the mix were to remain in place), even if the economy avoids recession and expands steadily. Second, the deficit is counter-cyclical, which means that it moves opposite to the business cycle. As noted already, when the economy grows, the deficit tends to shrink; and when the economy shrinks, the deficit tends to grow. Again, that occurs for two reasons. First, tax revenues are pro-cyclical – i.e., they increase when the economy is expanding, jobs are aplenty, and profits are rising. Second, safety-net spending is counter-cyclical because more people meet the eligibility requirements for programs like unemployment benefits and food stamps when the economy stagnates and unemployment increases.

These two aspects of the budget are illustrated by Figure 2.2, which shows the deficit as a percent of GDP from 1977 to 2017. The figure shows that the deficit tends to increase during recessions, which are shaded in the graph.[6] It also shows that the deficit tends to decrease during expansions – the periods in between recessions – and that the deficit rarely dips below 2 percent of GDP, even when an economic expansion is mature.

Note once again that the only period in which the government ran a surplus was 1998 to 2001. That occurred for two reasons. First, as discussed at greater length in Chapters 5 and 6, congresses and presidents in the late

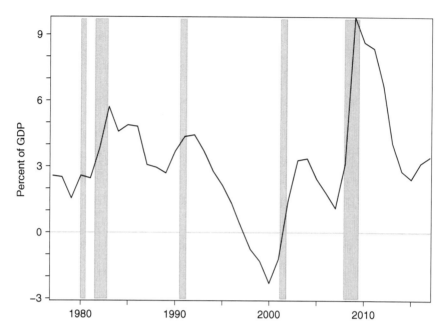

Figure 2.2 Budget deficits as a percent of GDP, 1977–2017.

Note: Shaded areas indicate that the economy was in recession, according to the National Bureau of Economic Research.

Source: Federal Reserve Bank of St. Louis.

1980s and 1990s spent years chipping away at the structural deficit. Second, the economy boomed in the 1990s. Note also that the surplus disappeared after 2001. That was partly due to a mild recession. But, more significantly, deficits returned because of budgetary decisions, especially large tax cuts, new wars in Iraq and Afghanistan, and, in 2003, a Medicare expansion.

A wholly separate point about the deficit is that its causal relationship with the economy is reciprocal. In other words, just as the economy affects the deficit, the deficit also affects the economy (albeit to a lesser degree). This is a point about macroeconomics – about the factors that affect the state of the economy – and it is something that we will discuss in the next chapter. But here is a brief explanation. When the economy is shrinking, people have less money to spend, business suffers, and the overall "demand" for goods and services in the economy falls. Counter-cyclical expenditures by the government moderate those slumps because they allow individuals, households, and businesses to cut back less than they otherwise would. Of course, that would not occur if the government cut some other program such that its total spending was left unchanged. Thus, the key is not counter-cyclical programs, per se, but the deficit. So, to be more accurate, counter-cyclical *deficits* dampen fluctuations in the economy. When the economy shrinks, the government borrows more money to finance a larger deficit, which counters the drop in demand and dampens the economy's slump. Similarly, when the economy expands, the deficit shrinks, which moderates the expansion.

In macroeconomic jargon, programs with counter-cyclical spending are often called *automatic stabilizers* because they can help moderate swings in the economy (if they are allowed to swell or shrink the deficit). The macroeconomic usefulness of counter-cyclical deficits is a core tenet of Keynesian economic philosophy, named after the British economist John Maynard Keynes (1883-1946). Keynesianism also emphasizes the usefulness of deficit-financed *fiscal stimulus* as a counter-recession measure. A deficit-financed fiscal stimulus can come in the form of either a tax cut, which puts more money in peoples' pockets, or extra government expenditures, especially on projects like highways and bridges that put people to work and advance economic productivity. (Expenditures are thought to be more effective because when people are given a tax cut there is no guarantee that they spend the money.) Of course, Keynesianism also maintains that the government should practice budget discipline when the economy is strong in order to contain government debt and moderate economic expansions. However, Congress's discipline during expansions has not been impressive. On many occasions, it has increased the deficit during an expansion in order to pay for goodies like tax cuts or government programs.

Financing Deficits

To borrow money and finance deficits, the Treasury Department sells various types of bonds, which pay interest, and which are known colloquially as Treasuries.[7] Treasuries are purchased and held by institutions all over the world. They are widely held because the dollar is the de facto reserve currency for international transactions and because Treasuries are deemed to be a safe investment – safer than other types of investments, including the debts of other governments.[8] US debt has been viewed as a safe investment because the nation's economy is large and strong and because the government has always paid its debts. A consequence of the high demand for Treasuries is that the government can issue them with low interest rates. That is, the United States borrows money cheaply.

Debt

Persistent deficits have caused the United States to accumulate a large debt, currently $21 trillion, which translates into about $65,600 for each of country's 320 million residents. As Figure 2.3 shows, the debt is about 105 percent of GDP, which is high by historical standards. However, it is not unprecedented – the debt was higher at the conclusion of World War II. The nation's debt burden (relative to GDP) fell through the 1950s, 1960s, and

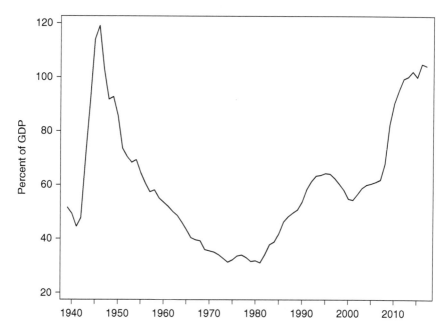

Figure 2.3 Federal debt as a percent of GDP, 1939–2017.

Source: Federal Reserve Bank of St. Louis.

1970s, even though the government ran many deficits during that time. That occurred because the economy grew faster than the government accumulated debt. By contrast, since about 1980, the government has accumulated debt faster than the economy has grown.

The difficulty of servicing or reducing the debt depends upon future fiscal decisions and rates of economic growth. Most people agree that fiscal adjustments are necessary and that future growth rates cannot be counted on to reduce the current debt burden. Of course, opinion varies on what to do. Some people prefer spending cuts to tax hikes; other people prefer the opposite.

The United States is not alone in accumulating debt in recent decades – most other developed countries have done the same. The debt burdens of the United Kingdom and France are also about 100 percent of GDP. Japan's debt load is much heavier, hovering around 200 percent of GDP. Germany's is lighter, near 50 percent of GDP.

Total Debt vs. Public Debt

Of the many institutions that own the debt, the largest is the government itself. In particular, the Federal Reserve and the Social Security Trust Funds hold large amounts of Treasuries. In 2015, Federal Reserve holdings came to about $2.5 trillion of regular Treasury bonds, and the Social Security Trust Funds holdings were about $3 trillion in special issue bonds.

The Fed's holdings skyrocketed in the wake of the 2008–2009 recession as the bank purchased about $2 trillion in Treasuries. As explained in the next chapter, the Federal Reserve purchases Treasuries to lower interest rates and boost the economy.

Social Security – the government's pension and disability program – collects taxes from wage earners and pays pensions to retired persons who previously paid into the program. To date, the program has raised more money than it has paid out, thus accumulating trust funds. Congress has required that those funds be invested in non-marketable, special issue Treasuries. In other words, the trust funds hold no cash – those monies are all given to the government in exchange for unmarketable IOUs. So, the government "owes" the Social Security funds.

The *public debt* (or "debt held by the public") is the portion of the *total debt* that the government owes to entities other than itself. The public debt is about 30 percent smaller than the total debt and amounts to about 70 percent of GDP. The owners of the public debt include domestic and foreign banks, investors, and governments. The largest foreign holder of Treasuries is China. In 2015, its holdings were $1.3 trillion.

The public debt represents promises to institutions and governments that have made loans to the United States. Similarly, the debt owed to Social Security represents promises that the government has made to American taxpayers. And the debt owed to the Federal Reserve has already been paid for in the form of *inflation*, which is an increase in the price level and corresponding decrease in the value of the dollar.[9] That occurs because the Federal Reserve purchases Treasuries by "printing money," which causes the dollar to lose purchasing power.

The Debt Ceiling

Congress has long had in place a *debt ceiling*, which is a legal limit on the government's debt.[10] In so far as it is intended to actually limit the debt, the ceiling has proved feeble. Every time that the limit has been reached, Congress has revised it upwards. That does not mean that the limit has done nothing to slow debt growth, but it certainly has not halted it.

Of course, Congress controls both the deficit and the debt ceiling. In effect, whenever the ceiling is reached, Congress has two opposing policies in effect: one is a mix of tax-and-spend policies that requires additional debt and the other is the ceiling that says that the government cannot go further into debt. If upon reaching the ceiling Congress were to abide by it (rather than raise it), the Treasury Department would be required to halt payments on government obligations. That could mean no Social Security checks to seniors or no wages to government employees or no payments to businesses that are owed government money. Or, the Treasury Department could default on debt payments (i.e., interest and principal payments on Treasuries). A default on the debt would likely change investors' feelings regarding US debt. In particular, the market would demand higher interest rates, so the government would have to pay more money to maintain the debt and run deficits. It would also send shock waves through the global economy, because Treasuries are so widely held and traded.

Taxes

The government's three main sources of revenues are: (1) income taxes on individuals, which includes taxes on wages and taxes on capital gains (e.g., investments), (2) income taxes on corporations, and (3) payroll taxes, which are taxes on employees and employers to fund social insurance programs, chiefly Medicare and Social Security. In 2014, 46 percent of federal revenues were from individual income taxes; 34 percent were from payroll taxes; and 11 percent were from corporate income taxes. Miscellaneous sources provided the rest.[11]

Relative to GDP, federal revenues have not changed much since World War II. They have hovered around 17 percent to 18 percent of GDP, ticking somewhat higher during expansions and dropping during recessions. However, the composition of revenues has changed (see Figure 2.4). In particular, payroll taxes grew from about 3 percent of GDP in 1960 to about

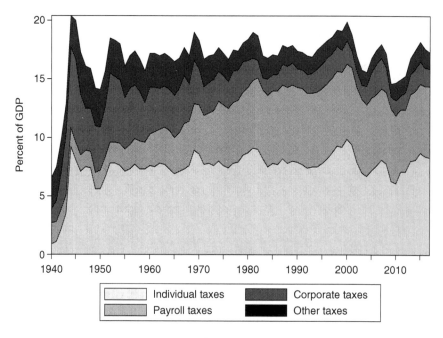

Figure 2.4 Tax sources as a percent of GDP, 1940–2017.

Source: Office of Management and Budget, Historical Tables: Table 2.3.

8 percent of GDP by 2010. Meanwhile, corporate income taxes shrank from about 5 percent to nearly 1 percent of GDP. Also, state and local taxes have roughly doubled since the 1950s, now accounting for about 15 percent of GDP. That change mirrors the growth in government over the same period, most of which has been at the state level.

Income Taxes on Individuals

Federal income tax rates on individuals are progressive: households with lower incomes are taxed at a lower rate than households with higher incomes. To illustrate, Table 2.1 lists the 2014 marginal tax rates on wage income for a married couple filing jointly. Under those rates, a couple with $50,000 in taxable income[12] would pay 10 percent of $18,150 and 15 percent on its remaining $31,850 in taxable income. So, their total tax would have been $6,592.50, or an effective tax rate of 13.185 percent on $50,000 in taxable income. The difference between a *marginal tax rate* and the *effective tax rate* is apparent: the former is a tax rate within a particular tax bracket, whereas the latter is the overall tax rate on a filer's taxable income.

Now consider the tax on a couple who reported $200,000 in taxable income, an amount which puts them in the fourth tax bracket. They, too, would pay 10 percent on $18,150; and they would pay 15 percent on $55,650 (their income in the second bracket, between the $18,150 and $73,800), 25 percent on $75,050 (third bracket), and 28 percent on $51,150 (the amount by which their income exceeded $148,850, where the fourth bracket starts). So, their total tax is $43,246.80, and their effective tax rate is 21.6 percent.

These examples illustrate the progressive nature of the income tax, but the tax code includes many other elements that influence effective income tax rates. In particular, there are tax breaks and credits for all manner of things, from education expenses to mortgage interest, all of which alter effective tax rates and some of which undermine progressivity because they disproportionally benefit middle-income or upper-income households.

Table 2.1 Marginal tax rates on wage income for a married couple filing jointly, 2014

Tax rate	On taxable income
10%	$0–$18,150
15%	$18,150–$73,800
25%	$73,800–$148,850
28%	$148,850–$226,850
33%	$226,850–$405,100
35%	$405,100–$457,600
39.6%	Over $457,600

Source: Internal Revenue Service.

Additionally, capital gains (e.g., income from the sale of an asset or investment) are taxed differently than wages. Specifically, most capital gains are taxed at 15 percent. One consequence is that someone who makes most or all of their income from capital gains can pay less tax than someone who makes their income from wages.[13] That is controversial because large capital gains are realized mostly by wealthy people, which means that the tax system taxes many wealthy households less than it does middle-income households.[14]

For those reasons, the average effective tax paid by individuals in the top 20 percent of the nation's income distribution in 2016 (all of whom had at least $147,700 in income) was 15.7 percent, which was considerably less than what was implied by the income tax rate alone. Meanwhile, the average effective income tax paid by middle-income-quintile Americans (incomes between $47,700 and $60,000) was 3.5 percent, and the similar figure for bottom-income-quintile Americans, who had incomes less than $24,600, was –4.8 percent. In other words, the income tax system is designed such that the nation's lowest-earning households receive money from (rather than pay tax to) the government when they file their income tax returns.[15]

Yet, that still does not provide a complete picture of the tax code as it applies to individuals. There are several other taxes on individuals, the most notable of which are the payroll taxes for Medicare and Social Security. The Medicare tax is mildly progressive, and the Social Security tax is mildly regressive. So, when those two taxes are factored in, the tax code is less progressive than implied by the income tax. (The Medicare tax is 2.9 percent of employees' earnings, half of which is paid by employers. So, each employee pays a tax of 1.45 percent, unless his or her income is over $200,000 (or $250,000 for a couple), in which case the rate is 2.35 percent. The tax for Social Security is 3.6 percent of income up to $117,000, after which there is no additional tax. Employers pay another 3.6 percent on employee income up to the same limit.)

And for a full picture of taxes on individuals and households we must factor in state and local taxes. State and local governments rely heavily on sales taxes, which are regressive because the poor spend a larger portion of their income on consumption, including food and housing. Thus, state and local taxes generally make the overall system of taxation in the United States less progressive than what is implied by the federal income tax on wages.[16]

Two final things to note about the income tax are the following. First, the rates reported in Table 2.1 are low compared those of several decades ago. In the 1950s, for example, the top marginal income tax rate exceeded 90 percent, and it was 70 percent or more throughout the 1960s and 1970s.[17] Second, the rates in Table 2.1 are no longer in effect. They were lowered and made less progressive by a tax reform in 2017 (see Chapter 8).

Corporate Taxes

We already noted that corporate taxes fell relative to GDP over the second half of the twentieth century. Here, we will add only that a 2017 tax reform thoroughly overhauled the corporate tax system, switching it from a progressive tax with a top marginal rate of 35 percent to a 21 percent flat tax, a move that is expected to decrease the government's revenues. It is also worth noting that the pre-reform tax rates were high relative to other countries, which led some firms to relocate to other countries or declare their profits in other countries. One goal of the 2017 reform was to reverse those trends.

Tax Breaks and Tax Expenditures

The federal tax code includes myriad tax credits, exemptions, and deductions on various types of income for various types of filers. Many of those tax breaks are constructed to benefit narrow groups of individuals or companies. For example, the tax code includes (or has recently included) tax breaks to benefit NASCAR racetrack owners, fishing companies, energy companies, rum producers, tobacco producers, film production companies, and importers of Chinese ceiling fans.[18] All told, a rough estimate of the costs of all such specialized tax breaks is in the "tens of billions of dollars."[19]

The complexity of the tax code also stems from a variety of more general-interest tax breaks. For example, the code as of 2008 contained "at least 11 incentives to encourage taxpayers to save for and spend on education," and each of those provisions had different "eligibility requirements, definitions of common terms, income-level thresholds, phase-out ranges, and inflation adjustments ... "[20]

The largest tax breaks are often called *tax expenditures*, and they function like social programs because they affect broad classes of citizens and are designed to promote certain types of activities or to provide relief to certain types of taxpayers. The largest tax expenditure by cost is the tax exclusion for employer-subsidized health insurance, which is estimated to have reduced government finances by about $250 billion in 2013 (see Table 2.2).

The tax deduction for mortgage interest provides a tax break to homeowners with mortgage debt. It is effectively a subsidy for homeowners that is not available to renters. Because the deduction is for interest payments, it is tied to home prices, and thus it primarily benefits middle-income and upper-income households. The deduction costs the government about $70 billion a year, which, depending on the year, is similar to or considerably larger than the government's expenditures on food stamps for the poor.[21] Of course, those middle-income and upper-income homeowners are still likely to pay more taxes than food stamp recipients because of the progressive nature of the income tax. But the comparison is still instructive.

Table 2.2 Selected tax expenditures, description, and cost in 2013

Tax expenditure	Estimated foregone revenues (2013) (billions)
Employer-sponsored health insurance. This tax exclusion allows employers to count only wages, and not health insurance, as part of their labor costs for payroll taxes. Employees also do not have to pay income taxes on "income" received in the form of employer-sponsored health insurance. This tax exclusion is credited with increasing the number of employers that subsidize health insurance for their employees.	$248
Pension contributions and earnings. Net pension earnings and contributions may be treated as tax-free income, and so may be employers' contributions to employee pensions.	$137
Mortgage interest deduction. Homeowners can deduct their mortgage interest payments from their taxable income. The deduction may encourage home ownership over renting. The deduction primarily helps upper-income mortgage holders more than lower-income mortgage-holders since the latter often claim the "standard deduction" when filing their taxes, in which case the mortgage interest deduction provides no benefit.	$70
Earned-Income Tax Credit (EITC). The EITC tax credit is for employed, low-income individuals and families. The tax credit is refundable, which means that households with very low incomes may pay negative income taxes. The EITC aims to alleviate poverty while encouraging work. It is meant to discourage low-income people from dropping out of the workforce and living entirely on government assistance.	$61
Child tax credit (CTC). The CTC is a nonrefundable credit that reduces a household's tax bill. The credit is $1,000 per qualifying child under the age of seventeen, and it phases out for households with income above $110,000, with households that make above $150,000 receiving no credit.	$57

Source: budgetary figures from Congressional Budget Office (2013).

Of all the tax expenditures listed in Table 2.2, the only one that benefits the poor more than upper-income taxpayers is the Earned Income Tax Credit (EITC), which is itself the most expensive of all of the government's anti-poverty programs.[22] The EITC is also the main reason why low-income households pay negative income tax.

Of course, each tax expenditure could be restructured as a social program that is funded from the expenditure side of the budget. For instance, in place of a tax deduction for mortgage interest, Congress could direct the Treasury Department to send a check to households that pay mortgage interest. Congress's use of the tax code may be given an administrative rationale – the tax code already contains a large number of credits and deductions and an agency to oversee them (the Internal Revenue Service – IRS), so additional credits are not that expensive or difficult to administer. It may also have a political rationale – it is easier for Congress to create "programs" via tax credits and much more difficult to create new programs on the expenditure side of the budget. To see why, just imagine which the public would find more objectionable: (a) the government agency that cuts checks to people with mortgages, but not other people, or (b) the IRS including in its individual tax forms a line by which homeowners can subtract their mortgage interest from their taxable income.

Spending

There are three big items on the expenditure side of the government's budget: defense, health care programs, and Social Security. In 2016, those three categories combined for over $2.6 trillion and 66 percent of all outlays (see Table 2.3). The next largest category is a collection of safety-net programs, including unemployment compensation, food assistance, and housing assistance.[23] None of those programs is very large by itself. None costs half as much as annual interest payments on the debt, which cost $240 billion

Table 2.3 Federal budget outlays and composition, 2016

Program or Category	Expenditures (billions)	Percent of total*
Health care programs (Medicare, Medicaid, other health care)	$1,106	28%
Social Security	$916	23%
National defense	$593	15%
Income security / safety-net programs (including unemployment insurance, food stamps, cash welfare payments, and housing assistance)	$514	13%
Interest payments on debt (net of interest received)	$240	6.0%
Veterans' benefits	$175	4.4%
Education, training, and social services	$110	2.8%
Transportation	$93	2.3%
Administration of justice (federal courts and law enforcement)	$56	1.4%
International affairs (including foreign aid)	$45	1.1%
Everything else (energy, agriculture, natural resources, scientific research, etc.)	$134	3.3%

Source: Office of Management and Budget, historical tables: Table 3.2.

*Does not total 100% because of rounding.

a year – at least 6 percent of the budget. Items like education, energy, veterans' benefits, foreign aid, the justice system, and transportation infrastructure are smaller still.

Health Care Programs

On the tax side of the budget, the federal government has two health care "programs." One is the tax exemption for employer-subsidized health insurance. The other is the Obamacare tax credit for private insurance that is purchased on the individual market. On the spending side of the budget, the federal government has three main health care programs: Medicare for seniors, Medicaid/Children's Health Insurance Program (CHIP) for low-income families and children, and the Veterans' Health Administration (VHA) for veterans.[24]

The VHA differs from Medicare and Medicaid in that it is a government-run health care system – i.e., the doctors and care providers are government employees who work in government facilities. By contrast, Medicare and Medicaid are systems of government-financed care that is provided privately by for-profit or non-profit health care providers.

Medicare provides health care to nearly all Americans over the age of 65.[25] It also provides benefits to some disabled persons under 65. Medicare is partially (40 percent) funded by a payroll tax; the remaining 60 percent of costs is paid by general government revenues, by patient premiums and copays, and by other funds. As noted above, the payroll tax is 2.9 percent of employee earnings, half of which is paid by the employer with the other half coming out of employees' wages. The tax is flat except for a tax surcharge on households with incomes over $200,000 (individuals) or $250,000 (couples): they pay an extra 0.9 percent of income (i.e., 2.35 percent instead of 1.45 percent). In practice, Medicare has redistributed wealth from the young to the old because seniors have received more in benefits than they paid in taxes.[26]

Medicaid varies from state to state because it is administered by state governments. CMS oversees Medicaid programs, but states have wide discretion to determine eligibility, costs, and payments. The federal government shares the costs with the states via a matching grant: for each $1 a state spends on its Medicaid program the federal government will match that spending by at least $1. (In lower-income states, the federal government pays more, up to $3 per $1.) Medicaid expenditures increase during recessions because more people meet the eligibility requirements when unemployment is high.

CHIP was created in 1997 to provide health care to children and pregnant women in households whose incomes are modest but too high to qualify for Medicaid. The program is funded by a block grant (i.e., a lump sum in the discretionary budget); however, the federal government provides matching funds to states for enrolling and covering eligible persons. When created,

Table 2.4 Federal health care programs and expenditures, 2016

Program	Population (millions)	Federal expenditures (billions)
Tax exemption for employer-subsidized health insurance	155	$266
Tax subsidies for exchange-purchased health plans	10	$32
Medicare	57	$592 (net of offsetting receipts)
Medicaid / CHIP	68	$360 (excludes expenditures by state governments)
Veterans' Health Administration (VHA)	9*	$70

Sources: Congressional Budget Office (2016). Centers for Medicare and Medicaid Services (2016). Veterans' Health Administration (2016). Bagalman (2014).

*2014.

CHIP was authorized for a ten-year period, in accordance with budget rules at the time. It was reauthorized in 2007, 2009, 2013, and 2015, with Congress introducing various revisions along the way.

Combined, the government's five major health care "programs" – summarized in Table 2.4 – form the core of all health insurance coverage in the United States, which in 2016 covered 92 percent of citizens and legal residents. The remaining 8 percent were uninsured.

The Issue of Costs

Public sector and private sector spending on health care grew rapidly over the past half century. In part, that growth was driven by medical advances that came to market and enabled heart surgeries, knee replacements, cancer treatments, and much more. The growth was also due to consumption, much of which was related to lengthening lifespans and the aging of the population. Those trends continue, and so the budgetary pressure on the public health care systems continues to mount.

Another reason for fast-rising expenditures on health care has been wasteful inefficiencies in each of the health care systems. For example, one estimate suggests that the government loses $100 billion a year to people who defraud the government's health care systems.[27] The inefficiencies in the private marketplace may be more costly than that. Two facets of the system – the fact that consumers are insulated from costs because they are borne by insurance companies, and the market leverage that providers have over insurance companies – combine to allow health care providers to charge incredible sums for their services. Outrageous costs abound, one example being the hospital that charges insurance companies $18 per dose of aspirin.[28] The private marketplace is also characterized by high administrative costs, as insurance companies spend enormous resources haggling with customers and providers. The public systems have proved more efficient on account of lower administrative costs and the ability to exert more cost pressure on providers.[29]

Those inefficiencies are a good part of the reason why the United States spends an outsized proportion of its national income on health care. In 2015, the figure was 17.8 percent of GDP, an amount that far surpassed what countries like the United Kingdom, France, and Canada spent on health care.[30] The inefficiencies are also part of the reason for skyrocketing insurance costs. In 2015, the average annual premium for employer-subsidized insurance surpassed $17,000 per family – a huge cost for employers and employees to share. And copays and deductibles increased the cost further.[31]

In 2016, the government took a modest step to control public health care costs with trial programs that would to shift Medicare from a fee-for-service model, in which the government pays health care providers for each service they provide, to a fee-for-outcome model, in which the government pays health care providers for outcomes (e.g., healthy patients). A similar push was underway in some parts of the private marketplace, with the hope that it would make providers more mindful of costs and the number of tests and procedures that they recommend.

A Brief History of the Health Care Systems

Table 2.2 noted that the tax expenditure for employer-subsidized health care is partially responsible for the prevalence of employer-subsidized health insurance in the United States. The tax expenditure is also part of the reason why the United States has such a complex patchwork of federal health care programs rather than a single, coherent system that provides universal coverage.[32]

The tax expenditure emerged rather by accident – as a tax loophole – during World War II, when the government instituted a freeze on wages and prices. The government's edict did not clarify whether it applied to fringe benefits like health insurance, which were then very uncommon. Perhaps without considering the consequences of its decision, the War Labor Board ruled that the freeze did not apply to fringe benefits.[33] Although the decision was not very consequential at the time, it became so later. More and more employers started providing health coverage to its high-skilled, managerial, and unionized employees. Other segments of the population – particularly seniors and people with low-wage or non-union jobs – remained uninsured. And their lack of coverage became more financially threatening as health care became more expensive.

Reformers who pushed the idea of a universal health care system faced opposition not only from conservatives but also from unions and other wage-earners who already enjoyed health insurance.[34] Such groups had little reason to embrace a new health care system, and many were worried that their coverage would be more modest if their private, employer-sponsored plans were replaced by a government plan.[35] In the face of that opposition, Lyndon Johnson's push for broader coverage only succeeded in creating a health care plan for seniors (Medicare) and a system for the poor (Medicaid).[36]

Three decades later, the Clinton White House made a push to establish a universal health care system to provide insurance coverage to the considerable slice of the population that still lacked it and to ensure that covered employees did not lose insurance if they lost their jobs. . The Clintons' proposal was somewhat similar to the ACA of 2010 in that it mandated health insurance and provided subsidies to individuals who could not afford the full sticker price of an insurance plan. But it also gave the government considerable powers to contain health care prices, including regulatory powers over the prices of insurance plans and regarding the compensation to doctors for health care services. The plan drew strong opposition from those interests, and it was defeated.

A few years later, a divided government created CHIP to provide care for children and pregnant women who did qualify for Medicaid. As noted above, CHIP was created as a block grant, and it has been reauthorized several times since the first grant ended in 2007. At that time, more than seven million children were enrolled in CHIP.[37]

In 2003, Republicans passed the Medicare Modernization Act (MMA), which added a prescription-drug benefit to Medicare in order to help seniors defray the fast-rising cost of prescription drugs. Like CHIP, Medicaid, and the rest of Medicare, the new program shifted costs to taxpayers and did little to address health care costs. In fact, the MMA included a provision that safeguarded pharmaceutical companies' profits by forbidding the government from using its large-buyer power to demand low, wholesale prices.[38]

The next major health care overhaul came seven years later. As noted already, the Affordable Care Act (ACA or Obamacare) of 2010 mostly ignored the problem of health care costs and focused instead of covering the uninsured. Again, the law's main elements included a Medicaid expansion, an employer mandate, and the three-legged-stool system to expand the individual market. It also established insurance "exchanges." These are websites, managed either by the federal government or a state government, where individuals can compare and purchase private insurance plans. As individuals shop on the exchanges, governments identify people who qualify for subsidies.

Immediately after Obamacare became law, the Supreme Court ruled against one of its Medicaid-expanding provisions. The ACA had two provisions to induce states to expand their Medicaid rolls: a carrot and a stick. The carrot was that the federal government would cover 100 percent of the cost of expansion for the first two years, after which its contribution would fall to 90 percent. The stick was that the federal government would have the power to withhold all Medicaid funds from states that chose *not* to pursue the Medicaid expansion. In 2012, the Supreme Court ruled that the government could not penalize states in that way.[39] As a result, states could choose not to expand their programs without penalty, and many Republican-controlled states that were publicly opposed to Obamacare chose to pass on the Medicaid expansion. The ACA's insurance coverage expansion was thus less than intended, but it still lowered the uninsured rate for adults between the ages of 18 and 64 from 22.3 percent to 11.9 percent.[40]

Since 2010, health care costs and premiums have continued to increase, including those sold on the Obamacare exchanges. In addition, many localities were underserved on the Obamacare exchanges, which meant that they lacked coverage options and faced especially high costs. In 2017, a unified Republican government failed in its attempt to repeal Obamacare, but it did repeal the individual mandate (see Chapter 8). Also, President Trump moved to cut some of the Obamacare subsidies and to loosen some of the regulations the Obama administration had placed on insurance companies in order to implement the ACA. Those moves weakened the law's three-legged-stool system, thus making it likely that the individual market would shrink, and the uninsured rate would rise.

Social Security

Three programs that were collectively called Social Security were created during the Great Depression. Two focused on needy children and the disabled. The third and much larger program, formally called Old Age, Survivors and Disability Insurance (OASDI), was created in order to prevent poverty among the elderly and to safeguard workers against disabilities that could prevent them from working until late in life. All three programs continue to exist in some form, but when people speak of "Social Security," they usually refer only to this pension and disability system (OASDI). This book does similarly.

The disability component of Social Security can be described as an insurance program. People pay taxes and are insured against work-ending disabilities. The much larger pension component of the program can be described as a forced retirement-savings program. The government taxes people in their working years, and upon the age of 67 it starts paying them a monthly pension, which they receive for the rest of their lives.[41] Each person's pension is proportional to his or her lifetime FICA tax payments. However, the system is also progressive, providing a larger pension-to-tax amount for those who "contributed" less during their lifetimes, and that is because its primary goal is to keep seniors out of poverty. The FICA tax – a payroll tax paid by employees for Social Security – is a flat 6.2 percent tax on wage income up to an inflation-adjusted wage base, after which there is no additional tax. In 2014, the wage base was $117,000.

The pension system can alternatively be described as a transfer from workers to seniors. Although the Social Security Administration tracks how much people pay in FICA taxes over their lifetimes, it does not have millions of over-stuffed safe-deposit boxes for the country's future seniors. Instead, FICA revenues become part of the government's general revenues. To date, the government has paid out less in Social Security's benefits than it has collected in FICA taxes. However, demographic projections suggest that that will reverse over the next couple of decades. Thus, if the government wants to maintain the balance between Social Security expenditures and FICA revenues, it can do something like increase the FICA tax rate or raise the age at which people can start receiving the pension.

In 2012, the government spent $773 billion to provide Social Security benefits to 59 million people.[42] The average monthly pension was $1,294, a figure that was not much higher than the federal poverty line.[43]

Other Welfare Programs

To this point, we have noted nine major social programs: five related to health care (two of which are tax expenditures), four other major tax expenditures (including the EITC), and Social Security. This section briefly explains six other safety-net programs of note.

Supplemental Security Income

SSI is one of the three Social Security programs created during the Great Depression. It provides modest monthly cash assistance to people who are both very poor and disabled, blind, or elderly. In 2012, about eight million people received SSI benefits, and the program cost the government $50 billion.[44]

Temporary Assistance to Needy Families (TANF)

The third Social Security program was called Aid to Dependent Children (ADC). It was created to help state governments provide financial assistance to "needy children who had been deprived of parental support or care because their father or mother was absent from the home, incapacitated, deceased, or unemployed."[45] States structured and administered their own versions of the program under federal guidelines, and the federal government provided a matching grant to states to share the financial burden. From its creation until 1996, federal matching outlays tended to increase during recessions when more people would require financial assistance.

In 1996, the program was fundamentally restructured and renamed Temporary Assistance to Needy Families (TANF). The programs still provide cash and other benefits, like child care financing, to poor families with children, and they are still means-tested, which means that eligibility depends on having a sufficiently low income. The programs also remain structured and administered by state governments, but the 1996 restructuring changed two key aspects. First, they were redesigned to provide only temporary assistance. Federal rules now prevent families from receiving TANF benefits for more than sixty months during their lifetimes, though there can be some exceptions to this rule. Rules also require beneficiaries to spend time looking for a job. TANF programs also can (and do) spend money on job-training activities and on programs that are meant to discourage out-of-wedlock pregnancies. Second, federal funding was switched from a matching grant to a block grant. Furthermore, since 1996 outlays have stayed constant at $16.5 billion, failing to increase during recessions and declining in value over time due to inflation. State funds for TANF programs summed to about $15 billion in 2013.[46]

In 2014, the average TANF program provided about $428 in monthly cash assistance to a family of three with no income – an amount equivalent to about a quarter of the federal poverty level. TANF recipients may also draw on other types of support, like food stamps.[47]

Supplemental Nutrition Assistance Program (SNAP)

The food stamp program, SNAP, is a means-tested program run by the Department of Agriculture that provides food assistance to low-income households.[48] The assistance increases with family size and decreases with household income. Most adults without children are limited in the number of months during which they can receive food stamps.

Although SNAP spending is mandatory, the program is subject to periodic reauthorizations by Congress. Specifically, SNAP is usually reauthorized by Congress in a five-year Farm Bill that also includes a host of agricultural policies, including crop subsidies and insurance for farmers.

In 2015, SNAP spending was $74 billion.[49] In the average month of that year, almost 46 million Americans received food stamps – nearly 15 percent of the population.[50] The average amount of monthly food assistance given to a family of three was $378, and the maximum amount allowed under the law was $511 (or $170 per person).[51]

Housing Assistance

Within the discretionary budget are several means-tested programs to help low-income people afford housing, including a voucher program to subsidize rent in private units, a program that subsidizes apartments in privately owned housing developments, and a fund to support public housing developments. Overall, federal rental assistance helps some ten million low-income people afford housing.

Unemployment Insurance (UI)

UI systems are run at the state level, and they are mostly funded by states, although there is some federal funding for the programs, and there is a federal UI payroll tax that is paid wholly by employers. UI programs provide cash to workers who have been laid off. To receive benefits, recipients must actively look for new employment. In most states, benefits are available to individuals for up to six months. The size of the monthly benefit varies with prior income and household size, but it is capped at a modest amount.

Federal UI expenditures averaged $33 billion per year in the years leading up to the Great Recession, when they increased fivefold, to $155 billion in 2010.[52] Of course, part of that increase was because unemployment spiked during the recession. However, it was also because the federal government passed a temporary expansion of states' programs so that people could draw UI benefits for a longer period of time.

Defense

Most of the base budget for national defense consists of: (a) pay and benefits for active duty officers and enlisted members of the armed forces, (b) operation and maintenance, including salaries for civilian members of the armed forces, (c) procurement of weapons and equipment, and (d) technological research and development. The remainder is spent on construction, family housing, and other items. Some defense-related items are not included in the budget for the Department of Defense (DOD). For example, nuclear weapons and naval nuclear reactors are funded by the Department of Energy.[53]

None of the DOD's base funds are for war operations. Rather, they are to have the military prepared and ready in case war should arise. To fund war and other foreign operations, Congress provides additional funds in the form of an Overseas Contingency Operations (OCO) fund. Each year, between 2003 and 2012, the fund received an amount in excess of $100 billion to fund the war efforts in Iraq and Afghanistan.[54] More recently, Congress has included some non-operational items in the OCO fund in order to get around its self-imposed limits on the DoD budget.

Congress's appropriations for DOD are largely based on recommendations and requests from the Pentagon; and Congress and the Pentagon put defense strategies front-and-center in the budget. However, the budget also reflects the particularistic nature of Congress. Members of Congress like to see expenditures for bases and contractors in their districts, and sometimes Congress funds procurements that the DOD does not request.[55]

Everything Else

We have not reviewed the budgets of most cabinet-level departments, including Energy, Education, Agriculture, Transportation, Treasury, Commerce, Labor, State, Justice, Interior, Veterans Affairs, and Homeland Security. Those departments run an untold number of programs and agencies, including everything from the Forest Service and foreign aid to Amtrak and the arts. However, all of those programs are dwarfed by the items we have discussed, so we will move on to regulations.

First, however, a few words about pork. Typically, Congress allows its members to earmark funds for projects and initiatives in their districts; often they are infrastructure projects or grants for research centers or historical institutions.[56] These pork-barrel[57] projects get singled out for attention because they symbolize to many the idea that politicians waste tax dollars on unnecessary items for their own electoral benefit. That characterization is not inaccurate, but three considerations put the issue in proper perspective. First, the cost is not as large. Indeed, according to the conservative group Citizens Against Government Waste (2016), pork spending peaked at $28 billion in 2006, which was only 1 percent of the budget. Moreover, the charge of economic inefficiency can be leveled at other programs, too. Indeed, pork spending is small relative to fraud and inefficiencies in the health care systems. Second, pork projects are meant to return tax dollars to districts for projects that are usually meant to be "visible," in contrast to policies like tax breaks for special interests. And, third, pork can serve a useful purpose in the legislative process. Specifically, it can facilitate the passage of general-interest legislation by encouraging members of Congress to take electoral risks they otherwise might not.

Regulation

Hundreds of federal agencies regulate nearly every sector of the economy. Some sectors, like energy and commercial aviation, are heavily regulated. The "regulatory state" that exists today was built over time. One notable period of regulatory expansionism was the Progressive Era (early twentieth century), when the government first imposed a minimum wage, a forty-hour work week, prohibitions on child labor, and many other economic regulations. The Great Depression was another notable period of expansionism, most notably regarding banking. The 1970s was a third major era of regulatory expansionism. During the early part of the decade, laws such as the Clean Air Act Amendments (1970), Occupational Safety and Health Act (1970), Endangered Species Act (1973), and Education for All Handicapped Children Act (1975) greatly expanded the government's regulation of economic activities.

Regulations have social and economic costs as well as benefits; and they have distributive consequences. For example, minimum-wage hikes help low-wage workers, but they increase the costs of all goods and services that are produced with low-wage work. Likewise, EPA regulations to cut air pollution trade short-run costs for long-run benefits, and they favor cleaner energy sectors (e.g., wind, solar, natural gas) over dirtier energy sectors (e.g., coal). Similarly, rules that require new pharmaceutical drugs to go through a rigorous testing process before they are marketable protect consumers, but they raise the price of drugs as well as deny treatments to individuals while the testing period is on-going.

In at least some shape or form, regulations begin in Congress, since the legislature specifies regulatory agencies' goals and powers. However, agencies specify the details of regulations, and they have some ability to influence how strictly they are enforced. Industries and interest groups lobby policymakers – in both agencies and Congress – in order to influence regulations, and policymakers actively seek their input, in part to regulate in a way that is effective and sensible. Also, when agencies draft new regulations, they usually must do so via a process that is open to public examination and comment. That checks against ill-advised or very unpopular regulations, and it allows information about draft regulations to be brought to Congress's attention. When agencies consider regulatory changes, they usually must estimate the costs and benefits and publish those estimates along with draft regulations in the *Federal Register*.

Regulators in the Executive Branch

Many regulatory bodies are part of the executive branch, which means that they are directed by the president. The president can influence their actions, goals, and priorities to the extent allowed by law. Regulatory agencies in the executive branch include the Environmental Protection Agency (EPA), the Federal Aviation Administration (FAA), and the following:

- Federal Transit Administration (FTA), an agency of the Department of Transportation that regulates public transportation systems.
- Food and Drug Administration (FDA), an agency of the Department of Health and Human Services that regulates foods, food production, and drugs.
- Occupational Health and Safety Administration (OSHA), an agency of the Department of Labor that regulates businesses to ensure that they engage in workplace practices that do not endanger the health and safety of workers.
- The Bureau of Ocean Energy Management (BOEM) and the Bureau of Safety and Environmental Enforcement (BSEE), which are units within the Department of the Interior that are responsible for monitoring offshore oil and gas operations.

In some cases, the implementation and monitoring of regulations are overseen by special entities or courts. Two such examples include:

- The Federal Mine Safety and Health Review Commission, which serves as a special court to review the mining regulations that are created by the Department of Labor.
- The Equal Employment Opportunity Commission (EEOC), which seeks to combat workplace discrimination. It receives and investigates complaints from workers who believe they have been subject to unlawful discrimination.

Independent Regulatory Commissions

Other regulatory agencies are placed outside the executive branch, or they are designed in a way to give them greater independence from elected officials. The Federal Reserve is a prominent example (see Chapter 3). It and other independent commissions are made independent in part by giving their board members terms of at least five years – i.e., longer than the term of the president who nominates them. Other examples of these "independent regulatory commissions" are:

- The Securities and Exchange Commission (SEC), which aims to prevent insider trading and to produce transparent, well-functioning trading exchanges for stocks and bonds.
- The Federal Deposit Insurance Corporation (FDIC), which regulates retail banks and provides insurance on depositors' money (up to $250,000).
- The Commodity Futures and Trading Commission (CFTC), which regulates the trading of various commodities (oil, gas, corn, cotton, copper, gold, etc.).
- The Federal Communications Commission (FCC), which regulates television, radio, broadband, and more.
- The Federal Trade Commission (FTC), which aims to protect consumers from deceptive and fraudulent practices by businesses.
- The Consumer Product Safety Commission (CPSC), which regulates a variety of consumer products, from infant car seats and automobiles to swimming pools and carbon monoxide detectors.
- The Consumer Finance Protection Bureau (CFPB), created in 2010, which aims to assist and protect consumers with financial products, including credit cards and mortgages.

Conclusion

This chapter provided a cursory review of the government's budget, tax code, and regulatory agencies. Six key points can be reemphasized.

1 The budget deficit is structural and counter-cyclical.
2 The three largest components of the budget are the health care programs, Social Security, and defense. All other items are small by comparison. So, to really reduce the structural deficit, policymakers must cut or reform one or more of those programs; or they must raise taxes.
3 Over the past couple of decades, the cost of the health care programs has risen rapidly – much faster than inflation.
4 The tax system is not just for revenues; it is also used to provide distributive benefits and to pursue policy objectives. Of particular note are the various broad-based tax expenditures that function like social welfare programs. Those tax expenditures modify income tax progressivity.
5 The federal government regulates most sectors of the economy, some heavily.
6 All economic policies have distributional consequences.

The fact that economic policies have distributional consequences immediately raises questions of politics. That is the subject of Chapter 4. First, however, we consider the government's influence on macroeconomic phenomena, like unemployment and economic growth.

Notes

1 Cohen, Martinez, and Zammitti, 2014.
2 OECD, 2016. General government spending (indicator). Retrieved from: doi: 10.1787/a31cbf4d-en (accessed December 5, 2016).
3 The term "entitlement program" is sometimes meant pejoratively, as a means to highlight the notion that social security or social welfare programs create a sense of individual entitlement to government benefits. In this book, the term is used without any normative judgment. Note also that the term entitlement program is almost always used in reference to programs on the expenditure side of the budget, and not tax expenditures like the Child Tax Credit.
4 Since 1921, Congress has mandated that the president prepare a draft budget, a task that is performed by the White House's Office of Management and Budget.
5 During the year, actual expenditures on programs (called outlays) may be smaller than what Congress has appropriated.
6 The official starting and end dates of recessions are determined by the National Bureau of Economic Research.
7 Depending on their date to maturity, different types of Treasuries are referred to as T-bills, T-notes, or T-bonds. The Treasury Department sets a nominal interest rate that it thinks the marketplace will be willing to pay, and it then auctions the bonds. The higher the demand for new bonds, the higher the price they will fetch the Treasury, and thus the lower the real interest rate. For example, say the Treasury offers a $100 ten-year bond with 2% interest. The bond will pay $2 a year for ten years, so if a bank buys the bond at auction for $100, it will receive the nominal (i.e., 2%) interest rate for the bond. If, however, the bank buys the bond for $101, the $2 a year corresponds to a real interest rate of 1.98%. In that case, the bank accepts a lower real interest rate while the US government pays a smaller real interest rate.
8 This remained the case even after the dramatic increase in debt after the recession of 2008–2009.
9 Note that when a Federal Reserve-owned Treasury note matures, the Treasury Department does not pay back the principal. Instead, the bank simply purchases new Treasuries. Thus, Federal Reserve purchases have a permanent effect on the currency. Also, the bank does not retain the interest payments on its Treasuries – it returns them to the Treasury Department. That means that a sizable portion of the US debt is interest free. Again, however, the public still pays for the debt in the form of inflation.
10 For a history of the debt ceiling, see Austin and Levit, 2013.
11 Tax Policy Center, 2017.
12 Taxable income is less than gross income. Two key reasons for that are the "personal exemption" and the "standard deduction," which are flat sums that individuals can deduct from their gross income. In 2014, a married couple filing jointly would be able to deduct two personal exemptions, totaling $7,900, and apply the $12,400 standard deduction. The personal exemption increases tax code progressivity because it exempts more income from lower-income households than from higher-income households. The standard deduction would do similarly, except that higher-income households are more likely to itemize their deductions and deduct more than the standard deduction.

13 See Buffett, 2011 for commentary.

14 Note, however, that the taxation of capital gains presents a number of challenges, including the fact that investors choose when to realize their capital gains. Debates about capital gains taxation also center on saving and investment, which facilitate economic growth. Certainly, a very high rate of capital gains taxation would raise concerns about economic growth. See Bartlett, 2012.

15 Tax Policy Center, 2018.

16 The federal government does not levy a sales tax; although it does levy a tax on cigarettes and a per gallon tax on gasoline. Many countries have national sales taxes, typically in the form of a value-added tax (VAT). Countries with a VAT tend to have more progressive income tax systems than the US in order to compensate for a VAT that is regressive. See Wilensky, 2012.

17 Bartlett, 2012, Appendix II.

18 The Chinese ceiling fans information is from Alexander, Mazza, and Scholz, 2009, p. 401. The information on fishing, alcoholic beverages, and tobacco quota-holders is from Clausing, 2004. The information on rum producers and films shot in the US is from National Public Radio, 2013, January 7.

19 According to Professor Victor Fleisher (National Public Radio, 2013, January 7).

20 Taxpayer Advocate Service, 2008.

21 It is also useful to contrast the "visibility" of these tax expenditures with programs like SNAP and TANF. Whereas the latter are administered by government agencies and their costs are listed in the government's budget, tax expenditures seem somewhat invisible. Voters are less aware of their size and importance, so they focus on them less. Hacker (2002) and Mettler (2011) consider the political implications of the "hidden" welfare state.

22 A study of the distributional effects of tax expenditures is provided by the Congressional Budget Office (2013).

23 In 2007, before the recession, those programs constituted 13.2% of the budget.

24 Other federal health care programs include a system for civilian federal employees and a system within the Department of Defense for active duty and retired military personnel.

25 Medicare contains four main parts, and each is financed differently. Part A covers hospital and hospice care. Part B covers doctor visits and other types of outpatient care. Part C is the Medicare Advantage program through which people can enroll in a private health insurance that includes Part A and Part B benefits, as well as outpatient prescription drugs. Part D is the outpatient prescription drug plan that was added in 2003.

26 See Steuerle and Carasso, 2003.

27 This figure includes the amount of money the government pays to catch fraudsters (*The Economist*, 2014).

28 Examples of such pricing abound. This example is from National Public Radio, 2009. See also Brill, 2015.

29 Regarding Medicaid, the Center on Budget and Policy Priorities (2016a) noted:

> It costs Medicaid substantially less than private insurance to cover people of similar health status. This is due primarily to Medicaid's lower payment rates to providers and lower administrative costs. That is, private insurance is less efficient than Medicaid and it pays doctors and providers more money for the same type of care.

Furthermore, many health care providers refuse to accept Medicaid patients on account of the lower payments they receive in exchange for their services. As a result, it often can be difficult for Medicaid patients to find health care providers.

30 See Reid, 2009 for a comparison of US health care with peer countries. The 17.8% figure is from Centers for Medicaid and Medicare Services, 2015. Congressional

Budget Office, 2007 notes the growth in Medicare and Medicaid spending as a percent of GDP. In 1980, fifteen years after they were created, the programs spent about 1.5% and 1% of GDP. By 2005, each was about 3% of GDP.

31 Kaiser Family Foundation, 2015.

32 Peer countries provide universal coverage in different ways. In the United Kingdom, universal health care is provided by a government department. In Canada, universal health care is financed by taxes but provided by a private marketplace. And in France, universal health care is provided mostly by private insurance companies. See Reid, 2009.

33 The decision was perhaps "the easy way out" because it would have been difficult for the War Labor Board to freeze fringe benefits and because it followed an IRS rule that treated fringe benefits as non-taxable (Helms, 2008, p. 7).

34 Also, when President Truman sought to create a national health insurance system he faced strong opposition from the American Medical Association (Brill, 2015, p. 439).

35 Brill, 2015, pp. 20–23.

36 Johnson's attempt to create a system for both seniors and the poor was blocked by southern senators who did not want to create a generous health care system for blacks. As a result, Medicaid emerged as a separate system that would be managed and partly financed by state governments.

37 Note also that some of the enrollment in CHIP came at the expense of private insurance plans. Perhaps up to 50% of CHIP enrollees had had private insurance (Congressional Budget Office, 2008).

38 Gellad et al. (2008) estimate that the provision costs taxpayers $22 billion annually.

39 *National Federal of Independent Business et al. v. Sebelius* 132 S. Ct. 2566 (2012). The case also upheld the constitutionality of the individual mandate.

40 Garfield and Damico, 2016. About 2.6 million more people would have received insurance if all states pursued the Medicaid expansion (Cohen, Martinez, and Zammitti, 2014).

41 The basic eligibility requirement for the pension is ten years of Federal Insurance Contribution Act (FICA)-tax-paying employment. The pension can be drawn at age 67 (for people born after 1960). For people born before 1938, the "full retirement age" at which one became eligible for pension benefits was 65. For people born between 1938 and 1960, there is a sliding scale making their full retirement age somewhere between 65 and 67.

42 Social Security Administration, 2014.

43 The Center on Budget and Policy Priorities (2014) estimates that the Social Security lifts more than fourteen million seniors out of poverty.

44 Center on Budget and Policy Priorities, 2014.

45 Department of Health and Human Services, 2009. Aid to Dependent Children (ADC) was renamed Aid to Families with Dependent Children (AFDC) in 1962.

46 Congressional Budget Office, 2015.

47 Floyd and Schott, 2014.

48 The nation's first food stamp program was created during the Great Depression, though it ended during World War II. A new food stamp program was created in the 1960s, and the program has seen many reforms and changes since.

49 Department of Agriculture, 2017.

50 Those numbers were down slightly during the post-recession years of 2012–2014, but they were still much larger than the pre-crisis years of 2006–2007. See Congressional Budget Office, 2012c.

51 Center on Budget and Policy Priorities, 2016b.

52 Carrington, 2013.

53 Tyszkiewicz and Daggett, 1998.
54 Davidson and Brooking, 2015.
55 In his 1961 presidential farewell address, President Eisenhower famously warned about the potential for a "military-industrial complex," in which a defense industry exerts too much influence over the government's budget and in which the military, defense contractors, and allies in Congress form a "sub-government" or "iron triangle" that directs policy in a way that may not align with the public interest.
56 In 2011, Congress sharply curtailed members' abilities to earmark funds, and the longstanding practice has yet to be fully reinstated. However, there is also evidence that members of Congress have found work-arounds. See Chapter 7 and Mills, Kalaf-Hughes, and MacDonald, 2016.
57 The term pork-barrel

> came into use as a political term in the post-Civil War era. It comes from the plantation practice of distributing rations of salt pork to slaves from wooden barrels. When used to describe a bill, it implies the legislation is loaded with special projects for Members of Congress to distribute to their constituents back home as an act of largesse, courtesy of the federal taxpayer.
> (Kernell et al., 2018, p. 229)

References

Alexander, Raquel, Stephen W. Mazza, and Susan Scholz. (2009). Measuring rates of return on lobbying expenditures: An empirical case study of tax breaks for multinational corporations. *Journal of Law and Politics*, 25, 401–458.

Austin, D. Andrew, and Mindy R. Levit. (2013). The debt limit: History and recent increases. Washington, DC: Congressional Research Service Report RL31967.

Bagalman, Erin. (2014). The number of veterans that use VA health care services: A fact sheet. Washington, DC: Congressional Research Service Report R43579.

Bartlett, Bruce. (2012). *The benefit and the burden.* New York, NY: Simon & Schuster.

Brill, Steven. (2015). *America's bitter pill: Money, politics, backroom deals, and the fight to fix our broken health care system.* New York, NY: Random House.

Buffett, Warren. (2011, August 14). Stop coddling the super-rich. *The New York Times.*

Carrington, William. (2013). The unemployment insurance system. Congressional Budget Office. [Web log comment]. Retrieved from: www.cbo.gov/publication/44041 (accessed December 18, 2016).

Center on Budget and Policy Priorities. (2014). Introduction to Supplemental Security Income. Retrieved from: www.cbpp.org/cms/index.cfm?fa=view&id=3370 (accessed March 29, 2017).

Center on Budget and Policy Priorities. (2016a). Policy basics: Introduction to Medicaid. Retrieved from: www.cbpp.org/research/health/policy-basics-introduction-to-medicaid (accessed May 22, 2018).

Center on Budget and Policy Priorities. (2016b). Introduction to the Supplemental Nutrition Assistance Program (SNAP). Retrieved from: www.cbpp.org/research/policy-basics-the-supplemental-nutrition-assistance-program-snap (accessed June 28, 2017).

Centers for Medicaid and Medicare Services. (2016). Research, statistics, data & systems. Retrieved from: www.cms.gov/Research-Statistics-Data-and-Systems/Research-Statistics-Data-and-Systems.html (accessed May 22, 2018).

Citizens Against Government Waste. (2016). Pig book and historical trends. Retrieved from: www.cagw.org/reporting/pig-book#historical_trends (accessed October 9, 2017).

Clausing, Kimberly A. (2004). The American Jobs Creation Act of 2004: Creating jobs for accountants and lawyers. *Tax Policy Issues and Opinions*. Vol. 8. Washington, DC: Urban–Brookings Tax Policy Center.

Cohen, Robin A., Michael E. Martinez, and Emily P. Zammitti. (2014). Health insurance coverage. Early release of estimates from the National Health Interview Survey, 2011. Washington, DC: National Center for Health Statistics.

Congressional Budget Office. (2007). The long-term outlook for health care spending. Retrieved from: www.cbo.gov/sites/default/files/110th-congress-2007-2008/reports/11-13-lt-health.pdf (accessed September 9, 2018).

Congressional Budget Office. (2008). Covering uninsured children in the State Children's Health Insurance Program. Testimony of CBO Director Peter R. Orszag Subcommittee on Health Care Committee on Finance of the United States Senate, April 9, 2008.

Congressional Budget Office. (2013). The distribution of major tax expenditures in the individual income tax system. Retrieved from: www.cbo.gov/publication/43768 (accessed September 9, 2018).

Congressional Budget Office. (2015). Temporary assistance for needy families: spending and policy options. Retrieved from: www.cbo.gov/publication/49887 (accessed September 9, 2018).

Congressional Budget Office. (2016). Federal subsidies for health insurance coverage for people under age 65: 2016–2026. Retrieved from: www.cbo.gov/publication/53091 (accessed September 9, 2018).

Davidson, Janine, and Emerson Brooking. (2015, June 16). How the overseas contingency operations fund works – and why Congress wants to make it bigger. [Web log comment]. Retrieved from: http://blogs.cfr.org/davidson/2015/06/16/how-the-overseas-contingency-operations-fund-works-and-why-congress-wants-to-make-it-bigger/ (accessed March 29, 2017).

Department of Agriculture. (2017). Supplemental Nutrition Assistance Program participation and costs. Retrieved from: www.fns.usda.gov/pd/supplemental-nutrition-assistance-program-snap (accessed June 28, 2017).

Department of Health and Human Services. (2009). Aid to Families with Dependent Children (AFDC) and Temporary Assistance for Needy Families (TANF) – overview. Retrieved from: http://aspe.hhs.gov/hsp/abbrev/afdc-tanf.htm (accessed May 22, 2018).

The Economist. (2014, May 31). The $272 billion swindle.

Floyd, Ife, and Liz Schott. (2014). TANF cash benefits have fallen by more than 20 percent in most states and continue to erode. Center on Budget and Policy Priorities. Retrieved from: www.cbpp.org/research/family-income-support/tanf-cash-benefits-have-fallen-by-more-than-20-percent-in-most-states (accessed June 28, 2017).

Garfield, Rachel, and Anthony Damico. (2016). The coverage gap: Uninsured poor adults in states that do not expand Medicaid. *Kaiser Family Foundation*. Retrieved from: www.kff.org/uninsured/issue-brief/the-coverage-gap-uninsured-poor-adults-in-states-that-do-not-expand-medicaid/ (accessed June 28, 2017).

Gellad, Walid F., Sebastian Schneeweiss, Phyllis Brawarsky, Stuart Lipsitz, and Jennifer S. Haas. (2008). What if the federal government negotiated pharmaceutical prices for seniors? An estimate of national savings. *Journal of General Internal Medicine*, 23(9), 1435–1440.

Hacker, Jacob S. (2002). *The divided welfare state: The battle over public and private social benefits in the United States.* Cambridge, UK: Cambridge University Press.

Helms, Robert. (2008). Tax policy and the history of the health insurance industry. In Henry J. Aaron and Leonard E. Burman (Eds.), *Using taxes to reform health insurance: Pitfalls and promises.* (pp. 13–35). Washington, DC: Brookings Institution Press.

Kaiser Family Foundation. (2015). 2015 Employer health benefits survey. Retrieved from: www.kff.org/health-costs/report/2015-employer-health-benefits-survey/ (accessed May 22, 2018).

Kernell, Samuel, Gary C. Jacobson, Thad Kousser, and Lynn Vavreck. (2018). *The logic of American politics* (8th ed.). Washington, DC: CQ Press.

Mettler, Suzanne. (2011). *The submerged state: How invisible government policies undermine American democracy.* Chicago, IL: University of Chicago Press.

Mills, Russell W., Nicole Kalaf-Hughes, and Jason A. MacDonald. (2016). Agency policy preferences: Congressional letter-marking and the allocation of distributive policy benefits. *Journal of Public Policy*, 36(4), 547–571.

National Public Radio. (2009, November 12). $18 for a baby aspirin. Retrieved from: www.npr.org/sections/money/2009/11/18_dollar_asprin.html (accessed June 28, 2017).

National Public Radio. (2013, January 7). Tax breaks extended for special interests. Retrieved from: www.npr.org/2013/01/07/168771104/tax-breaks-extended-for-special-interest (accessed May 22, 2018).

OECD. (2016). General government spending (indicator). Retrieved from: doi: 10.1787/a31cbf4d-en (accessed December 5, 2016).

Reid, T. R. (2009). *The healing of America: A global quest for better, cheaper, and fairer health care.* New York, NY: Penguin.

Social Security Administration. (2014). Basic facts. Retrieved from: www.ssa.gov/news/press/basicfact.html (accessed March 29, 2017).

Steuerle, Eugene and Adam Carasso. (2003). Lifetime social security and Medicare benefits. The Urban Institute. Retrieved from: www.urban.org/sites/default/files/publication/42731/310667-Lifetime-Social-Security-and-Medicare-Benefits.PDF (accessed March 28, 2017).

Tax Policy Center. (2017). Briefing book. Retrieved from: www.taxpolicycenter.org/briefing-book/background/numbers/revenue.cfm (accessed June 28, 2017).

Tax Policy Center. (2018). Average effective Federal tax rates: All tax units, by expanded cash income percentile, 2016. Retrieved from: www.taxpolicycenter.org/model-estimates/baseline-average-effective-tax-rates-march-2017/t17-0040-average-effective-federal (accessed May 18, 2018).

Taxpayer Advocate Service. (2008). 2008 Annual report to Congress. Retrieved from: www.irs.gov/pub/tas/08_tas_arc_msp_1.pdf (accessed June 28, 2017).

Tyszkiewicz, Mary T., and Stephen Daggett. (1998) A defense budget primer. Congressional research service report RL30002.

Veterans' Health Administration. (2016). Restoring trust in veterans' health care. Fiscal year 2016. Annual report. Retrieved from: www.va.gov/health/aboutVHA.asp (accessed May 23, 2018).

Wilensky, Harold L. (2012). *American political economy in global perspective.* Cambridge, UK: Cambridge University Press.

3   Government and the Economy

From late 2007 to mid-2009, the economy shrank. Individuals and businesses purchased fewer goods and services, and businesses cut their production and payrolls. By mid-2009, the economy was producing $600 billion less than it had been two years before, and millions of unemployed adults hunted for jobs that were in very short supply.

The federal government tried to revive the economy in several ways.[1] Congress's signature response was the American Recovery and Re-Investment Act, a grab-bag of new expenditures and tax cuts that amounted to $800 billion in new debt, a fiscal boost that was similar in magnitude to the economy's slump. The previous chapter noted how an increase in deficit spending can prop up demand and counter a recession. However, the "Recovery Act" did not exactly live up to its name. The nation's unemployment rate remained above 9 percent for more than a year after the stimulus was passed by Congress. Essentially, Americans did not "feel" the stimulus at all.

But that does not mean that it did not stimulate. Indeed, there is every reason to believe that it prevented a larger contraction and hastened the economy's recovery.[2] And it might have done more if its contents had been different. After all, one-third of the funds were less "stimulus" than "backstop" for state governments that faced sharply falling tax revenues.[3] And another third came in the form of tax cuts, which may be less effective than new expenditures as a means to spur the economy because households and businesses may use tax savings not for consumption but to pay down debts or shore up savings.

Still, the Recovery Act was a large fiscal boost, and the fact that it – and the government's other responses to the Great Recession – did not have a very noticeable effect on the economy underscores an important point: seldom do changes in federal laws or budgets have a major effect on short-run macroeconomic variables, like the nation's unemployment rate. By far the biggest exception to this rule occurred during World War II, when Congress's enormous spending spree – which nearly quadrupled federal spending as a share of GDP – caused America's long-depressed economy to roar to life. But nothing on that scale has happened since, and easily the government's most dramatic and frenzied action in the last seven decades was its flurry of responses to the Great Recession. So, indeed, the government's actions, as consequential as they may be, do not dictate the economy's trajectory. America's economy is large and influenced by many other things, including global politics, financial speculation, and the weather; and its fluctuations often have little to do with the actions of the current administration or Congress.

As important as these points are, we should not let them blind us to some other important truths. One is that the government's influence is modest by choice. Congress and other policymaking institutions normally make only incremental changes to policy, and the major reforms that Congress enacts are usually focused on particular programs or sectors. In contrast, we would anticipate a noticeable macroeconomic effect if Congress were to sharply raise import tariffs, double the federal minimum wage, or radically alter something else of systemic importance.

A second truth is that many "small" policies can have large effects over the long run. For example, today's public investments in research and infrastructure can have outsized effects on the economy's performance a decade or two in the future. The accumulation of debt and the government's management of the money supply also have long-run implications, and so do the government's policies surrounding investment and innovation. Put another way, the decisions of today's businesses and investors that will shape tomorrow's economy are structured by today's policies and political climate.

This chapter unpacks these points to explain the government's general influence on both the business cycle and the long-run economy. It is not a primer on macroeconomics, and it does not survey that discipline's concepts, models, and debates. Instead, it concentrates on the federal government's influence on the macroeconomy. After brief discussions of fiscal policy and monetary policy, the chapter turns to political business cycles, the political independence of the Federal Reserve, and the political determinants of long-run economic growth. Later chapters will touch on some related subjects, including trade, income inequality, and the origins of the 2008 financial crisis.

Fiscal Policy

In macroeconomics, *fiscal policy* refers to the effect of government deficits on the economy. We have already provided an example (the Recovery Act), and the previous chapter already explained the gist of how it works. To elaborate slightly, consider again the Great Recession. From 2007 to 2009, aggregate demand in the economy fell: businesses and individuals reduced their demand for goods and services. Linked with that – as cause, effect, or both – was a drop in aggregate supply: businesses cut production and payrolls. Thus, the economy assumed a lower equilibrium level of output (GDP). In that situation, the government can help to restore the prior, higher-output equilibrium with increased deficit spending. By borrowing money to do something like upgrade infrastructure or give households a tax break, the government can increase aggregate demand and thus aggregate supply and output. Likewise, the government could attempt to increase supply directly by, say, extending a tax break to businesses that expand their payrolls or productive capacities.

While the Recovery Act was a deliberate attempt to counter the recession, any change in the deficit constitutes a type of fiscal policy, whether it is intended that way or not. In other words, any increase in deficit spending constitutes an expansionary fiscal policy that fuels the economy, whereas any decrease in deficit spending constitutes a contractionary fiscal policy that reduces aggregate demand and supply.

Note that an expansionary policy only works to expand the economy when the economy is producing below its potential. If the unemployment rate is already very low and if businesses can not readily expand output through increased employment, then an increase in the budget deficit will do little to increase production and employment. In other words, the added debt will provide no macroeconomic benefit.[4]

However, when the economy is operating below its potential, a fiscal boost can improve the economy by more than its size. The ratio of GDP change (over some period of time) to the size of the fiscal boost is called the fiscal multiplier, and during a recession it may be greater than one, such that a boost of $100 billion will translate into a GDP increase of more than that amount.[5] That is possible because the extra $100 billion does not just "sit still" after the government spends it. Rather, after it is transferred to households and businesses, they spend that income, which in turn supports other businesses and households, and it continues to ripple through the economy. The full output effect of a fiscal stimulus takes some time to materialize – perhaps a year or two. And that is one source of controversy about fiscal policy: by the time a fiscal stimulus is felt, the economy might begin to recover on its own.

Third, and more importantly, the government seldom pursues an active fiscal policy.[6] Congress usually allows the budget deficit to grow or shrink via automatic stabilizers – i.e., safety-net programs that automatically shrink or grow with opposing changes in the economy (see Chapter 2). Beyond that, Congress rarely takes specific measures to counter recessions, and it leaves macroeconomic policy to the Federal Reserve. Also, Congress's most significant fiscal decisions tend to be in pursuit of non-macroeconomic objectives. For example, Congress may add to the deficit to pay for health care or tax cuts. The fiscal boost that may accompany such reforms is usually a secondary issue – an added benefit, perhaps.

Monetary Policy and the Federal Reserve

Monetary policy influences the supply of money and interest rates, and in turn the amount of borrowing, spending, consumption, and production in the economy. Consider first the effects of the money supply and interest rates, before we turn to how they are influenced by monetary policy. In brief, when the money supply expands, there is more money available for households and businesses to borrow, which causes interest rates to fall. That encourages borrowing, and more borrowing means more spending, because the money that households and businesses borrow they spend on cars, furniture, construction materials, and the like. That spending benefits businesses, and as businesses increase production to meet demand, they need more workers. So, when the economy is in a slump, an increase in the money supply can boost demand and supply (and output and employment) back toward their potential levels.

However, an expansion of the money supply also implies inflation, an increase in prices. At its simplest, this effect can be understood via supply and demand. If the money supply increases, then the purchasing power of each monetary unit (i.e., dollar) will fall as people demand more monetary units per good or service (i.e., they raise prices). Alternatively, the effect can be understood via the dynamics of economic expansion. As spending ramps up, prices can increase to reflect higher demand; and, as businesses increase production and unemployment falls, employers may need to increase wages, the cost of which may be passed on to consumers in the form of higher prices.

Inflation can be self-perpetuating. As prices rise, workers demand higher wages; and as businesses face higher personnel costs, they raise their prices. Also, inflation expectations can be self-fulfilling. If employees, banks, borrowers, and other parties to economic contracts expect future inflation, they will want to structure their contracts to account for expected future prices. Yet, as they build future wages and prices into their contracts, they cause that inflation to come into being. Of course, that only occurs if it is done on an economy-wide scale, because inflation is by definition an increase in prices for a broad range of goods and services.

Slow, steady inflation of about 2 percent or 3 percent per year is not problematic. In fact, it is desirable because it facilitates effective monetary policy. However, high inflation complicates all types of economic activity and discourages long-term contracts and investments, which undermines economic growth. Also, disinflation, or reducing the inflation rate, is difficult because it is not easy to alter expectations about future inflation. Disinflation is also painful, because it requires an economic slowdown and unemployment.

In other words, the unemployment rate and inflation rate are inversely related. As such, the Federal Reserve confronts a tradeoff in its dual mandate to maximize employment and maintain price stability. When the "Fed" acts to counter a recession with an expansion of the money supply, it fuels inflation. And when it acts to counter inflation, it slows economic activity and increases unemployment. Since 2012, the Fed has navigated this tradeoff by explicitly targeting an inflation rate of 2 percent.

As with fiscal policy, expansionary monetary policy can only improve output and employment when unemployment is high and the economy is producing below its potential. In other circumstances, an increase in the money supply will not bring any additional output or employment – it will only bring inflation. A related point is that the inverse relationship between unemployment and inflation is strictly a short-run phenomenon. An increase in the money supply can restore production and employment to their potential levels, but it does not bring a long-run increase in the economy's productive capacity. It does, however, introduce a higher price level that sticks around.[7]

Finally, note that the (short-run) tradeoff between inflation and unemployment has distributional consequences, and thus so does monetary policy. In particular, a high unemployment rate tends to hit unskilled laborers and the poor especially hard. Unskilled jobs are often the first to disappear in a recession, and the poor lack savings on which to live while they are unemployed. High inflation affects a broader swath of the public, and especially pensioners and people with savings. Additionally, faster-than-expected inflation benefits debtors, such as homeowners, because the value of their debts declines over time, whereas creditors benefit from slower-than-expected inflation and from deflation (i.e., a decrease in the price level), both of which increase the value of their loan assets.

Monetary Policy

The Fed's primary instruments of monetary policy are *open market operations*, which are simply the buying and selling of Treasury bonds from commercial banks. Those actions influence the supply of credit (money) because banks are subject to Federal Reserve regulations that require them to hold a certain ratio of their liabilities (e.g., customer deposits) as reserves. The process works as follows. When the Fed wants economic activity to tick up, it buys Treasuries from commercial banks by crediting their accounts with more reserves. That allows banks to extend more loans and still meet their required *reserve ratio*. Banks then extend credit to put their resources to work, which constitutes an expansion of the money supply. That puts downward pressure on interest rates, which motivates economic activity.[8]

In other words, the Fed buys Treasuries when it pursues an expansionary (or loose) monetary policy. It does the reverse for a contractionary or tight monetary policy – i.e., it sells Treasuries to banks and debits their bank accounts. In that case, banks need to reduce their loans to meet the reserve ratio, and the contraction in the money supply results in higher interest rates.

Note that when the Fed buys Treasuries and credits banks' accounts, it does not actually transfer any funds. Instead, it simply declares that the banks have more reserves. In effect, it "prints" money.[9] That is not costless, because it causes inflation.

The Fed has two other tools by which it can affect interest rates. First, it can change the reserve ratio, though it seldom does that. Second, the Fed can change the discount rate, which is the interest rate for Fed loans to banks that need money to meet their reserve ratio. When the Fed increases the discount rate, banks increase the interest rates that they offer to their customers.

Nearly all of the Fed's decisions are open to some criticism, and that is not only because they have distributional consequences. The economy is complex, always evolving, and difficult to forecast. Thus, even people with similar views on policy priorities can disagree about what policy is best at a particular time. However, some critics make a more sweeping charge and allege that the Fed cannot help but react too slowly to changes in the economy, and thus that its actions exacerbate rather than attenuate swings in the economy.

Federal Reserve Independence

The Federal Reserve acts independently of the elected branches. However, that independence is not total, and it can be revoked. In particular, Congress could at any time abolish or reform the Fed. Also, the Chair of the Federal Reserve Board, who serves four-year terms, is chosen by the president.[10] So, a Fed Chair who wishes to keep his or her job may be sympathetic to the president's interests regarding macroeconomic policy, which are invariably to keep the economy humming through the next election. Although recent presidents have largely steered clear of trying to influence Fed policies, Fed Chairs know that if they depart too much from the president's preferences they are likely to encounter political pressure. And, like the Supreme Court, the Fed knows that its independence depends upon its own restraint. If its policies too frequently clash with the interests of the elected branches, it may see its power curtailed.

Central bank independence is advantageous for monetary policy and macroeconomic performance. When politicians control monetary policy, there is a distinct possibility that they might ignore the dangers of inflation in pursuit of a fast-growing economy that helps their short-term reelection prospects. Indeed, many countries have experienced damaging periods of high inflation because their governments have used monetary policy for purposes other than economic stability. Of course, central bank independence may not be sufficient to ensure monetary stability, and that is not only because the bank may make mistakes. It is also because the elected branches control the budget and fiscal policy, which gives them the ability to manipulate (or mismanage) the economy.

The Federal Reserve came under much criticism in the wake of the 2008 financial crisis. In particular, the Fed was blamed for maintaining an overly loose monetary policy and overly lax regulatory approach in the years preceding the crisis. However, from the early 1980s until the crisis, the Fed enjoyed a very favorable reputation, and its independence was virtually unchallenged by politicians. That was a departure from the 1970s, and that shift merits a brief telling.

At the start of the 1970s, the price level was increasing nearly 6 percent per year. Public polices were to blame, especially timid monetary policies and budget deficits that had swelled to fund new social programs and the Vietnam War.[11] A temporary tax hike in 1968–1969 to fund the war balanced the budget, and it contributed to a recession in 1970, which reduced inflation. But then the Fed bowed to President Nixon's demand to keep the economy humming in 1972, an election year.[12] The Fed's loose policy helped the economy surge and Nixon win his reelection campaign, but it set the stage for faster inflation in 1973. In that year, a coalition of oil-producing countries, OPEC, began an oil embargo on the United States, which caused inflation to spike and the economy to slow. That combination, dubbed "stagflation," was a tricky problem to address with monetary policy because of the tradeoff between inflation and unemployment. Any attempt to revive the economy would increase the inflation rate, and any attempt to reduce inflation would intensify and prolong the recession.

Inflation remained high in the years that followed. It averaged 8.5 percent per year from 1974 through 1979, when President Carter nominated Paul Volcker to chair the Fed. Carter chose Volcker because he promised to whip inflation, but that presented political risks for Carter, who was up for reelection in 1980. Sure enough, Volcker's Fed immediately hiked interest rates, a recession began a few months later, in January 1980, and Carter lost his reelection bid later in the year.

Volcker's Fed maintained its aggressive fight against inflation in the Reagan years. Its policies were initially threatened by Reagan's early budgetary moves, which combined a large tax cut with a boost in defense expenditures. However, in the face of criticism about the deficit, Reagan agreed to delay some of his tax cuts, which allowed the Fed's tight monetary policy to do its work. The economy contracted sharply in 1981 and 1982, and so did the inflation rate. In 1983, inflation was near 3 percent, a long way from the double-digit rates of 1979 and 1980.

The year 1983 would later be marked as the beginning of a long period of sustained economic growth and low inflation. Over the next quarter-century, until the financial crisis in 2008, real (i.e., inflation-adjusted) GDP per capita grew by 75 percent, and the economy experienced only two mild recessions. Economists dubbed the period the Great Moderation, and the Fed's dual mandate of high employment and low inflation was being fulfilled better than it had been in decades. Volcker and his successor, Alan Greenspan, were widely praised for their management of the economy – the former was hailed as the tough guy who saved the country from inflation, and the latter was called the "maestro" for his ability to keep the economy on an even keel. Later, when the 2008 financial crisis struck, Greenspan's reputation took a hit. But by that time the Federal Reserve had a new place in America's political system. In particular, presidents relegated their enthusiasm for expansionary macroeconomic policies to central bank independence and price stability.

One illustration of this deference occurred in the late 1980s when Greenspan tightened policy to cool the economy and forestall inflation. The tightening contributed to a recession in 1990, which threatened Bush I's reelection bid. President Bush kept his complaints private, however, and he reappointed Greenspan when his term was up in 1991.[13] Then, after he lost his reelection campaign, Bush made his complaints public, but in the post-inflation 1990s, the Fed and its leader, Greenspan, were revered and presidential gripes about Fed policy were rather taboo. Bush's successor, Clinton, provided another illustration: he twice reappointed Greenspan as Fed Chair, despite the fact that Greenspan was a libertarian-minded Republican. Also, Clinton chose to back down on some of his campaign pledges after Greenspan threatened to raise interest rates if Clinton were to pursue them via deficit spending.[14] In other words, whereas the Fed Chair had once deferred to Nixon's political demands, Bush and Clinton practiced deference to the central banker.

That new norm of presidential politics was followed by the next two presidents, Bush II and Obama. But President Trump acted differently. In the summer and fall of 2018, he publicly criticized the Fed's rate hikes. He gave no indication that he would do anything further to undermine or pressure the bank, but the words were an important break with modern tradition, and they could potentially come to be marked as a pivot point in the elected branches' posture towards the bank.

Political Business Cycles?

It was emphasized above that the government's powers to accelerate or stabilize the economy are ultimately powers of the elected branches, and especially the congress. We have also noted that politicians generally prefer expansionary policies, because a growing economy buoys their reelection chances. That raises a few questions. In particular, to what extent *do* the elected branches try to boost the election-year economy? And, to what extent do they succeed, thus inducing a *political business cycle*, in which the economy's oscillations are driven by the electoral cycle?[15]

Several preceding observations are relevant for these questions. First, the change in political behavior vis-à-vis the Federal Reserve, which replaced Nixon's opportunism with Carter's deference, has meant that monetary policy is not available to the elected branches as a means to boost the election-year economy. Second, we have noted that Congress rarely makes policy changes that are big enough to jolt the economy and rarely pursues an active fiscal policy, which itself illustrates a measure deference towards a bank that could counter expansionary fiscal policy with tight monetary policy.[16] And there is one other reason why we should expect no more than a modest or irregular political business cycle: divided government. Indeed, Congress may be disinclined to boost the election-year economy if there is a chance that it may help an opposing-party president win reelection, and especially because the state of the economy matters less to congressional elections than to presidential elections. (Even so, we can imagine a Democratic Congress increasing spending or a Republican Congress cutting taxes in an election year even if it might buoy the economy and an opposing-party president at the polls.[17])

Still, what about actual experience? In short, the answer is that most recent elections do not exhibit the hallmarks of opportunism (i.e., election-motivated boosts to the economy), and the economy's fluctuations have not resembled a political business cycle. In fact, since 1980, only one presidential election – 2004 – resembles opportunism. In the lead-up to that election, the Fed kept interest rates low to help the economy continue its recovery from the mild recession of 2001. Meanwhile, from 2001 to 2004, Congress enacted increasingly large budget deficits to fund two rounds of tax cuts, the wars in Iraq and Afghanistan, and a Medicare expansion.[18] The second round of tax cuts, in 2003, were opposed by President George W. Bush's Treasury Secretary, Paul O'Neill, and by the Fed Chair, Alan Greenspan. But Greenspan did not respond with interest rate hikes, so both monetary policy and fiscal policy were expansionary in the 2004 election year.

Other elections since 1980 offer a contrast. As we have noted, the Fed pursued a tight policy in the lead up to the 1980 and 1992 elections, and Congress adopted a contractionary or steady fiscal policy in three elections that were held during divided government (1996, 2000, and 2012). Evidence of a political business cycle is also weak, given that four elections (1980, 1992, 2008, and 2012) occurred when the economy was in recession or in a sluggish recovery. Two of those (1980 and 2008) were held during unified government.

Those points notwithstanding, three contrasting arguments are worth considering. First, tendencies may have been different prior to 1980. Analyses that focus on those decades seem to identify a political business cycle,[19] although those results might turn heavily on a single data point, the 1972 election. Second, just because electoral opportunism has not been pronounced in recent decades does not mean that it will not be in the future. The inflation of the 1970s motivated a degree of fiscal restraint during the 1980s and 1990s; but as that experience moves further into the past it may become more likely for a government to relegate monetary stability to short-term political goals.

Finally, just because there is not a pronounced political business cycle does not mean that politicians do not time policy changes for maximum electoral benefit. Nor does it mean that they are equally disciplined about budget deficits in election years as they are in other years. On the contrary, the elected branches seemingly never construct policies and budgets that create unnecessary risks in an election year. While modern examples abound, the most vivid illustrations occurred in the 1960s and 1970s. In particular, Social Security checks tended to increase right before elections – until 1975, when they were indexed to inflation so that they would increase automatically.[20] Veterans' benefits exhibited a similar pattern.[21]

Partisan Cycles?

A different question is whether the economy performs better – or differently – when the government is controlled by one political party or the other. On the one hand, we might expect growth to be somewhat slower under Republicans given the party's greater interest in protecting higher-income Americans from inflation. On the other hand, we might expect faster growth under Republican rule if we think that their business-friendly policies are more conducive to economic growth than Democrats' pro-worker-and-welfare policies.

The historical record favors the first idea, although there are also good reasons to believe that the relationship may be spurious.[22] Any sweep of modern history is bound to note that (1) the nation's two biggest economic crises (in 1929 and 2008) occurred under Republican rule; (2) aside from the recessions that followed those crises, growth has been faster under Democratic presidents; and (3) inflation has been tamed when the president is Republican. The second observation reflects the fact that the 1960s and 1990s were periods of growth and rule by Democratic presidents, whereas the third observation reflects the disinflation of the early 1980s, when Reagan occupied the White House.

While each of those episodes is of great historical importance, a case can be made that things would have been no different had the other party been in power. The 1960s' boom, for example, occurred in nearly all Western economies,[23] and so it might have occurred if the Republicans had been in power. The case is more clear-cut regarding disinflation. The Fed was more responsible for that achievement than the Reagan White House. Indeed, Reagan's initial moves were inflationary, although he subsequently scaled back his tax cuts after they increased the deficit.

What about the two financial crises? Although Republicans' economic ideology deserves blame in both cases – because it put too much faith in the idea that markets do not need regulation because they are rational and self-correcting (see Chapter 7 on the 2008 financial crisis) – it can also be argued that Democratic politicians might not have taken sufficient steps to forestall either crisis.[24] Indeed, no politician or voter wants a boom economy to end, and before a bubble bursts it is difficult for people to see that the economy is headed for a crash. Governmental action often seems unnecessary until it is already too late.

Long-Run Growth

The performance of an economy over the long run has some relation to how well it performs over the short run. If recessions tend to be long, deep, or frequent, an economy will not perform well over the long run. However, there is much more that matters for the long run, and the primary drivers of long-run growth are wholly separate from those that dictate the economy's performance over the short run.

Before explaining that point, note that differences in long-run growth rates are the reason for the yawning gaps in wealth between "developed" and "developing" economies. The latter need higher long-run growth rates in order to close that gap, reduce poverty, and attenuate civil and political strife. Long-run growth is also important for developed economies like America's, for it allows improvements in health and education, eases the tackling of social, environmental, and fiscal problems, and permits younger generations to have more wealth than their parents.

Figure 3.1 shows the performance of four economies – those of the United States, France, Mexico, and China – from 1960 to 2016. The graphic shows the standard measure of an economy's level of wealth: real (i.e., inflation-adjusted) GDP per capita, in 2010 US dollars. Real GDP per capita does not account for many things. It does not account for differences in the cost of living (or "purchasing power"), which would reduce the gaps in the figure, because the cost of living is much lower in Mexico or China than in the United States or France. The measure also does not account for income inequality. All economies have income inequality, and where it is larger

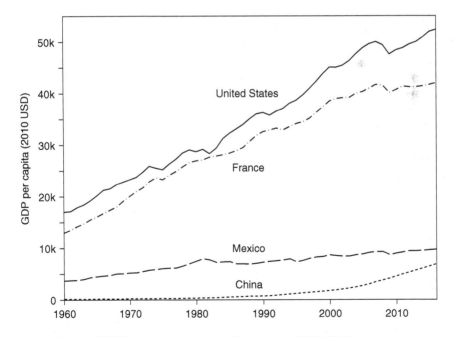

Figure 3.1 Real GDP per capita in selected countries, 1960–2016.

Notes: Data are adjusted for inflation (listed in 2010 $US) but not for different costs of living.

Source: The World Bank, 2018. World Development Indicators.

there will be a greater disparity between what the *median* citizen earns and what the economy produces for the "statistically average" person. Also, real GDP per capita is simply a measure of income or production. It does not capture many "quality-of-life" metrics like mental and physical health. Across countries, those measures are positively correlated with real GDP per capita, but not perfectly. Some poorer countries outperform some richer countries on various quality-of-life metrics.[25]

Nevertheless, real GDP per capita does capture something basic and important: the amount an economy produces on a per-person basis. And Figure 3.1 shows that in the half-century after 1960 all four economies grew. Note also that since the mid-1990s, when the North American Free Trade Agreement (NAFTA) went into effect between the United States, Canada, and Mexico, the growth rate in Mexico has been lackluster. In fact, real GDP per capita grew faster from 1994 to 2016 in the United States than in Mexico.[26] That disparity is not because NAFTA did not contribute to Mexico's output – it did. Instead, it reflects other things. One is the fact that Mexico was much wealthier than China, and so China benefited more from its opening to export-oriented industry. In other words, for many goods destined for the United States, it was still cheaper to produce in China and ship across the ocean than to produce right next door in Mexico. (However, as China has boomed, the production-cost gap between Mexico and China has shrunk.) In addition, Mexico's slow growth reflected the country's poor infrastructure and sub-optimal legal and banking systems.[27] In those respects, Mexico was not necessarily any worse than China, but Mexico was a middle-income country that required more than just export-oriented industry to grow. It also required systems that encouraged growth of the domestic economy.

Note that in 1960, before the modern trade boom, there was a wide development gap between countries like the United States and France and countries like Mexico and China. That gap was created by different rates of long-run growth, and it was primarily the result of different domestic institutions. That is, the United States and France had political and economic systems that were more conducive to economic growth. What were the key elements of those systems? What was it about the US political economy that was (and is) conducive to long-run growth? What hinders long-run growth?

What Drives Long-Run Growth?

Before we discuss political and economic institutions, note that the main driver – or, in fact, essence – of long-run economic growth is improved labor *productivity*, which is the amount of goods or services that a worker can produce per hour. Greater productivity means that an economy can produce more stuff with the same number of workers working the same number of hours ("worker-hours"). Productivity gains increase real GDP per capita.

A one-off increase in productivity implies a one-off improvement in growth, not an economy that experiences growth decade after decade.

For example, if some innovation allows workers to produce 120 rather than 100 widgets per hour, then the economy's total production will have grown on a per worker-hour basis. However, without additional improvements in productivity, there will be no additional growth. Productivity must be *constantly* increasing for per capita production and income to increase over time.

A similar point is that an economy can produce more in a year if the average worker works more hours over the course of the year. However, the increased production would be a one-off improvement that is maintained only so long as the number of worker-hours remains at the higher level. That observation underscores that productivity – not hours worked – is the main driver of long-run growth.[28] Over the past 150 years, the American economy was transformed from an agricultural economy into a rich and productive hi-tech economy not because the average worker logged more work-hours each passing year, but because capital, technology, and education increased productivity.

Indeed, productivity growth stems from three things:

1 *Increasing amounts of physical capital per worker.* Physical capital includes things like tools, machines, and computers; it also includes things like buildings, transportation systems, and other types of infrastructure. If workers have more, bigger, and more powerful tools to bring to production, and if infrastructure improvements ease the efficiency of transport, markets, and communication, then the economy can produce more per worker-hour.
2 *Increasing amounts of human capital.* The term human capital refers to the education and knowledge of the workforce, and increasing human capital allows increasing productivity because the workforce can utilize more-efficient production techniques and tools.
3 *Technological advances and innovations.* Many types of innovations and technological advances are relevant for productivity. Some are tangible and come to mind quickly, including inventions like the light bulb, the combustion engine, and the semiconductor. Others that are less tangible and obvious include innovations like Henry Ford's assembly line and digital systems for inventory control and manufacturing supply-chain management. What these various productive "technologies" have in common, however, is that they consist of a new idea, practice, or system that improves the economy's productivity. New technologies are the most important of the three drivers of productivity growth; without them, growth is limited by the diminishing returns to capital accumulation. For example, once a new technology is put to use throughout the economy there is little to be gained from the additional spread of the technology. Or, as Evsey Domar put it, capital accumulation without new production technologies is like "piling wooden plows on top of existing wooden plows."[29]

Now we can consider what sort of political economy fosters rising productivity. Put differently: what are the key reasons why the United States and other Western nations experienced long-run growth over the nineteenth and twentieth centuries? The answer boils down to two main components:[30]

1 *A competitive marketplace.* In competitive markets, enterprises are forced to be efficient (and to improve their efficiency) or else they will be beaten by competition that is able to offer lower prices. Market competition creates an incentive for productivity; and economies that are marked by open competition are poised to exhibit faster productivity gains.

   Governments can impede growth if they bestow advantages such as unfair, anti-competitive advantages on certain firms, including licensing regulations that effectively bar competition. Of course, in the political arena, firms seek such benefits and lobby for them.[31] So, the maintenance of open, fair markets is not automatic, and it is only likely to succeed to the extent that government resists special interests and safeguards competition and consumer power.

2 *Incentives to save, invest, and innovate.* These incentives are a function of many things. At the most general level, they depend upon political stability, which itself depends upon many things. One condition for political stability that deserves mention is that the benefits of long-run growth are widely distributed among the population. The trouble is that competitive, market-driven economies – which are necessary for growth – have the potential to generate vast disparities in wealth. This suggests that government may need to redistribute the market's distribution of wealth in order to maintain a political economy that is conducive to growth.[32]

   Similarly, saving and investment depend on the government providing *sound management of the financial system and the money supply* so that the economy does not experience instability, crisis, or hyperinflation. Long-run growth depends upon well-functioning credit and financial systems, because they channel savings into investments and business ventures. If the government poorly regulates those sectors – either by undermining their efficient operation or by failing to prevent systemic problems – then the economy's long-run potential is threatened. And if today's government is too careless about inflation, people will not make long-term investments that can yield innovations and more productive technologies.

   Savings, investment, and innovation also depend upon the establishment and enforcement of *property rights*. This means many things, including (a) the government protects property from theft, (b) the government restrains itself from confiscating property (only doing so rarely and under due process of law), and (c) the *legal system* works well to formally recognize property rights and to provide a neutral, non-corrupt arena by which property disputes can be adjudicated. If property rights are not well established and protected, individuals and businesses will be discouraged from making investments and from using their property to its full economic potential. That limits the accumulation of physical capital and the potential for technological innovation.

In a similar vein, it is useful to have a *patent system* or some other means to encourage innovation and protect *intellectual property* (IP) rights. Patents and intellectual property rights constitute a government-protected temporary monopoly for new inventions that allows innovators to reap all possible rewards from their inventions for some period of time.[33] If there is no such system and new ideas can simply be copied by others, then there will be less innovation and technological advancement. Of course, for an IP system to be socially useful, the monopoly must last long enough to provide the inventor ample rewards but not so long that it leads to excessive costs on the part of consumers.

In addition to maintaining competitive markets and establishing systems and policies that encourage investment and innovation, the government can assist long-run growth by making public investments in scientific research, public education, and infrastructures like energy grids, communications systems, and transportation systems. Indeed, such investments contributed to America's tremendous economic growth during the twentieth century. Of course, the private sector also makes important investments in research and infrastructure, and in theory its investments could replace those of the public sector, and perhaps even improve upon them. As a historical matter, however, government investments in research, education, and infrastructure made large contributions to the economic growth of all developed nations.

Although long-run growth is facilitated by institutions that safeguard competitive markets and encourage investment and innovation, no set of institutions can guarantee growth, because productivity gains are very much the product of invention. In a related vein, it has been argued, most notably by Robert J. Gordon in his 2016 book, *The rise and fall of American growth*, that future economic growth in the United States will be slow because the productivity gains of the industrial and technological revolutions have already been realized and because future advances are likely to do much less to improve productivity. Such arguments should be treated with caution, because history is replete with similar prognostications that did not come to pass. Still, Gordon's argument is plausible and important. Gordon also makes two compelling arguments about demographics and "headwinds" facing the modern economy. First, he argues that two key sources of economic growth in the twentieth century – the spread of basic and higher education throughout the population and the entry of women into the workforce – cannot be replicated.[34] Second, Gordon argues that the aging of the population and the accumulation of government debt will slow the country's growth rate. The former will occur simply because there will be fewer worker-hours per person as more of the population enters retirement or cuts back on work, and the latter will occur because the government may have to forego making some investments in infrastructure, systems, and people that would be beneficial for future growth.[35]

Note a few other things about the basic institutional determinants of long-run growth. First, a pro-growth environment depends on a small set of important systems and structures – not on policy minutiae. Of course, policy details do matter. Growth is jeopardized if banks are poorly regulated, the money supply is poorly managed, or tax policies discourage investment. And it is possible for very "small" policies to greatly retard economic growth. However, there are so many policies that matter, each with so many relevant details, that to focus on them is to miss the bigger picture. The bigger picture has to do with the country's overall economic framework and political economy. Does the government safeguard open markets, or does it favor established interests and support crony capitalism? Does the government safeguard financial and monetary stability, or does it poorly regulate finance and brazenly accumulate debt? Those are the essential questions, at least in a broad sense.

Government regulations are often cited for being a drag on growth. The charge has merit, although it is often too sweeping. Individual regulations and the overall regulatory burden on businesses hinder long-run growth to the extent that they discourage investment and competition; and research suggests that countries that frustrate business-formation with a heavy regulatory burden do experience lower growth rates.[36] However, some regulations improve markets and financial stability and thus facilitate growth over the long run. Many environmental regulations might do similarly. Indeed, it can be argued that long-run growth requires long-run environmental sustainability, in part because air and water pollution have future costs in terms of clean-up and health. In any event, long-run growth is more about investment and productivity than it is about a mix of current costs and future cost savings, which are the main points of contention in debates about environmental regulations and business costs.

A similar point is that growth can proceed even in a context of a considerable redistributive taxation. Indeed, the most economically developed countries in the world happen to be those that combine a market system with heavy doses of taxation, redistribution, and regulation.[37] Of course, there are limits; and it matters *how* the government taxes and spends. Growth is hindered if tax policies discourage investments and government expenditures are wasteful. Growth is favored if the government uses taxes to build infrastructure, spread economic opportunity, and increase human capital.[38]

A final point is that whereas the fundamental aspects of a nation's political economy seldom change rapidly, no political system permanently safeguards a pro-growth environment. Economic interests are forever seeking government protections and subsidies, not competitive markets. And, in a democracy, policy is made by elected officials, who are accountable to voters, and both they and their representatives may be too focused on short-run considerations to worry about long-run investments.

Inequality and Growth

Other chapters touch on the topic of income inequality in various ways. The previous two chapters discussed public policy and inequality, and Chapter 5 will study the growth of income inequality since the 1970s. In this chapter, inequality is relevant because of its reciprocal relationship with economic growth. In one direction, the two are related because economic growth tends to increase inequalities in income and wealth. That tendency relates to core features of pro-growth market economies – chiefly, markets reward productivity-enhancing innovations, and the profits accrue to those who finance those experiments. The results are illustrated by Thomas Piketty in *Capital in the twenty-first century*, a data-rich analysis of capitalism and inequality that suggests that the rate of return on capital tends to exceed the rate of economic growth. Put another way, the norm in capitalist economies seems to be that the riches of the wealthy accumulate faster than the wages of the multitudes.[39]

In the other direction, high levels of income inequality can hinder economic growth by causing social strife, encouraging capital flight to foreign countries, and undermining investment in the economy's core productive industries.[40] Of course, high levels of inequality are unwelcome, regardless of their effects on growth. High levels of inequality cause social polarization and conflict, and the concentration of wealth sits uneasily with the principle of political equality that undergirds democratic rule.

Conclusion

The introduction to this chapter noted that changes in laws or budgets only rarely have a noticeable effect on the short-run economy. By contrast, the effects of economic fluctuations on politics, elections, and budget deficits are unmistakable. Yet, the government can and does influence the economy, over both the short run and the long run, and it is important to understand how and to what extent it does.

One key observation is that the government's influence over the short-run economy is limited because its policy changes are usually incremental or focused on particular sectors or programs. However, even modest monetary policy adjustments by the Federal Reserve have an important effect on the short run, and its power and priorities relate to the authority and latitude it has been granted by the elected branches.

Although markets, investment, and innovation are the engines of economic growth, they depend upon politics and government much more than is often recognized. While all sorts of policies matter, including things like the specifics of the tax code, the most essential ingredients of a pro-growth environment are more general things like financial sector stability, monetary stability, the absence of major social unrest, the maintenance of open and competitive markets, intellectual property rights, a well-functioning legal system, and investments in infrastructure and human capital.

Some fortunate political circumstances allowed the United States to become an economic super-power. The Constitution's protections of property rights and insistence on due process were consequential, and so was the fact that the political system frustrates policy change. Also, the major expansions in regulation and redistribution that have occurred across history proved more beneficial than harmful. Progressive Era reforms expanded public education and facilitated competitive markets. New Deal reforms added banking regulations and social protections that enhanced economic stability and social security. And the government's later investments in infrastructure and research contributed to the economy's post-war boom.

Of course, the nation's economic future will be shaped by the politics and polices of today, and there is no guarantee that they will do so positively. Economic interests demand policies that advance their bottom line, not a level playing field or system-wide stability. Elections focus attention on short-term considerations, not long-term investments. And policies are crafted in the political system, where ideas and interests collide, and compromises are made. These points do not suggest that the nation's political system should be reformed to prioritize long-run growth, especially if such reforms would curtail routine elections or streamline the consensus-oriented policymaking process. But they do underscore the importance of politics for economic policies and outcomes, and it is to those politics that the next chapter turns.

Notes

1 Chapter 7 discusses more aspects of the 2008 financial crisis and Great Recession, and the federal government's contributions and responses.
2 This conclusion is supported by Congressional Budget Office, 2012; Chodorow-Reich et al., 2012; and other analyses.
3 See Becker, 2010 and PGPF, 2010. Also, Krugman (2012) argues that the stimulus was too small.
4 Theoretically, the debt could provide a long-term benefit if it is used for investments (like infrastructure) that help long-run growth. However, a recession is better timing, because it then also provides a short-run benefit. Moreover, there is a cost to deficit spending: persistent or increasing deficits can elevate interest rates, which can result in a "crowding out" of private investment – i.e., foregone investment by the private sector that is not undertaken because of the rise in interest rates. That, in turn, can negatively affect the economy's future growth. And that is another reason why expansionary policies are not recommended during economic expansions.
5 During expansions, the fiscal multiplier may be less than one (Batini et al., 2014).
6 Prior to 2009, Congress did not pass a major stimulus to counter any of the recessions of the past several decades. However, as explained in Chapter 2, the budget

almost always has a deficit. And, as explained later in this chapter, Congress's fiscal policies from 2001 to 2004 were expansionary. We can also find earlier examples of expansionary fiscal policy, including tax cuts in the mid-1960s. Meanwhile, tax hikes in 1968 and defense spending cuts in the 1950s might have contributed to recessions. See Bartlett, 2012, p. 8 and Blinder and Watson, 2016.

7 Economists thus draw a distinction between the "short-run Phillips curve" and the "long-run Phillips curve," both named after the economist A.W.H. Phillips (1914–1975), who recognized the short-run tradeoff. The long-run curve implies no tradeoff. Graphically, the relationship between the inflation rate (vertical axis) and the unemployment rate (horizontal axis) is downward sloping over the short run and vertical over the long run.

8 More precisely, open market operations influence the federal funds rate, which is the interest rate that banks charge each other for short-term loans so that they can meet their reserve requirements. As that interest rate falls, banks also lower the interest rates that they charge to other customers. Fed policy usually seeks to move the federal funds rate to a target level, and it does that mostly via open market operations.

9 When it does so, it expands the monetary base, which is the amount of bank reserves and currency in circulation. Changes in the monetary base have a multiplicative effect on the money supply. A full explanation is outside the scope of this text, but it hinges on the fact that when banks' reserves are increased by X they can extend loans by an amount larger than X and remain in compliance with the reserve ratio.

10 Members of the Federal Reserve's Board of Governors are nominated by the president and serve 14-year terms. The Chair is a Board member, and her four-year term is renewable so long as she is a member of the Board.

11 The inflation rate had been well below 3% for most of the 1950s and 1960s. At that time, the Federal Reserve was emerging as an independent institution, after it played a subservient role to the Treasury during World War II. As inflation ticked up after 1964, the Fed tightened policy, but very gradually. The Fed's tightening in 1965 enraged President Johnson (Fessenden, 2016), and perhaps that was the reason why the Fed did not raise rates more rapidly.

12 Abrams, 2006.

13 Mallaby, 2016.

14 Mallaby, 2016.

15 This type of political business cycle (PBC) is frequently called an "opportunistic" PBC to differentiate it from a "partisan" PBC. Opportunistic cycles are driven by a universal tendency, among all governing parties, to boost the election-year economy. Partisan cycles occur if right-leaning and left-leaning parties manipulate the economy in different ways that cater to their primary electorates.

16 Or, following the "rational expectations" school in macroeconomics, they might anticipate that financial markets will anticipate expansionary policies and respond in ways that happen to reduce their effectiveness.

17 Tufte (1978, p. 54) remarked similarly: "Perhaps the best time for a liberal Congress to increase beneficiary payments in the face of a veto by a conservative president is during an election year, especially one in which the president is seeking re-election."

18 Chapter 6 puts these policies and budget deficits in context.

19 See Nordhaus, 1975; Tufte, 1978; Alesina, Roubini, and Cohen, 1997; Faust and Irons, 1999; and Drazen, 2000.

20 See Tufte (1978, p. 32), who also documented that the first Social Security checks after the benefit increase were accompanied by a note saying that the president himself had authorized the increase – lest any beneficiary forget to appreciate the president.

21 Keech and Pak, 1989.
22 Studies that emphasize the connection between Democratic rule and growth include Hibbs, 1989; Wilensky, 2012; Bartels, 2009; and Blinder and Watson, 2016.
23 Nearly all of those economies also hit more troubled waters in the 1970s and 1980s, and in each case that facilitated the rise of an opposition party.
24 See McCarty, Poole, and Rosenthal, 2013.
25 For this reason, researchers and organizations have built alternatives to GDP. One is the Human Development Index, which combines education, life span, inequality, and GDP data into a general measure of "development."
26 The average annual growth rate in real GDP per capita from 1994 to 2016 was 1.4% in the United States and 1% in Mexico. Meanwhile, it was 8.6% in China.
27 Haber et al., 2008.
28 That point is relevant in a comparison with France's economy. France has a lower GDP per capita than the United States (see Figure 3.1), but the difference has less to do with productivity than with the French working fewer hours. The standard work week in France is thirty-five hours in contrast to America's forty-hour routine; and the French take about twice as many vacation days as Americans, including longer summer vacations. Essentially, compared to America, France trades some wealth for more leisure. See Krugman, 2007.
29 Domar's words, penned in 1961, are cited by Gordon (2016, p. 569).
30 For a fuller exposition of this argument, and to refer to the book on which this section borrows most heavily, see Acemoglu and Robinson, 2012.
31 The economist Joseph Schumpeter (1883–1950) famously described change in competitive market economies as being characterized by "creative destruction," in which old technologies and firms are replaced by new ideas and more efficient modes of production. A challenge, however, is that established firms often want to enlist the power of government to prevent creative destruction.
32 See Acemoglu and Robinson, 2012 and Ostry et al., 2014.
33 Article I of the Constitution specifically grants Congress the power to create a patent system.
34 Along with that, Gordon also emphasizes many inventions that improved productivity around the home – like electricity, kitchen appliances, and washing machines – that enabled more people to take employment opportunities outside the home.
35 On debt-driven economic crises, see Reinhart and Rogoff, 2009.
36 See Djankov et al., 2006 and Nicoletti and Scarpetta, 2003. Those studies use World Bank data regarding the "cost of doing business" due to regulation. It is significant that the World Bank data focuses on phenomena like how long it takes to open a business or to get a government permit. Those are among the types of regulations that can stymie market competition.
37 The United States exhibited rapid economic growth through the twentieth century, despite the tremendous growth of government in the form of regulations and redistributive social programs. Even after the regulatory expansion of the 1960s and 1970s, private investments (and fortunes) were made, innovations were made, and the economy grew. Other countries became rich following a similar trajectory, including several that implemented greater levels of redistributive taxation. In particular, the "social democratic" economies of northern Europe bloomed at the same time that their governments hiked taxes to pay for robust social welfare states, including full public financing of health care and college education. By contrast, governments that pursued state socialism saw very poor results. Socialism is incompatible with economic growth because it does not harness the power of market competition and because it does not encourage investment and innovation. While it is true that the Soviet Union was

able to industrialize its economy through its command-and-control socialism, its economy was hollow, and that is why the super-power collapsed. Additionally, the system was terribly repressive and not respectful of democratic rights and individual freedoms.
38 Bruce Bartlett (2012, p. 49) put the matter this way: "the issue of taxation cannot be viewed in isolation from how the revenues are used. Some kinds of spending stimulate growth; some kinds retard it."
39 See Piketty, 2014.
40 For more, see Acemoglu and Robinson, 2012 and Ostry et al., 2014.

References

Abrams, Burton A. (2006). How Richard Nixon pressured Arthur Burns: Evidence from the Nixon tapes. *Journal of Economic Perspectives*, 20(4), 177–188.
Acemoglu, Daron, and James Robinson. (2012). *Why nations fail: The origins of power, prosperity, and poverty*. New York, NY: Crown Business.
Alesina, Alberto, Nouriel Roubini, and Gerald D. Cohen. (1997). *Political cycles and the macroeconomy*. Cambridge, MA: MIT Press.
Bartels, Larry M. (2009). *Unequal democracy: The political economy of the new gilded age*. Princeton, NJ: Princeton University Press.
Bartlett, Bruce. (2012). *The benefit and the burden*. New York, NY: Simon & Schuster.
Batini, Nicoletta, Luc Eyraud, Lorenzo Forni, and Anke Weber. (2014). Fiscal multipliers: Size, determinants, and use in macroeconomic projections. Technical Notes and Manuals, 14(4). Washington, DC: International Monetary Fund.
Becker, Gary. (2010). Fiscal stimulus packages: What are their effects? [Web log comment]. Retrieved from: www.becker-posner-blog.com/2010/03/fiscal-stimulus-packages-what-are-their-effects-becker.html (accessed May 29, 2018).
Blinder, Alan S., and Mark W. Watson. (2016). Presidents and the US economy: An econometric exploration. *The American Economic Review*, 106(4), 1015–1045.
Chodorow-Reich, Gabriel, Laura Feiveson, Zachary Liscow, and William Gui Woolston. (2012). Does state fiscal relief during recessions increase employment? Evidence from the American Recovery and Reinvestment Act. *American Economic Journal: Economic Policy*, 4(3), 118–145.
Congressional Budget Office. (2012). CBO's estimates of ARRA's economic impact. [Web log comment]. Retrieved from: www.cbo.gov/publication/43014 (accessed May 29, 2018).
Djankov, Simeon, Caralee McLiesh, and Rita Maria Ramalho. (2006). Regulation and growth. *Economics Letters*, 92(3), 395–401.
Drazen, Allan. (2000). The political business cycle after 25 years. In Ben S. Bernanke and Kenneth Rogoff (Eds.), *NBER Macroeconomics Annual*, 15 (pp. 75–137). Cambridge, MA: MIT Press.
Faust, Jon, and John S. Irons. (1999). Money, politics and the post-war business cycle. *Journal of Monetary Economics*, 43(1), 61–89.
Fessenden, Helen. (2016). 1965: The year the Fed and LBJ clashed. *Econ Focus*, 3Q/4Q, 4–7.
Gordon, Robert J. (2016). *The rise and fall of American growth*. Princeton, NJ: Princeton University Press.
Haber, Stephen H., Herbert S. Klein, Noel Maurer, and Kevin J. Middlebrook. (2008). *Mexico since 1980*. Cambridge, UK: Cambridge University Press.

Hibbs, Douglas A. (1989). *The American political economy.* Cambridge, MA: Harvard University Press.

Keech, William R. and Kyoungsan Pak. (1989). Electoral cycles and budgetary growth in veterans' benefit programs. *American Journal of Political Science,* 33(1), 901–911.

Krugman, Paul. (2007). *The conscience of a liberal.* New York, NY: W.W. Norton & Company.

Krugman, Paul. (2012). *End this depression now!* New York, NY: W.W. Norton & Company.

Mallaby, Sebastian. (2016). *The man who knew.* New York, NY: Penguin Press.

Nicoletti, Giuseppe, and Stefano Scarpetta. (2003). Regulation, productivity and growth: OECD evidence. *Economic Policy,* 18(36), 9–72.

Nordhaus, William D. (1975). The political business cycle. *The Review of Economic Studies,* 42, 169–190.

Ostry, Jonathan David, Andrew Berg, and Charalambos G. Tsangarides. (2014). Redistribution, inequality, and growth. IMF staff discussion note SDN1402. Washington, DC: International Monetary Fund.

PGPF (Peter G. Peterson Foundation). (2010, November 2). A report on fiscal stimulus. Retrieved from: www.pgpf.org/analysis/a-report-on-fiscal-stimulus (accessed June 1, 2018).

Piketty, Thomas. (2014). *Capital in the twenty-first century.* Cambridge, MA: Belknap Press.

Reinhart, Carmen M., and Kenneth S. Rogoff. (2009). *This time is different: Eight centuries of financial folly.* Princeton, NJ: Princeton University Press.

Tufte, Edward R. (1978). *Political control of the economy.* Princeton, NJ: Princeton University Press.

Wilensky, Harold L. (2012). *American political economy in global perspective.* Cambridge, UK: Cambridge University Press.

4 The Politics of Economic Policy

The longest government shutdown in US history spanned twenty-one days over the end of 1995 and the beginning of 1996. It occurred a few weeks after a related, five-day shutdown in November. The shutdowns were the result of a budget battle between President Clinton and the Republican-controlled Congress, led by House Speaker Newt Gingrich. The battle centered on what was essentially a left–right issue: Congress sought significant cuts to social programs, including and Medicare and Medicaid, and Clinton objected. As the shutdowns dragged on, the public came to side with Clinton and blame Gingrich for the impasse, and Gingrich eventually agreed to scale back the budget cuts. The resulting budget was farther to the left than what Republicans' had sought, but it remained to the right of what most Democrats would have preferred. In that respect, it was exactly the type of budget we would expect to see when the government is under divided party control.

Two years later, a Clinton veto on a defense budget bill was overridden by a broad coalition of Republicans and Democrats. The veto at hand was actually a collection of 38 *line-item* vetoes. Clinton could veto specific lines in legislation because in 1995 the Republican Congress had passed legislation to give the president line-item veto power as a means to check some of the unnecessary projects and expenditures that members of Congress like to insert into budget bills. In 1998, the Supreme Court ruled that the law was unconstitutional, and that line-item veto power could only be created via constitutional amendment. Before that ruling, however, Clinton exercised line-item veto power on several occasions, including the 1998 defense budget. He vetoed only a handful of the projects in the bill, but enough members were displeased that an override vote succeeded. Significantly, their gripes were not ideological – the debate was not a left–right disagreement on defense spending. Rather, it reflected an institutional difference between members of Congress and the president: members represent small districts or specific states, whereas the president does not. Thus, representatives are keen on bringing tax dollars to their districts, whereas the president may prioritize other concerns, like deficit control.

In combination, these two episodes from the Clinton years illustrate something important about economic policymaking: different types of policies solicit different types of politics. Of course, the politics of policymaking can also change as the political environment changes – say, from divided government to unified government. This chapter surveys these varied politics. Its primary objective is to introduce a series of theoretical frameworks that help make sense of economic policymaking. Implicitly or explicitly, each approach focuses on Congress and the legislative process. While that is appropriate, we should also not lose sight of the fact that a great deal of policymaking occurs on a more routine basis as government agencies – most notably those under the president's management – adjust rules and priorities within the legal boundaries established by prior legislation. For that reason, this chapter begins with an overview of the president's policymaking powers.

The President and Economic Policy

In contrast to the sweeping powers that are granted by the Constitution to Congress – which allow it to specify any and all aspects of the budget, tax law, social welfare programs, and economic regulations – the Constitution grants to the president only the ability to veto Congress's bills.

Of course, the veto's power is more than the ability to block change, because it may allow the president to extract policy concessions from Congress.[1] In general, that will occur when three conditions are in place: (1) Congress anticipates a veto from the president unless it makes some sort of concession, which implies that Congress views any veto threat from the president as credible, rather than a bluff; (2) a vote to override a veto from the president would not obtain the necessary two-thirds of members in both chambers in order to succeed; (3) Chamber majorities would prefer to accommodate the president rather than let their legislative initiative fail and the status quo policy to stay unchanged. These three conditions exist regularly, especially during periods of divided government. However, even then the president's leverage is limited. Congress will accommodate the president only to the minimum amount that is necessary.

In his classic study of the presidency, Richard E. Neustadt (1960) recognized the president's limited power in the legislative process, and he emphasized that much of what constitutes presidential "power" is merely the office-holder's ability to charm and *persuade* others to adopt his positions and agenda. Powers of persuasion vary from individual to individual. They also depend on the political environment, and the mid-century political environment that Neustadt surveyed allowed more room for presidential persuasion than today's party-polarized environment.

Yet, the president's policymaking powers have grown in other respects since Neustadt's time, and that is because Congress has gradually delegated more powers to the executive branch.[2] Congress grants such authority for several reasons. On occasion, Congress does so because it finds it too politically difficult to specify the details of policies that it wants to advance. A well-known example pertains to Pentagon requests to close domestic military bases in order to reallocate defense resources. From prior experience, Congress knows that it would struggle to put together such packages itself, because specific base closures adversely affect specific congressional districts, whose representatives would seek to undo packages rather than see them get through the legislature. So, the legislature follows a procedure in which it cedes to a president-appointed commission the authority to determine which bases will be closed, reserving for itself only the power of an up-or-down vote on the entire proposal.[3] More routinely, however, Congress delegates authority to the executive branch for one of three reasons: to avoid spending time on details that are not of great political or economic consequence, to defer to agency expertise, or to allow some flexibility in policy design and implementation.

Presidents mostly shape discretionary economic policies indirectly, through the personnel they choose to direct agencies. Like-minded cabinet secretaries and department heads see to it that they use their agencies' available policy discretion to pursue the president's agenda. However, presidents also sometimes issue direct executive orders and presidential memoranda to provide specific and public direction to agencies. There is not a sharp or clear distinction between these two types of directives. Generally, presidential memoranda are used to provide more narrow and discrete instructions to agencies, whereas executive orders tend to be more sweeping and consequential.[4] Executive orders are often used to create investigative commissions and planning committees, to set foreign policies or sanctions, and to restructure government agencies. However, the most economically consequential orders are those that direct agencies to shift program priorities or economic regulations toward some social or ideological goal. Some examples are provided in Box 4.1.

Recent presidents have tended to issue about forty executive orders per year. Many of those are uncontroversial and receive little attention. However, others – especially those that are more substantive than symbolic – stoke controversy. In some cases, the controversies center on legal questions. Executive orders can be as sweeping as allowed by legislation and other law, but those limits are often ambiguous, so there may be legitimate questions about the president's authority to issue this or that order. Of course, the controversies are also political. Presidents want their actions to be significant and newsworthy, and the president's opponents are poised to criticize those actions.

Besides the power to veto legislation, the power to persuade, and the power to shape the policy discretion that can be exercised by executive branch agencies, the president enjoys three types of powers that can prove economically consequential. The first is what might be called administrative policy and refers to the president's managerial power over executive branch labor and contracting. For example, the president can alter pay and benefits for federal employees (including military personnel), and he can set standards of employment compensation and labor-management relations in firms that contract with the government.[5] For example, Obama's Executive Order #13706 required federal contractors to provide their employees with a certain amount of paid sick or medical-related leave, and his White House estimated that the order would expand sick-pay benefits for as many as 300,000 employees.[6] Also, following his predecessors, Obama changed the rules regarding contractors' treatment of labor unions and labor–management relations. Those rules have seesawed for decades, changing each time partisan control of the White House has changed.

The second avenue for economic influence is foreign policy. Generally speaking, the president's room for maneuver in the conduct of foreign policy stems from legislation. For example, the president's ability to impose or remove sanctions on foreign entities originates in legislation, and a president's trade negotiations are conducted in lieu of processes created and maintained by Congress.[7] In some cases, however, the president's authority stems from congressional deference. For example, Congress tends to defer to the president as Commander in Chief in the initiation of combat exercises. (In the mid-1970s, Congress passed legislation that allowed the president to initiate combat authorizations without a prior declaration from Congress, but that legislation merely codified already existing practice.) In any event, foreign policies can be highly consequential for the domestic economy, especially trade policies and combat operations that require significant outlays.

The third type of economic influence occurs via the president's appointments to the Supreme Court, the Federal Reserve, and other independent agencies. Although members of these institutions are not responsible to the president, they have great and long-lasting influence over the nation's policies.

Box 4.1: Discretionary executive authority: Examples of policy influence

To appreciate the magnitude and scope of the president's ability to unilaterally change public policy via executive order, consider the following recent examples.

Example 1: Expanding the number of employees covered by overtime pay regulations. In 2014, Obama issued a presidential memorandum instructing the Department of Labor to update the criteria by which employees could be considered exempt from overtime pay requirements of the Fair Labor Standards Act (FLSA). The FLSA, which dates from 1938, establishes a national minimum wage and requires employers to pay overtime rates to employees who work more than forty hours per week. The law exempts from the overtime requirements employees who are "employed in a bona fide executive, administrative, or professional capacity,"[8] and it charges the Department of Labor (DOL) with establishing the specific criteria to identify those employees.

Prior to Obama, the criteria had last been set in 2004, when the minimum salary that could be considered overtime exempt was set to $23,660.

Obama's memorandum directed the DOL to raise the minimum overtime-exempt salary to over $50,000. After going through the standard rule-making process, during which the DOL issued a proposed rule and solicited public comment (over 270,000 comments were received, many from businesses and business groups), the DOL issued a "final rule" which raised the minimum overtime-exempt salary to $47,476.[9] The rule also established a process by which the threshold would be adjusted every three years for inflation. The Administration estimated that the rule change would extend overtime protection to an additional 4.2 million workers, including large numbers of employees in retail and food service industries.

In late 2016, before the rule went into effect, it was blocked by a federal court. In August 2017, the court ruled decisively against the rule, holding that the DOL attempted to raise the overtime-exempt salary more than is allowed under the FLSA. After the decision, the Trump administration was in the position of choosing whether to leave the minimum overtime-exempt salary at $23,660 or raise it to some amount below a maximum allowable that, as of early 2018, remained unspecified.

Example 2: Expanding assistance for student loan debtors. Obama's Department of Education (DOE) made a number of significant changes to federal student loan programs, including the income-based repayment program. The program, created by Congress in the College Cost Reduction and Access Act (CCRAA) of 2007, created two benefits for borrowers. First, it allowed borrowers experiencing "partial financial hardship" (PFH) to limit their monthly student loan payments to a percentage of their income. Second, it allowed borrowers who were in repayment for a long time (up to twenty-five years) to have their loans forgiven, in which case they would be paid off by the government.[10] The CCRAA granted the DOE some leeway to determine the details of those provisions. At first, the DOE set loan forgiveness at twenty-five years and monthly payments for PFH borrowers at 15 percent of their income in excess of the poverty line.

In 2012 and again in 2015, the Obama Administration altered the rules so that they would be more generous to borrowers.[11] In particular, borrowers became eligible for loan forgiveness after twenty years, and borrowers experiencing PFH could cap their payments at 10 percent of their poverty-line-exceeding income. Also, borrowers with Direct Loans (which are issued by DOE) could cap their monthly repayments at 10 percent of their poverty-line-exceeding income regardless of their personal financial status. The DOE estimated that two million borrowers would enroll in the reduced payment option on their Direct Loans, which would cost the government $15.3 billion over ten years.[12]

Example 3: On carbon emissions and energy production. In March 2017, Trump issued an executive order that saved the coal industry from Obama's moves to cut carbon emissions at power plants. In 2014, the Obama administration had issued two sets of regulations on the matter. One, dubbed the Clean Power Plan, was intended to reduce emissions from existing power plants. The other tightened emissions rules on new power plants, to an extent that would

> severely impinge on the viability of new coal-fired power plants. Obama's EPA claimed that the regulations would provide billions more in long-term savings on energy and health care expenditures than they would short-term costs on energy producers and consumers. Certainly, however, the implications for coal producers were considerable, as their opposition made apparent. Their challenges to Obama's orders succeeded in district court, but the nail in the coffin was the change of direction under Trump. His EPA estimated that the rule reversal would save industry up to $33 billion, a figure that was notably higher than what Obama's EPA had estimated the rules would have imposed.[13]

To make and coordinate economic policy – and to monitor and understand the economy – the president relies on an array of advisers, especially the Secretary of the Treasury, the Chair of the Council of Economic Advisers (CEA), and the Director of the National Economic Council (NEC).[14] The CEA and NEC are both are located within the Executive Office of the President (EOP), which means that they are part of the White House staff and work only for the president. (In other words, they are unlike cabinet secretaries, who run government departments and are charged with implementing programs within the parameters of the law.[15]) The CEA is the White House's "internal economics consulting shop" that is focused on monitoring and explaining the economy to the president, and the NEC assists the president with constructing and coordinating economic policies.[16] Other EOP offices that assist the president on economic policy are the Office of Management and Budget (OMB) and the US Trade Representative (USTR).

We can glean much about a president's take on economic policies by looking at whom he places in these managerial and advising roles. However, that still leaves many questions about presidential policymaking. For example, do presidents tend to prioritize policies that advance their ideological agendas? Or do they tend to prioritize political considerations, such as their public approval rating or the odds that they will win the Electoral College in their reelection campaign? Such questions motivate theorizing about presidents' behavior. The following section reviews some theories that might be applied to presidential policymaking. However, the theories focus on Congress and the legislative process, where the government's most consequential economic policies are fashioned.

Politics and Economic Policy: Theoretical Perspectives

Economic policies are not made by economists who seek to maximize the general welfare of the nation. They are made by elected officials and other policymakers who operate in a complex policymaking system and who must attend to political pressures and constraints. The political theories in this section attend to those pressures and constraints. They help us to understand the political logic of economic policies.

Spatial Voting and the Median Voter Theorem

Politics is routinely discussed in terms that imply that it takes place in an ideological space. For example, we say that politician A is to the *left* of politician B or that one budget proposal is to the *right* of another. *Spatial models* of politics focus on that idea, and they typically reduce politics to the positioning of proposals and the evaluation of alternatives on a single, left–right dimension. For example, in spatial voting theory each voter selects the candidate that is nearest to his or her "ideal point." If a voter is more conservative than all of the candidates on offer, she simply votes for the most conservative of the bunch, which is the candidate who is located farthest to the right. If the voter is centrist, she may need to figure out whether a candidate to her right or a candidate to her left is closer to her ideal point.

In his 1957 book, *An economic theory of democracy*, Anthony Downs advances a spatial theory of democracy in which voters are arrayed in one-dimensional policy space and two "office-seeking" parties compete for elected office, with the winner to implement its proposal. The office-seeking assumption means that the parties care foremost about winning the election, relegating all other objectives to a secondary concern. As such, both parties aim to construct the more popular proposal. Because voting is spatial and there are only two competitors, the model anticipates that both parties will adopt the *same* platform and that it will align with the preference of the *median* voter.[17] To appreciate this, imagine party A proposes platform M that corresponds to the preferences of the median voter, with exactly half of voters to the right and the other half to the left. Then, if party B proposes R that is to the right of M, party A will win the election because more voters are closer to M than R. That majority includes all voters to the left of M, which is half the electorate, plus all voters that are to the right of M but closer to M than R.

Downs' model has been used to explain many types of political phenomena. For example, it helps to explain why presidential candidates tack to the middle – advancing more moderate proposals – in general elections, after they have won their party's nomination. And it explains why congressional candidates in more liberal districts are more liberal than those in more conservative districts. Spatial models are also used to understand policy choices of governmental institutions such as a panel of regulators, a chamber of Congress, or the Supreme Court.

The type of economic policy that is most often analyzed with a Downsian model is redistributive taxation, which reflects the idea that the most general left–right issue pertains to how much the government should use taxes and transfers to reduce inequality, widen the distribution of resources, and assist the poor. To construct a Downsian theory of redistributive taxation, one must make some assumptions about voters and tax-and-transfer systems.[18] A basic and general idea is to posit that each voter's preference for redistribution is a function of her income, with poorer voters preferring more redistribution. Various hypotheses follow. First, government policy will conform to the preferences of the *middle-income voter*, who is probably a member of the lower-middle class. Second, redistributive taxation will increase if market inequality increases, as the median voter's economic position falls farther behind that of top earners. Third, redistributive taxation will increase after reforms that add more low-income voters to the electorate. (The Voting Rights Act of 1965 would be an example, because it greatly expanded the number of low-income voters in the electorate by dismantling literacy tests and other barriers to voting that had been used by southern states to disenfranchise black citizens.) And fourth, the government will do less redistributive taxation than what is preferred by the median *citizen* if poorer citizens are less likely to vote than wealthier citizens, because in that case the median *voter* who determines government policies is richer than the median citizen.

Now that we have connected the spatial model to some policy predictions, consider some of the ways that reality departs from Downsianism. First, one of Downs' main predictions does not obtain: the platforms of America's two parties are not identical, they are divergent. Second, many voters are not very knowledgeable about candidates' and parties' platforms, as the spatial model assumes. A third issue is that elections turn on more than just party platforms – candidates' personalities, campaign ads, the state of the economy, and many other things also matter. Another, more technical issue is that the median voter result does not emerge from a spatial model if the policy space is not unidimensional. Actually, if multiple policy spaces can be considered simultaneously – such as redistributive taxation *and* civil rights policy – then the model may yield no equilibrium platform or policy.[19]

These issues should not be considered shortcomings of the spatial model – *all* models are inaccurate oversimplifications. The usefulness of a model is less a function of how precisely it resembles the real world than of how it simplifies the world in order to reveal some important truths. If Downsian models help us to understand something about elections and public policies, then they are useful. Also, the "shortcomings" of Downsian models are useful departure points for thinking about other models. Indeed, a very large amount of political research has used those shortcomings as points of departure.

Retrospective Voting Models

One alternative to the Downsian framework assumes that voters are not *prospective* but *retrospective*. Whereas prospective voters choose parties and candidates that will give them the best future outcome, retrospective voters punish or reward incumbents according to their performance in office. Retrospective voters can base their judgments on various criteria. For example, they may be "pocketbook" voters who consider their own, personal finances. Or, they may be "sociotropic" voters who consider the performance of the wider economy.[20]

Retrospective voting models allow elections to be about much more than party platforms, including valence issues (i.e., matters on which everyone agrees) like whether or not the economy is strong, or whether or not the government is honest. They are also more realistic than prospective models in that parties are not bound by their campaign promises. Indeed, retrospective models tend to focus on the issue of electoral accountability, including questions like: under what circumstances can politicians break their campaign promises and "get away with it"? Can voters deter corruption? Do term limits worsen representation?[21]

Retrospective models have less to say about economic policies. Yet, one implication is fairly straightforward: parties will be keen on "delivering" in election years, which implies political business cycles and expansionary policies leading up to an election. That result may require a lack of sophistication on voters' part. If voters understand that politicians merely boost the economy for the election, and thus that the post-election period will feature higher inflation and more government debt, then they will be less inclined to reward politicians for election-timed expansions.

Voter Group Models of Distributive Politics

Another way to depart from Downsianism is to suppose that elections are not about broad ideological platforms and an ideologically minded electorate but rather about how might tax dollars be allocated across a variety of distinct voter groups, all of which are keen on maximizing their post-tax-and-transfer income. There are various theories of this type, which we may generally refer to as "group-targeting models of distributive politics." In general, they share six assumptions. First, parties offer distributive benefits to voter groups that vote prospectively.[22] Second, each group votes rather cohesively, whether it is a labor union, a group of farmers, or a demographic (e.g., African Americans). Third, each group is responsive to distributive policies like social programs and tax breaks that increase each member's post-tax income. Fourth, groups are differently attached to parties: some are "swing" groups that are not committed to one party or the other, whereas other, "core" groups are fairly committed to supporting a particular party. Fifth, parties promise benefits to groups in order to maximize votes or their probability of victory. And, sixth, parties face a budget constraint, which means that they cannot offer everything to everyone, and they need to determine how to "divide a fixed pie."

Of course, a key element in these models is groups' willingness to trade party allegiance for income, and many models reach the conclusion that "swing" groups receive larger transfers because they are more easily swayed. However, those results are typically based on a persuasion-only model, whereas winning elections in a non-Downsian environment is also a function of *mobilizing* and *coordinating* core supporters. In other words, if parties take their core groups for granted then those groups may abstain from voting or display intra-party disunity and support an independent or third-party candidate.[23] When those possibilities are considered, models tilt in favor of the hypothesis that core groups benefit more in the game of distributive politics.[24] That idea is supported by some empirical research. In particular, a study published in 2006 by Stephen Ansolabehere and James M. Snyder of Harvard University found that incumbent parties in US states tend to craft budgets that favor counties with more core supporters rather than swing counties with a more balanced electorate.

Public Choice and Special Interests

Whereas group-targeting models link distributive policies to parties' search for votes, another tradition links particularistic policies (including subsidies, tax breaks, and regulatory policies) to two phenomena that make narrow-interest groups more politically effective than broad groups like consumers or taxpayers. First, particularistic policies provide *concentrated benefits and diffuse costs*, which motivates different amounts of political pressure from beneficiaries as opposed to the broad groups who pay the price. For example, price supports for sugar provide a large benefit to a small group of farmers that is paid for by a nation of sugar consumers. Yet, consumers do not mobilize against the policy because the effort is not worth the potential gain for any individual consumer. By contrast, individual sugar farmers have much on the line, and they are willing to provide votes and campaign cash to members of Congress who defend the policy.[25] For office-seeking members of Congress, the political calculus is simple: they should help the group that cares greatly about the policy and not worry about the broader group that will exert no counter-pressure.

It is worth noting that this phenomenon also accompanies non-economic issues, where the difference in political pressure is related to intensity of feeling rather than monetary costs and benefits. For example, a majority of Americans has long favored stricter laws on the sale of firearms, but that has not translated into policies because opponents are more passionate and vocal.[26] The difference in intensity is well known, and it can be illustrated by pointing to the fact that there is a significant slice of the electorate that is almost singularly focused on protecting gun freedom. By contrast, there are hardly any "single-issue voters" for a pro-control agenda.

A further point is that special interests differ in the source of their political influence: some have voter power, others have money. For example, the NRA's political influence is primarily a function of the group's large membership, which is active in primary and general elections. By contrast, the pressure power of pharmaceutical companies is tied to their economic resources, which they can use for campaign contributions, political ads, and lobbyists. Pharmaceutical companies also partner with other businesses and industries in large pressure groups like the National Association of Manufacturers and the Chamber of Commerce. Because those groups have notable membership organizations in every congressional district, they may be able to exert great pressure on general issues that matter for employers and manufacturers. However, they do not exert pressure on issues that matter only to particular sectors or businesses.

The second phenomenon in favor of narrow groups is related to the first issue but centers more on the size of the competing groups and the challenges of cooperative collective action. In particular, larger groups face greater difficulties mobilizing because they face a more severe *free-rider problem*. The free-rider problem stems from individuals recognizing that their contributions to a collective good are too small to "make a difference" to the successful provision of the good. As a result, they do not contribute. Of course, the collective dilemma is that everyone else does similarly, and so the group is much smaller and less influential than it might be and the collective good that it desires may be under-provided. More succinctly, free-rider incentives undermine collective mobilization and the provision of collective goods.

Free-rider problems are ubiquitous in politics. Would-be activists free ride by not joining social movements; citizens who want democratic elections can be said to free ride on others whenever they fail to turn out to vote; and members of Congress free ride on their colleagues when they vote against something like raising the debt ceiling that they think should pass but is politically costly to support. Also, if not for the legal sanctions that apply to tax evasion, the free-rider problem would sharply curtail the government's revenues, because most Americans would keep their tax dollars if given the choice.

Small groups are better able to overcome free-rider problems because shirkers can be identified and pressured. Additionally, each member's contribution constitutes a larger share of the total effort in a small group, so each shirker can appreciate that his behavior will jeopardize the collective good. For these reasons, small groups can be more politically effective than large groups.

These arguments about cost diffusion, collective action, and political pressure were elaborated by Mancur Olson in his 1965 book, *The logic of collective action*. Olson's work – along with that of Anthony Downs and economists such as Kenneth Arrow, James Buchanan, and Gordon Tullock – became the foundation for new fields of research that applied the tools of economics to the study of politics. One variant that was very active in the 1970s and 1980s is known as "public choice" and focuses heavily on the undersupply of public goods and the oversupply of policies that benefit narrow commercial interests.[27]

Public choice arguments about the success of narrow groups hinge on the assumption that elected officials are office-seeking or "rent-seeking," which means that they seek to enrich themselves. And they assume that voters, like politicians, are rational, self-interested utility maximizers. Voters who are rational in that sense calculate the costs and benefits of both voting and paying attention to politics, and they conclude that there is insufficient reason to do either because the chance that their vote will change an election outcome is too small. Therefore, as Chapter 1 noted, citizens are expected to abstain from voting and to be "rationally ignorant."[28] As such, this economic approach to the study of voter turnout in elections tends to ponder "why is turnout so high?" rather than "why is turnout so low?"

Public choice analyses – like contemporary models of retrospective voting and electoral accountability – also emphasize that voters may be poorly served by elected officials because they encounter difficulties with monitoring and sanctioning their representatives. In the terminology of *principal–agent theory* – a tool that is used in accountability models – voters are "principals" who delegate governing tasks to elected representatives. The representatives thus act as voters' "agents," and voters experience *agency loss* to the degree that their representatives pursue actions that do not perfectly conform to voters' preferences.[29] Agency loss occurs because agents have their own preferences and because there is asymmetric information between principals and agents. In particular, principals do not know everything that their agents do, and agents do not know everything that their principals want.

Principal–agent theory considers various ways that principals can control their agents, and many of those controls can be useful for reducing agency loss. In the electorate–representative relationship, however, those mechanisms are not very effective, and the potential for substantial agency loss remains.[30] Principal–agent theory is useful for highlighting that fact, and it offers another lens by which to consider the success of special interests at the expense of broad groups. Still, any explanation of that phenomenon must point to the fact that special interests offer something of value that is not matched by broad voter groups. The public choice approach does that by emphasizing special interests' superior resources, organization, and attentiveness.

Partisan Legislatures and Policies

Public choice models provide a useful way to think about some political phenomena, but they fail to explain other important things, above all the existence of general-interest legislation. To explain the provision of programmatic policies by a legislature that is pulled in various directions – with each member having his or her own programmatic and particularistic priorities – our attention is drawn to two legislative institutions: political parties and the agenda control mechanisms that they employ to stay united and effect a programmatic agenda.

Theories of legislative parties are built upon the notion that parties serve an electoral function for their members. By way of illustration, note that parties would be electorally unnecessary if members of Congress could be reelected purely on the basis of pork projects and the support of narrow interest groups, for in that case all members could ensure their reelection simply by allowing each other to earmark some pork and special-interest giveaways. But, to the extent that members seek to enact programmatic policy, they would be hamstrung by particularistic pressures and the prospect of endless tinkering and coalition-making. Indeed, theories of institutionless legislatures predict intractable indecision and policy instability.[31]

The solution is to form a standing coalition – a party – that takes control of the chamber and advances a programmatic agenda. As it implements its platform, each member of the coalition is able to claim some credit for the accomplishments, and voters can reward them with reelection. The arrangement also allows voters to hold the majority collectively accountable for its performance and to replace it with the minority party if it underperforms. That, in turn, provides an important check on unwanted outcomes like excessive spending, corruption, and the under-provision of public goods. Put another way, we can view legislative parties as a response to voters' demand for programmatic policies and collective accountability, and parties allow those goods to be provided to an extent that would be unachievable in their absence.

As Chapter 1 noted, a majority party's ability to focus legislative activity on its program is highly dependent on its control of the legislative agenda. If the majority does not control the agenda, the minority party can propose bills or amendments that command support from some members of the majority party and generate policy successes that align more with it than with the majority party. By controlling the agenda, the majority ensures that those things do not happen. The only proposals that receive consideration are those of its choosing, and that gate-keeping safeguards the party's interests and allows it to amass its own record of accomplishment.[32] To be clear, agenda control does not imply that the majority will succeed in everything that its members may propose. On the contrary, the party often may be "disappointed," failing to muster enough votes to pass its proposals. Rather, agenda control implies that the party will never lose to a coalition that includes the minority party plus some majority party defectors. More specifically, if the majority never allows votes on legislation that is opposed by a majority of its members, then it will never be "rolled," in which a proposal passes against a majority of the majority.

To put these points another way, a majority party's legislative success vis-à-vis the minority has less to do with its numerical advantage on policy votes than its control of the chamber's agenda and procedures. And, if we return to the idea that legislative parties are created in order to establish a record that benefits its members, then we can consider agenda control to be something that is more than just a convenient tool. In a more fundamental sense, it is the reason for parties' existence. In other words, we can say that legislators form parties in order to control the legislative agenda, and they do that to establish a record that helps them curry favor with voters.

This particular theory of legislative parties is elaborated by Gary Cox and McCubbins (2005), who also identify the policy consequences of partisan agenda control.[33] Specifically, their model implies that new policies are unlikely to be counter to the preferences of a majority of the majority party. (In other words, the majority party will not be rolled.) A second implication is that new policies (on the core, unidimensional axis of partisan conflict) will reflect the preferences of the majority party's median member – not those of the chamber median, as a Downsian model without majority party agenda control would anticipate. A third and more basic hypothesis is that the chamber will be able to pass general-interest legislation.

In the House of Representatives, the majority's control of the agenda is secured by various rules and institutions, most notably the gate-keeping and procedural powers that are exercised by the Committee on Rules. The Rules Committee, as it is more frequently called, determines which bills will be considered by the floor (i.e., the entire chamber) and which amendments members can propose to modify a bill that is under floor consideration. The Rules Committee is stacked two-to-one in favor of the majority party, and its majority party members understand that their main responsibility is to protect and advance the interests of the party. Their success is illustrated by the fact that the majority party is almost never rolled on the floor of the House.[34]

There are some House rules that create the potential for minority party interference. For example, when legislation is drafted in the chamber's standing committees, it is normally the case that any committee member can offer an amendment.[35] However, committee chairs, who are always members of the majority party, are otherwise able to exert agenda control. Of course, the Rules Committee serves as a backstop in the event that a committee advances legislation that is not well received by the House majority. But such an event is unlikely, because committee chairs who do that are liable to be removed from their positions by the party or its leadership.

It is worth noting that the House has worked somewhat differently in other eras. In particular, in the middle of the twentieth century, before southern realignment and the polarization of the parties (see Chapters 5 and 6), House leadership was more easygoing about its grip on process and structure. For example, it would frequently allow legislation to be considered under an "open rule," in which any and all germane amendments can be offered from the floor. In addition, committee chairs held their positions on account of their seniority, and they were able to keep their positions even if they created routine headaches for their parties. The Democratic Party started to make the House more streamlined in the 1970s, in response to liberals' longstanding frustrations with southern Democrats. In later decades, as the parties became more polarized, House control became even more centralized. These days, the majority firmly secures its control of House process and structure, and open rules from the Rules Committee are exceedingly rare.[36]

With respect to present discussion, the Senate differs from the House in two important respects. First, it has long allowed filibusters, which allow a member to indefinitely stall a vote unless three-fifths of the chamber votes for cloture.[37] In practice, that means that new policies have some minority party support because the majority is seldom sixty members strong. As noted in Chapter 1, however, the majority sometimes considers budget or tax bills via budget reconciliation rules that do not allow filibusters. Those rules are especially useful when both chambers are controlled by the same party, because then the congressional majorities can advance bills without the need to win any support from minority party senators.

The second difference is that normal Senate rules allow all members to offer amendments on the floor. With nothing like the House Rules Committee to control amendments, minority party senators can frustrate and embarrass the majority, and they can steer policy proposals in their direction. Interestingly, however, Senate legislation often seems to reflect interests that align well with the majority party. According to Chris Den Hartog and Nathan W. Monroe (2011), two scholars of the Senate, the reason why is simply that the majority party commits to voting as a block on minority party amendments. That is costly because it requires some members to vote against proposals that they would like to support, but it is the only way to limit minority party interference in a setting where standing parliamentary rules allow all members to offer amendments.

In terms of policy outcomes, this makes the Senate similar to the House, except that under normal rules (i.e., filibusters are allowed) the majority needs to craft proposals that will win enough support from the minority to invoke cloture. More specifically, successful proposals will tend to have a majority party tilt, but not so much as in the House, where the majority does not require minority support for its proposals.[38]

Inter-Branch Bargaining

In the legislative process, Congress has the power to propose legislation and the president has the power to veto those proposals. Given that arrangement, what can we infer about policy? To pursue the question, we first consider a non-partisan spatial model. Then, we consider the question from a partisan perspective in order to contrast unified and divided government.

A basic, non-partisan spatial model of the policymaking process places actors and policies in a unidimensional left–right policy space and represents Congress as a single institution (ignoring bicameralism).[39] Then, with Congress as the agenda setter that makes proposals that the president chooses to accept or reject, we consider different locations of proposals,

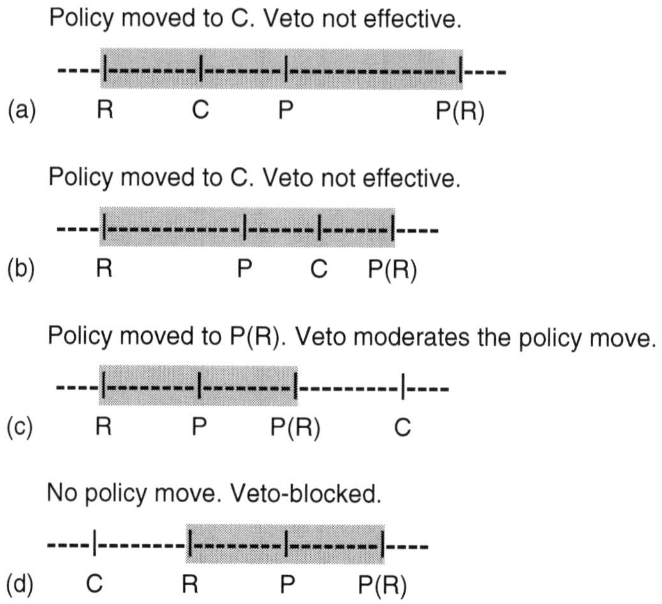

Policy moved to C. Veto not effective.

(a) R C P P(R)

Policy moved to C. Veto not effective.

(b) R P C P(R)

Policy moved to P(R). Veto moderates the policy move.

(c) R P P(R) C

No policy move. Veto-blocked.

(d) C R P P(R)

Figure 4.1 Spatial models of inter-branch policymaking.
Source: Author.

status quo policies, and ideal points. To illustrate, Figure 4.1 provides four configurations. In each, C is Congress's ideal policy (which can be thought of as the ideal point for the median member of Congress), P is the president's ideal policy, R is the status quo or reversion policy (i.e., the policy that exists if there is no change in policy), and P(R) stands for the president's "indifference point," which is the point that is equidistant from P as R, such that the president is indifferent regarding the two policies. In other words, the president would prefer P, or at least something closer to P than R or P(R), but if the choice is between P and P(R), then she is indifferent about which is chosen.[40] Therefore, the range between P and P(R) is what the president is willing to accept in place of R. All other policy proposals will be met with a veto.

Note that in configuration 1 Congress is able to move policy from R to C. Although the president would prefer a policy further to the right, a veto threat would not be credible. So, C is proposed and becomes the new policy, and the president's veto power does not help her. Veto power is also ineffective in configuration 2, where the president and Congress both want to move policy in the same direction and P is closer to C than R. In the third configuration, however, Congress's ideal policy is farther from P than R, so the president's veto is credible. As a result, Congress proposes P(R) because it is the best outcome it can obtain. Finally, configuration 4 predicts no policy change. Congress prefers to move policy one direction, but the president prefers to move in the other direction. If Congress proposes legislation, the president vetoes. R remains the government's policy.[41]

This model illustrates two basic points about the president's veto power. First, there are instances in which veto threats are not credible, and in those cases the president's veto power gives her no leverage in the policymaking process. The second point is that when a veto is credible, the president can block or moderate change, but in neither case is she made better off than under the status quo. Moreover, the veto's effect – to block or moderate change – depends not on the president's negotiating strategy but on the ideological location of the president's ideal policy vis-à-vis that of both Congress and the status quo.

Regarding policy, the spatial model supports two conclusions. First, and rather obviously, the status quo is unchanged whenever Congress and the president want to move policy in different directions. Second, if Congress and the president want to move policy in the same direction, new policies will reflect Congress's ideal point – *unless* that is too far of a departure from the status quo for the president to accept, in which case Congress moderates the policy to the minimum amount that is necessary.

That outcome is a serviceable description of the 1995 budget deal that was reviewed at the beginning of this chapter. However, note that the budget process is somewhat different than the ordinary legislative process in that the true reversion outcome is not the status quo budget but a government shutdown.. That may give the president some leverage in the budget game, especially if the public sides with the president in the budget impasse. That is what occurred in 1995, and so Congress faced pressure to modify its proposal. When it did so, it proposed a budget that was less of a departure from the previous year's budget and closer to the president's position.

Note that our simple spatial model does not incorporate veto overrides, although it could do so easily.[42] Nor does the model consider line-item vetoes or the possibility that Congress and president differ on non-ideological, particularistic grounds, as occurred in Congress's successful veto override in 1998.

Let us now move from a purely spatial model to one that considers political parties and the difference between unified government and divided government. We are inclined to think that configuration 4 in Figure 4.1 depicts divided government, whereas the other configurations depict unified government. Thus, we anticipate no policy movement (gridlock) under divided government.

Although that expectation is reasonable, there is one confounding issue: divided governments can be quite productive. In fact, there has been some debate among political scientists about whether the production of "significant" legislation is at all slowed by divided government. The most noteworthy study on this topic is David Mayhew's *Divided we govern*, a book that was first published in 1991 and updated in 2005 and that made a strong case that just as much "significant" legislation is passed during periods of divided government as during periods of unified government.[43] More recent experience suggests that Mayhew's argument no longer holds true. As the parties have become more polarized and the nation's political battles have become increasingly unidimensional, divided governments have been less productive.[44]

Even so, the passage of *any* significant legislation by divided governments raises the question of why experience departs from the predictions of the spatial model. Two possibilities exist. One is that divided governments succeed on issues that are not on the main axis of party competition and that enjoy considerable bipartisan support.[45] For example, legislative accomplishments may consist of things like trade agreements and regulatory overhauls that can be hailed as both pro-producer and pro-consumer.

The second possibility is that the parties "logroll" – i.e., they trade wins and losses with each other in a piece of legislation. For example, if Congress moves to reduce the budget deficit its solution may include both taxes and spending cuts so that the pain is not felt entirely on either side of the budget. Likewise, if Congress is in a spending mood, it may couple tax cuts with a boost to social spending, or tax cuts for the rich with tax credits for the poor, or greater social spending with greater military spending, or all of the above.

These logroll possibilities suggest a hypothesis: divided governments will generate larger, more-persistent budget deficits than unified governments.[46] Two ideas drive this hypothesis. First, deficit reduction may be more challenging during divided government because each party will try to limit policy changes that are averse to its core interests and ideological positions. By contrast, a unified government might be able to take a more aggressive step toward deficit reduction. Second, unified governments may have a greater interest in limiting budget deficits because any concerns among the public about budget deficits will be focused only at the governing party. During divided government, the parties can take comfort in the idea that neither is wholly responsible for the deficit.

Major pieces of legislation that are enacted during divided government – be they logrolls or agreements that are off the main axis of party contestation – are also likely to be greased by particularism and pork. Going further, we may hypothesize that divided governments will enact more particularistic policy and pork than unified governments, and that particularism and pork may be most abundant when Congress is itself divided, with each party in control of one chamber. The general argument here is that legislative processes that have more "veto players" – a generic term for any institution that can veto a policy move – generate more particularism because each veto player may require or demand some particularism for legislation to move forward.[47] In addition, as particularism and pork are added to bipartisan initiatives, both may tend to swell far beyond what is necessary in order to win majority support in each chamber because there is no reason for the enacting coalition to deny goodies to would-be supporters. Under unified government, by contrast, there is a greater incentive for the enacting coalition to keep a lid on particularism.

It is difficult to test these hypotheses, and it is possible that they are false or overstated. However, it is less difficult to appreciate how party polarization and a unidimensional policy space affect policymaking in partisan legislatures. Put simply, polarization makes logrolls more difficult, and unidimensionalism precludes the possibility of bipartisan reforms of off-axis policies. In other words, they cause the legislature to become gridlocked and status quo policies to become inalterable. In addition, the contrast between divided government and unified government may intensify. Indeed, although unified governments are also frustrated by party polarization and unidimensional politics, they have means to break the impasse. In particular, they may use budget reconciliation rules to get around the filibuster on tax or budget issues. More dramatically, the senate majority could break the logjam entirely by reducing the cloture threshold to a simple majority.[48] In that case, the government could be very productive, and it could decisively move all sorts of policies to the left or right.

Economic Theories of Politics

The various theories surveyed above consider the most salient features of the policymaking environment, and they help explain various aspects of economic policy. Of course, we have not considered every potentially relevant aspect of the political system. For example, we did not explore the Senate's overrepresentation of low-population states.[49] Nor did we consider differences between the branches regarding targeted spending, like that which led Congress to override Clinton's line-item vetoes in 1998.

To review, our theories linked the content of general-interest policies to the median voter, the median-income citizen, the median member of the majority party in Congress, and inter-branch bargaining games in which Congress is the agenda setter. Meanwhile, our theories of special-interest policies focused on free-rider problems and the asymmetric distribution of policy benefits and costs across narrow and broad groups. We also considered models of distributive politics in which parties distribute resources to core groups and swing groups, and we conjectured that the amount of particularism may relate to the number of veto players in the legislative process and that divided governments may produce larger and more persistent budget deficits.

Each framework that we considered is rooted in "rationalist" or "economic" schools of politics. The hallmark of these models is an assumption that actors (e.g., politicians, voters) respond rationally to beliefs about how they may reach their goals (e.g., electoral victories, policy influence).

The most common assumption about politicians is that they are office-seeking. The use of that assumption does not imply that real-world politicians do not have other goals. Sometimes, politicians cast votes for legislation that they know will make it more difficult to win their reelection campaigns but that they believe to be good policy. However, the office-seeking assumption is reasonable because politicians are highly focused on winning and retaining office and because they cannot shape policy unless they win their elections. More importantly, the assumption allows us to devise clear and cogent theories of political behavior. The median voter theorem is a good example. Although it is a gross over-simplification of electoral behavior and party platforms, it helps us understand politics and policy in a two-party system.

Economic Influence on Politics

Some of the theories that we have considered are economic in another sense, in that they identify ways that economic groups and phenomena influence politics and policies. Three of our theories fit that description.

First, the public choice tradition considers the relative influence of different economic interests, highlighting in particular the disadvantages of consumers vis-à-vis producers. Many types of producers may be privileged in that respect, including large and well-financed corporations. But recall that interest group influence is not only about money. It is also about the votes that they can supply in elections, and it is about the likelihood that consumers will attend to relevant policies. Consumers can and do attend to issues about product costs and safety, and that can translate into policy successes – not because they overcome the free-rider problem, but because political parties are keen on servicing them. So, the type of producer that may be the most politically influential, at least in a general sense, may be those that interact little with the public or those whose interactions with the government attract little public scrutiny. Examples include defense contractors and the sugar farmers we have repeatedly highlighted.

Commercial farmers, more generally, are poised to be politically effective because they operate in rural districts with electorates that are attentive to agricultural policies, and that attentiveness is not matched by urban consumers, whose policy interests are more varied. For that matter, any commercial enterprise that dominates the economy of an electoral district is likely to be relatively successful in the policymaking system, because representatives of that community will care greatly about policies that favor the industry.

Another theory of ours posits that changes in income inequality affect redistributive taxation via the preferences of the median-income citizen. The theory is purely spatial, and it assumes that citizens vote and are knowledgeable about party platforms and policies. If we relax those assumptions, we can identify some reasons why the theory's prediction – that an increase in income inequality will lead to greater redistribution – may not occur in the real world. Possibilities include: poorer citizens are less likely to vote, voters do not understand how policies affect inequality, and voters also attend to social and other issues. Additionally, and moving farther from spatial theory, we can again emphasize the organizational advantages of narrow, wealthier groups over broad, poorer groups, including the argument made by Madison in *Federalist #10* that a large republic makes it especially difficult for the poor to organize. We will revisit some of these points in Chapter 6, but for now we simply note that Downsian theories of redistribution are important for identifying a means by which the economy shapes politics and policy.

Finally, we have noted that the state of the economy affects incumbents' electoral fortunes. In this chapter, that idea was linked to retrospective voting. Earlier, in Chapter 1, the phenomenon was described as an empirical tendency: historically, a fast-growing economy with low unemployment tends to favor the president and his party, whereas a sluggish economy with high unemployment bodes well for the party that does not control the presidency. Figure 4.2 illustrates the strength of the relationship. The figure shows the economy's growth rate in the year leading up to an election and

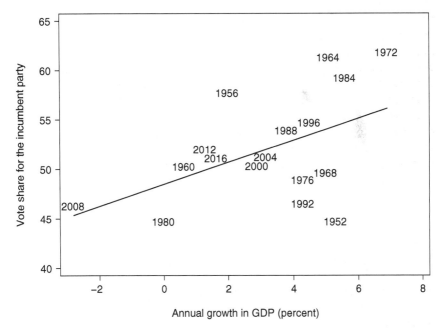

Figure 4.2 Economic growth and presidential election outcomes, 1952–2016.

Notes: The x-axis shows the annual change in GDP as measured on October 1 of the election year. The y-axis shows the share of the two-party vote received by the party that controlled the presidency at the time of the election. The line is an ordinary least squares regression.

Sources: Federal Reserve Economic Data (FRED), Federal Reserve Bank of St. Louis; The American Presidency Project: http://www.presidency.ucsb.edu/elections.php.

the percent of the two-party vote received by the incumbent party. The data show a clear positive relationship. A simple regression analysis suggests that each 1 percent increase in the growth rate tends to correspond to a 1 percent increase in the vote share for the incumbent party. It also suggests that the incumbent party and opposition party are likely to obtain an equal share of the vote if the growth rate is around 1.8 percent per year. Faster growth implies the odds are in the incumbent party's favor, and slower growth implies that the odds are in the opposition's favor. Of course, these estimates merely represent a historical average, and they will change if we bring other variables into the analysis. Some studies that do that suggest that the effect of economic growth is stronger.[50]

Even so, it is important to note that economic conditions are not deterministic. Indeed, whereas Figure 4.2 shows an unmistakable trend, it also shows that election results can depart significantly from the average or predicted result. Only at a very high or very low growth rate can we offer a rather safe prediction about an election outcome. Put another way, there are many other things that matter in presidential elections.

Conclusion

This chapter had three main threads. First, it reviewed the scope and means of the president's influence on economic policy and the economy. Second, it introduced a series of political theories, each of which helps explain economic policies. And, third, it reviewed three ways that the economy influences politics and policy, at least in theory.

In the chapters that follow, we adopt a different, historical perspective on the nation's political economy. The theories that we sketched in this chapter will help to make intelligible the complex and sometimes unexpected changes in policy that occurred along the way.

Notes

1 For a thorough analysis of veto power, see Cameron, 2000.
2 It is perhaps the case that contemporary laws tend to give less discretionary power to the executive branch than the laws of earlier times. However, the growth in programs over time has led to an increase in the scope and number of policy domains in which the president may have some room for maneuver on policy. In that sense, Congress has gradually delegated more powers to the executive branch.
3 The process was established in 1988 and legislated in the Defense Base Realignment and Closure Act of 1990.
4 Mayer, 2002, p. 35.
5 Some of the president's authority over administrative policy stems from the McNamara–O'Hara Service Contract Act of 1965 and the Davis Bacon Act of 1931.
6 Liptak, 2015.

7 Put differently, contemporary trade agreements are not negotiated under the treaty provisions of the Constitution, by which the president submits an agreement to the Senate, which then ratifies them only with a two-thirds vote. Instead, they are treated like legislation, and Congress grants the president trade promotion authority (which was previously called fast-track authority) under temporary legislation. The president then submits implementing legislation to Congress for an up-or-down (no amendments allowed) majority vote in both chambers.

8 FLSA, Section 13(a)(1).

9 Trottman and Morath, 2016.

10 A separate, less-generous program, called Income-Contingent Repayment, dates from 1994.

11 The 2015 changes came in response to Obama's Presidential Memorandum of June 9, 2014.

12 Stratford, 2015.

13 Revesz and Lienke, 2017.

14 This group mirrors the president's team of national security advisers, which includes the Secretaries of State and Defense, the Joint Chiefs, the directors of Homeland Security and the CIA, and the National Security Advisor.

15 However, per legislation, the heads of CEA, OMB, and USTR must be confirmed by the Senate.

16 Hennessey, 2010.

17 Another assumption that is necessary for this result is that voters' preferences are "single-peaked" (Downs, 1957). Downs' model is built on earlier models of committee decision-making by Black (1958) and of two-firm competition in a one-dimensional town by Hotelling (1929).

18 See Londregan, 2006 for a review of the literature and Meltzer and Richard, 1981 for a well-known spatial model of redistributive taxation.

19 The proofs of these propositions appear in Arrow, 1963 and McKelvey, 1976.

20 Are voters primarily prospective or retrospective? A survey of the relevant research concludes that voters tend to "react to past (retrospective) events more than to expected (prospective) ones, but the difference is small" (Lewis-Beck and Paldam, 2000, p. 114).

21 Retrospective voting analyses date to Key, 1966 and Fiorina, 1981. More recent work tends to assume that voters look at the past in order to choose the best outcome in the future – that is, they are retrospective in order to vote prospectively. See Ashworth, 2012 for a review of the literature on accountability. Classic works on accountability include Barro, 1973 and Ferejohn, 1986. A more recent contribution is Besley, 2006.

22 For an overview of these models, see Londregan, 2006.

23 Note that these theories are not about congressional *districts*. Parties certainly target swing districts in order to win a legislative majority. Rather, the theories are about which groups within a district are favored.

24 Cox, 2009.

25 The sugar farmers are called a "privileged group" if one or more members of the group have incentives to provide the good for the whole association because the costs of their actions outweigh the benefits that they receive.

26 Surveys consistently show that a majority of Americans supports stricter laws on the sale of firearms (Gallup News, 2017).

27 For a comprehensive review of public choice, see Mueller, 2003. The public choice genre continues to this day, but its modern variants tend to use more of a "political economy" framework, which is marked by stronger assumptions and game-theoretic analysis. A recent work focused on special interest politics is Grossman and Helpman, 2001.

28 These ideas about voters originate with Downs (1957).

29 Representative democracy is built upon delegation. Voters delegate policymaking to elected representatives, who in turn delegate policy refinement and implementation to agencies. There is agency loss each step of the way. Representatives may choose policies that differ from what their constituents would prefer, and bureaucrats may implement policies in a way that differs from Congress's preferences.

30 A general solution to the agency loss problem is pay for outcomes, which frees principals from having to monitor everything that their agents do. Instead, principals simply need to evaluate the outcomes they care about, and the burden of asymmetric information falls upon agents, who need to figure out what their principals want and make it happen. The pay-for-outcome solution may work well in the case of some principal–agent relationships, like the employer–employee relationship. But there are several aspects of the electorate–representative relationship that allow for agency loss, even if voters focus on simple outcomes like whether the education system was improved or whether the economy expanded. One is that voters may not have uniform or clear preferences about outcomes. Another is voters would consider not just the incumbent's performance but also the expected performance of the challenger.

31 Only if the policy space is restricted to a single dimension is an institution-less legislature capable of producing stable policy (corresponding to the preferences of the median legislator). On instability, see Arrow, 1963 and McKelvey, 1976.

32 There are two types of agenda control. The type emphasized here is called "negative" agenda control and consists of the ability to block the consideration of items. "Positive" agenda control is the ability to determine which sorts of policy issues will be considered.

33 Cox and McCubbins, 2005. See also Cox, 2006b.

34 Cox and McCubbins, 2005.

35 Another procedure that can help the minority is the discharge petition. It allows a majority of House members to bring a bill to the floor without a veto by the Rules Committee. The procedure is very rarely used, and its existence does not imply that the majority party is not able to control the House agenda via ordinary rules and procedures.

36 See Aldrich and Rohde, 2005.

37 Filibusters have been allowed under Senate rules since 1806, but no filibusters were attempted until decades later. The cloture rule was added in 1917, and the cloture threshold was dropped from two-thirds to three-fifths in 1975.

38 For a spatial theory of the Senate and the US policymaking system, see Krehbiel, 1998. Krehbiel's theory does not attend to the majority party's agenda control, so it reaches different conclusions about policy than those offered here.

39 Romer and Rosenthal (1978) first used this type of model. For a review of the subsequent literature, see de Figueiredo, Jacobi, and Weingast, 2006 and Cameron, 2006. See also Shepsle and Weingast, 2012.

40 The "P(R)" notation is from de Figueiredo, Jacobi, and Weingast, 2006.

41 A Congress that is purely focused on policy outcomes would not bother making a proposal if it would be met with a veto, and so vetoes would never happen. In the real world, vetoes may occur because Congress wants to make a political point or because Congress and the president are using hardball tactics in budget negotiations.

42 Krehbiel's (1998) spatial model considers veto overrides.

43 See Mayhew, 2005.

44 See Howell et al., 2000, Binder, 2004, McCarty, Poole, and Rosenthal, 2006 and McCarty, 2007.
45 A separate hypothesis about divided government is that it may lead Congress to delegate less to the executive branch. See Epstein and O'Halloran, 1999 and Huber and Shipan, 2006.
46 McCubbins, 1991.
47 This argument is made by Cox and McCubbins (2001), who also note the importance of other veto players, like the Supreme Court.
48 For a review of the procedural and systemic consequences of polarization, see Lee, 2015 and McCarty, 2007.
49 On how Senate malapportionment may benefit low-population states, see Hauk and Wacziarg, 2007; Lee, 1998; and Ansolabehere, Snyder, and Ting, 2003.
50 Kramer, 1971; Hibbs, 2000, 2006.

References

Aldrich, John H., and David W. Rohde. (2005). Congressional committees in a partisan era. In Lawrence C. Dodd and Bruce I. Oppenheimer (Eds.), *Congress reconsidered*. Vol. 8 (pp. 249–70). Washington, DC: CQ Press.

Ansolabehere, Stephen, and James M. Snyder. (2006). Party control of state government and the distribution of public expenditures. *The Scandinavian Journal of Economics*, 108(4), 547–569.

Ansolabehere, Stephen, James M. Snyder, and Michael M. Ting. (2003). Bargaining in bicameral legislatures: When and why does malapportionment matter? *American Political Science Review*, 97(3), 471–481.

Arrow, Kenneth. (1963). *Social choice and individual values*. New Haven, CT: Yale University Press.

Ashworth, Scott. (2012). Electoral accountability: Recent theoretical and empirical work. *Annual Review of Political Science*, 15, 183–201.

Barro, Robert J. (1973). The control of politicians: An economic model. *Public Choice*, 14(1), 19–42.

Besley, Timothy. (2006). *Principled agents? The political economy of good government*. Oxford, UK: Oxford University Press.

Binder, Sarah A. (2004). *Stalemate: Causes and consequences of legislative gridlock*. Washington, DC: Brookings Institution Press.

Black, Duncan. (1958). *The theory of committees and elections*. Cambridge, UK: Cambridge University Press.

Cameron, Charles M. (2000). *Veto bargaining: Presidents and the politics of negative power*. Cambridge, UK: Cambridge University Press.

Cameron, Charles M. (2006). The political economy of the US presidency. In Barry R. Weingast and Donald Wittman (Eds.), *The Oxford handbook of political economy* (pp. 241–255). New York, NY: Oxford University Press.

Cox, Gary W. (2006b). The organization of democratic legislatures. In Barry R. Weingast and Donald Wittman (Eds.), *The Oxford handbook of political economy* (pp. 141–161). New York, NY: Oxford University Press.

Cox, Gary W. (2009). Swing voters, core voters, and distributive politics. In Ian Shapiro, Susan C. Stokes, Elizabeth Jean Wood, and Alexander S. Kirshner (Eds.), *Political representation* (pp. 342–357). Cambridge, UK: Cambridge University Press.

Cox, Gary W., and Mathew D. McCubbins. (2001). The institutional determinants of economic policy outcomes. In Stephan Haggard and Mathew D. McCubbins (Eds.), *Presidents, parliaments, and policy* (pp. 21–62). Cambridge, UK: Cambridge University Press.

Cox, Gary W., and Mathew D. McCubbins. (2005). *Setting the agenda: Responsible party government in the US House of Representatives.* Cambridge, UK: Cambridge University Press.

Den Hartog, Chris, and Nathan W. Monroe. (2011). *Agenda setting in the US Senate: Costly consideration and majority party advantage.* Cambridge, UK: Cambridge University Press.

Downs, Anthony. (1957). *An economic theory of democracy.* New York, NY: Harper & Row.

Epstein, David, and Sharyn O'Halloran. (1999). *Delegating powers: A transaction cost politics approach to policy making under separate powers.* Cambridge, UK: Cambridge University Press.

Ferejohn, John. (1986). Incumbent performance and electoral control. *Public Choice,* 50(1), 5–25.

de Figueiredo, Rui J. P., Tonja Jacobi, and Barry R. Weingast. (2006). The new separation-of-powers approach to American politics. In Barry R. Weingast and Donald Wittman (Eds.), *The Oxford handbook of political economy* (pp. 199–221). New York, NY: Oxford University Press.

Fiorina, Morris P. (1981). *Retrospective voting in American national elections.* New Haven, CT: Yale University Press.

Gallup News. (2017, November 9). Guns. Retrieved from: http://news.gallup.com/poll/1645/guns.aspx (accessed November 9, 2017).

Grossman, Gene M., and Elhanan Helpman. (2001). *Special interest politics.* Cambridge, MA: MIT Press.

Hauk, William R., and Romain Wacziarg. (2007). Small states, big pork. *Quarterly Journal of Political Science,* 2(1), 95–106.

Hennessey, Keith. (2010, September 22). Roles of the President's White House economic advisors (updated) [Web log comment]. Retrieved from: http://keithhennessey.com/2010/09/22/economic-roles-updated/ (accessed November 14, 2016).

Hibbs, Douglas A. (2000). Bread and peace voting in US presidential elections. *Public Choice,* 104(1), 49–180.

Hibbs, Douglas A. (2006). Voting and the macroeconomy. In Barry R. Weingast and Donald A. Wittman (Eds.), *The Oxford handbook of political economy* (pp. 565–586). New York, NY: Oxford University Press.

Hotelling, Harold. (1929). Stability in competition. *Economic Journal,* 39, 41–57.

Howell, William, Scott Adler, Charles Cameron, and Charles Riemann. (2000). Divided government and the legislative productivity of Congress, 1945–94. *Legislative Studies Quarterly,* 25(2), 285–312.

Huber, John D., and Charles R. Shipan. (2006). Politics, delegation, and bureaucracy. In Barry R. Weingast and Donald A. Wittman (Eds.), *The Oxford handbook of political economy* (pp. 256–272). New York, NY: Oxford University Press.

Key, V. O. (1966). *The responsible electorate.* New York, NY: Vintage Books.

Kramer, Gerald H. (1971). Short-term fluctuations in US voting behavior, 1896–1964. *American Political Science Review,* 65, 131–143.

Krehbiel, Keith. (1998). *Pivotal politics: A theory of US lawmaking*. Chicago, IL: University of Chicago Press.

Lee, Frances E. (1998). Representation and public policy: The consequences of senate apportionment for the geographic distribution of federal funds. *The Journal of Politics*, 60(1), 34–62.

Lee, Frances E. (2015). How party polarization affects governance. *Annual Review of Political Science*, 18, 261–282.

Lewis-Beck, Michael S., and Martin Paldam. (2000). Economic voting: An introduction. *Electoral Studies*, 19(2), 113–121.

Liptak, Kevin. (2015, September 8). New Obama order requires contractors to pay for sick leave. CNN. Retrieved from: www.cnn.com/2015/09/07/politics/obama-mandatory-sick-leave/ (accessed December 1, 2017).

Londregan, John. (2006). Political income redistribution. In Barry R. Weingast and Donald A. Wittman (Eds.), *The Oxford handbook of political economy* (pp. 84–101). New York, NY: Oxford University Press.

McCarty, Nolan. (2007). The policy effects of political polarization. In Paul Pierson and Theda Skocpol (Eds.), *The transformation of American politics: Activist government and the rise of conservatism* (pp. 223–254). Princeton, NJ: Princeton University Press.

McCarty, Nolan, Keith T. Poole, and Howard Rosenthal. (2006). *Polarized America: The dance of ideology and unequal riches*. Cambridge, MA: MIT Press

McCubbins, Mathew D. (1991). Government on lay-away: Federal spending and deficits under divided party control. In Gary W. Cox and Samuel Kernell (Eds.), *The politics of divided government* (pp. 113–153). Boulder, CO: Westview Press.

McKelvey, Richard D. (1976). Intransitivities in multidimensional voting models and some implications for agenda control. *Journal of Economic Theory*, 12(3), 472–482.

Mayer, Kenneth R. (2002). *With the stroke of a pen: Executive orders and presidential power*. Princeton, NJ: Princeton University Press.

Mayhew, David R. (2005). *Divided we govern: Party control, lawmaking and investigations, 1946–2002* (2nd ed.). New Haven, CT: Yale University Press.

Meltzer, Allan H., and Scott F. Richard. (1981). A rational theory of the size of government. *Journal of Political Economy*, 89(5), 914–927.

Mueller, Dennis C. (2003). *Public choice III*. Cambridge, UK: Cambridge University Press.

Neustadt, Richard. (1960). *Presidential power*. New York, NY: John Wiley & Sons.

Olson, Mancur. (1965). *The logic of collective action: Public goods and the theory of groups*. Cambridge, MA.: Harvard University Press.

Revesz, Richard L., and Jack Lienke. (2017, October 9). The E.P.A.'s smoke and mirrors on climate. *The New York Times*. Retrieved from: www.nytimes.com/2017/10/09/opinion/environmental-protection-obama-pruitt.html (accessed December 1, 2017).

Romer, Thomas, and Howard Rosenthal. (1978). Political resource allocation, controlled agendas, and the status quo. *Public Choice*, 33(4), 27–43.

Shepsle, Kenneth A., and Barry R. Weingast. (2012). Why so much stability? Majority voting, legislative institutions, and Gordon Tullock. *Public Choice*, 152(1), 83–95.

Stratford, Michael. (2015, October 28). Obama's income-based repayment expansion finalized. *Inside Higher Ed*. Retrieved from: www.insidehighered.com /quicktakes/2015/10/28/obamas-income-based-repayment-expansion-finalized (accessed December 1, 2017).

Trottman, Melanie, and Eric Morath. (2016, May 17). Obama Administration extends overtime pay to millions. *The Wall Street Journal*. Retrieved from: www.wsj.com/articles/obama-administration-set-to-extend-overtime-pay-to-millions-1463502142 (accessed December 1, 2017).

Part II

The Evolution of US Political Economy

5 Neoliberal Shifts and the Reagan Era

During his 2016 election campaign, Donald Trump railed against American companies that moved production to Mexico, where they could make use of lower-cost labor. One company he singled out for abuse was Ford, which was then considering moving production of a Lincoln car from Kentucky to Mexico. Ford subsequently decided against the move, and Trump declared victory on behalf of American workers. However, the victory was more symbolic than substantive. For one, Ford's decision actually had no effect on the Louisville plant, which would have stayed in production regardless.[1] More importantly, Ford's decision had no practical effect on long-term trends. For almost two decades, automobile manufacturers had been shifting production to Mexico, and for longer than that they had been doing something similar: moving production facilities away from the Midwest and into states like Kentucky and Tennessee, where labor costs and unions were less burdensome. Indeed, for nearly half a century, workers at established domestic plants had felt the pressure of out-of-state plants that could offer their workers lower wages.

The market pressures that drove those trends intensified in the 1970s when Japanese automakers made fast inroads into America's market – their share of the market surging from 3 percent to 18 percent over the decade. Fearing a further loss of market share, domestic automakers sought government help, and in 1981 the Reagan administration responded by pressuring Japan to curb auto exports. Japan obliged with modest "voluntary export restraints," which in turn led Japanese automakers to hasten their plans to move production stateside. Honda was the first Japanese manufacturer to assemble a car in America. Its 1982 plant in Ohio was soon followed by a Nissan plant in Tennessee and a Toyota plant in Kentucky.

Domestic automakers increasingly favored those states, too, and to manage costs in their established manufacturing sites they adopted a harder line toward labor unions. Their efforts succeeded, and GM, Ford, and Chrysler – America's "Big Three" – emerged as more attractive and competitive companies in the 1990s. Consumers also benefited, and they continue to benefit from market pressures that motivate companies to innovate and control costs. However, their empowerment has meant some measure of decline for the manufacturing communities of the Midwest, where wages have stagnated, and jobs have disappeared.[2]

Of course, the government's role in this decades-long story was not limited to export pressure on Japan in the early 1980s. In fact, Reagan's more emblematic policy – and the one that fit more squarely with his anti-government, pro-market agenda – was to shift the government's position in labor-management disputes in favor of the latter. The change in posture helped companies at a time when they needed to cut costs in order to compete with foreign competitors and weakened unions at a time when they were already under great pressure.

Indeed, the government's new posture affected more than just the auto industry, and it was not just auto manufacturers who were prodded by economic globalization. The great expansion of trade in the final decades of the century touched virtually every corner of the economy, and coinciding *neoliberal* changes in policy tended to compound the effects of globalization for both consumers and workers.

The term neoliberal is often treated as a synonym for conservative, but more precisely it pertains to a post-1960s economic philosophy that emphasizes free markets but allows social insurance and welfare programs. Above all, neoliberalism emphasizes a regulatory regime and trade regime that are liberal in the classical sense, with minimal government interference.

America's political economy became more neoliberal in the 1980s and 1990s as the government pursued trade liberalization and deregulation. The period contrasted sharply with the late 1960s and early 1970s, when the government greatly expanded its regulatory agencies and functions. The neoliberal reforms over the next three decades were arguably less sweeping, but the trend was unmistakable, and rapid economic change followed the deregulation of sectors such as banking, transportation, and telecommunications.

To be sure, the post-1970s trajectory was also conservative in a broader sense, as taxes and welfare programs were cut, and social conservatives won some victories on issues like gun rights and abortion restrictions. However, the neoliberal label is still useful – in part because the term has been widely used since the 1970s, when the philosophy gained purchase, and in part because the adjustments to tax policies and social programs were less consequential than the massive economic changes that accompanied market liberalization and globalization.

To understand the economy's development in the neoliberal era one must appreciate that it was borne of both politics and economics. That is, as important as the policy changes were, the economy's development was also partly its own making. In particular, the growth in trade and the decline of unions were economic phenomena that were well underway before Reagan took office and accelerated them. It is for that reason that this chapter reviews economic developments first, before it turns to politics and policy. However, we should not underestimate the importance of policy changes, nor of the monumental changes in the nation's politics that helped deliver them. Indeed, those are the main subjects in this chapter and the next, which collectively trace developments from the 1970s until 2008, when financial crisis struck and called into question some neoliberal policies.

Because the history we review focuses on change over a particular period of time, it can leave the impression that a settled state of affairs existed before a period of transformation began. Although that depiction is accurate in some respects, a more general truth is that macro-level phenomena like the party system and the geography of jobs are forever being reshaped by slow-moving economic, political, and social change. It is also important to note that whereas some of the most important forces of change over the past half-century are exclusively modern, others – like trade, technology, and immigration – have been reshaping the nation's political economy for much longer.

Economic Developments

This section briskly reviews seven major economic developments of the late twentieth century, beginning with the growth in trade.

Trade

The simplest way to appreciate the dramatic growth of trade over the last several decades is to look at the value of imports as a share of GDP, which grew from 10 percent in 1980 to almost 16 percent in 2005 (see Table 5.1). Sixteen percent may seem modest, but it is not when you consider that the economy was becoming ever-more service-oriented, and services like

Table 5.1 Economic and demographic change, 1980–2005

Economic and demographic change	1980	1990	2000	2005	Percent change 1980–2005
1 Real GDP per capita (2009 $)	$28k	$36k	$45k	$48k	+70%
2 Imports as a percent of GDP	10.3%	10.5%	14.3%	15.5%	+60%
3 Manufacturing share of private sector	27.9%	21.7%	17.3%	13.2%	–53%
4 Union density (percent of workers in unions)	22.3%	15.5%	12.8%	12.0%	–46%
5 Percent of population that was foreign born	6.2%	7.9%	11.1%	12.1%	+95%

Sources: Line 1. US Bureau of Economic Analysis, US Census Bureau. 2. The World Bank. 3. US Bureau of Economic Analysis, NIPA 6.5 tables. 4. OECD and Visser, 2015. 5. US Census Bureau, except the statistic for 2005, which is from Camarota, 2005.

finance, legal services, health care, and education are mostly provided by domestic firms. Note also that the rise of imports did not crowd out many big-ticket items that are domestically produced, including military procurements, commercial planes, and infrastructure. Not surprisingly, then, the growth in imports is much more dramatic if we focus on consumer goods. To illustrate, the import share rose of clothing and footwear rose from 11.5 percent to 32 percent from 1979 to 2009, and over the same period the import share of household furnishings rose from 5.4 percent to 19.6 percent.[3] An even more dramatic illustration is provided by strolling through any big-box retail store, whose stock is almost entirely imported.

As far back as the 1960s, Americans were purchasing enough imports to cause large trade deficits with other countries. However, imports really accelerated in the 1990s and 2000s, for three reasons. First, the cost of transportation and logistics fell. Second, economic reforms in countries like China and Mexico opened their economies to investment and allowed them to capitalize on low-cost labor for export-driven economic growth.[4] And, third, the United States pursued free trade agreements that aimed to further reduce the barriers to international trade.

The trade boom had profound consequences for the economy. Two of the most notable were the increase in consumers' purchasing power and the jolt to domestic manufacturers. Many US firms lost market share to foreign competitors, and many others moved production to China or Mexico, where labor costs were much lower. Either way, domestic manufacturing jobs were lost, and America's unskilled and semi-skilled workers faced an increasingly difficult labor market, which meant wage stagnation.[5]

Sectoral Shifts and Consolidations

Ever since the end of World War II, manufacturing's share of the economy has given way to a growing service sector. Economic growth was the main reason why, because income growth allows households to spend less of their income on goods and more on services like health care, tourism, and yoga classes. However, trade accelerated the shift by moving low-skill manufacturing jobs abroad and depressing the prices of many consumer goods.

Two service sectors that grew especially rapidly after 1980 were health care and finance. As a percent of GDP, health care grew from 8.5 percent to 15 percent from 1980 to 2005, whereas finance grew from 5 percent to 8 percent. In other words, the two sectors came to account for more than one-quarter of the entire economy. The growth in health care was due to both consumption and costs. Chapter 2 reviewed the underlying forces, which included lengthening lifespans, improvements in care, technological advancements, and a health care financing model that encouraged excessive consumption and procedures.

Financial sector growth also had multiple causes. One was global economic liberalization. After the 1970s, countries all over the world, from

Argentina to Zambia, liberalized their economies, which in effect opened new markets for large financial firms headquartered in the United States and the United Kingdom. A second reason was economic growth, both at home and abroad, which increased the wealth that would be funneled through Wall Street and the financial sector. A third reason was the unequal distribution of growth in the United States, which mattered because the wealthy invest more of their income than the poor, who spend all of their incomes on consumption. And a fourth reason was the growth in consumer credit, which grew from 48 percent of GDP in 1980 to 99 percent in 2007.[6] To a notable degree, finance grew in part because the rich got richer and the middle class assumed more debt.

Much of finance's growth was in the "shadow banking system" – a term that refers to a varied set of lightly regulated financial markets and institutions, including hedge funds, private equity funds, and specialty finance companies. Although the shadow banking system was just getting started in the 1980s, it grew to be larger than the regulated part of the financial sector by the eve of the 2008 financial crisis.[7] That growth was partly due to policy – or, more precisely, the lack thereof. Hedge funds and private equity funds were investment vehicles of the wealthy, and the government took the view that such entities did not need regulation because the investors were sophisticated and the firms were not publicly traded.

Finance not only grew; it also consolidated. Megabanks did not exist in 1980, and even as late as 1994 there was not a single financial firm among the nation's top-twenty revenue-grossing companies. By 2005, however, the list included three banks (Citigroup, JP Morgan, and Bank of America) and two insurance companies (AIG and State Farm). Regulatory change was a primary impetus. In particular, the Riegle–Neal Interstate Banking and Branching Efficiency Act of 1994 repealed a regulation that had given states the power to control whether and how out-of-state banks could operate in their territories. With the repeal, regional banks merged and grew in order to have a national focus. Megabanks were born.

Another sector that consolidated was retail, as small retailers were rendered uncompetitive by big-box stores like Walmart. Large retailers had long had an advantage over small retailers due to economies of scale, and those grew more pronounced as technology advanced and trade expanded. Walmart capitalized on those developments most efficiently, as its spectacular growth made apparent. The company only first appeared on the Fortune 500 list of US companies in 1995, but by 2002 it topped the list. It has since kept that spot as the country's largest company by both revenues and employment.

The rise of megabanks and big-box retail outlets coincided with other developments that magnified the influence of corporate interests in the political system, especially policymakers' embrace of neoliberalism and their demand for campaign contributions, which was driven by the fast-rising cost of election campaigns – a topic that we take up in Chapter 6.

Regional Shifts

Since at least the 1960s, economic growth and demographic growth have been concentrated in the southern "Sun Belt" that ranges from Florida to California, whereas the northern "Rust Belt" states around the Great Lakes have stagnated. The Sun Belt's boom was related to the growing availability of air conditioning, a growing number of sun-seeking northern retirees, racial desegregation in the South, and business's aversion to states with strong unions. In Rust Belt states, where manufacturing had been the core of the economy, workers' wages were high, unions were strong, and laws were generally pro-union. By contrast, many states outside the Rust Belt, including all southern states, had "right to work" laws, which undercut unions by allowing employees to opt out of paying union dues. Once the Sun Belt became more hospitable on account of air conditioning and desegregation, manufacturers quickly displayed a preference for locating their factories there.[8]

The most obvious political consequence of the demographic shift was the increasing political power of Sun Belt states relative to Rust Belt states. Over the three decennial reapportionments of congressional seats between 1980 and 2000, New York, Pennsylvania, Michigan, Ohio, and Illinois lost a total of 30 congressional seats – nearly a quarter of their representation in the House of Representatives and Electoral College. Meanwhile, Texas, Florida, Arizona, and Georgia picked up twenty-five seats, which was nearly a 50 percent increase in their representation.[9] The shift affected national politics, not least because it put more House seats in Republican hands.

Deunionization

From 1980 to 2005, the percent of the workforce that belonged to a union fell from 22.1 percent to 12 percent. The decline was confined to the private sector, and it was especially pronounced within manufacturing, where the unionization rate fell from 33 percent to 13 percent. Meanwhile, the unionization rate in the public sector, encompassing government employees and teachers, remained steady.

Deunionization occurred for several reasons that we have already discussed, including trade pressures, the geographic movement of jobs, the relative decline of the manufacturing sector, and the post-1980 change in the federal government's posture vis-à-vis labor–management relations.[10] In addition, deunionization can be linked to non-unionization in the growing service sector, especially in retail and other low-skill service sector jobs. Walmart and other large employers fought unionization aggressively, and they were aided by local and federal policymakers.[11]

The demise of private-sector unions contributed to wage stagnation for unskilled and semi-skilled workers and for jobs that did not require a college education. And, in the political arena, it eroded a key source of votes, campaign finance, and political muscle for the (northern) Democratic Party.[12]

Rising Income Inequality

From 1955 to 1980, the nation's economic growth benefited the rich and poor equally, so income inequality did not increase. But, since then, incomes have diverged sharply. One indicator of those shifts is change in the share of the nation's pre-tax income that went to the top 1 percent of individuals. By that measure, inequality actually fell by three-and-a-half percentage points from 1955 to 1980, from 14.1 percent to 10.7 percent. However, over the next twenty-five years, the income share of the top 1 percent surged to 19.4 percent.[13] By 2014, it was higher still – at 20.2 percent.[14]

The growth in income inequality is also illustrated by Figure 5.1, which shows real average income (in 2015 dollars) for families in four slices of the income distribution: the bottom 20 percent, middle 20 percent, top 20 percent, and top 5 percent. The figure shows that top incomes grew much faster than others, and it illustrates that there was little or no wage growth for lower-income and middle-income households. Indeed, in inflation-adjusted terms, the average income in the bottom 20 percent did not change at all between 1980 and 2015 – it was essentially stuck at $17,500 for thirty-five years straight. Middle-income households fared a little better: their average income grew from $58,000 to $71,000, a 22 percent increase. But that paled next to the gains for the average household in the top 20 percent, whose income rose 66 percent, from $135,000 to $225,000. And within

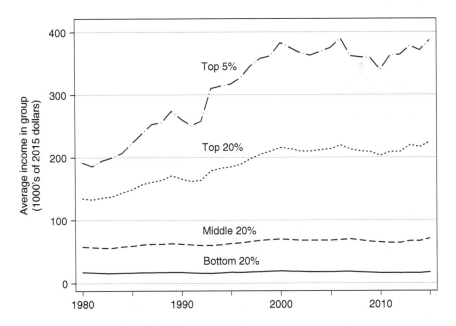

Figure 5.1 Income growth by income-distribution segment, 1980–2015.

Source: US Census Bureau.

that group the gains were skewed toward the richest. For example, the top 5 percent saw their incomes double.

Widespread income stagnation was made worse by two concurrent trends: an increase in the number of hours worked per family per year and rapidly accelerating costs of housing and health care. The first trend was due mostly to the increase in women's workplace participation, which was due to changing social norms and financial demands. In the mid-century economy, middle-class lifestyles could be achieved with only one wage earner. By the end of the century, however, many more families had two wage earners, and yet their total household incomes improved only slightly from 1980 to 2005. And while that occurred, the costs of housing and health care doubled and quadrupled, respectively.[15] That bred widespread frustration. The frustration was greatest among low-skilled men of prime working age, whose incomes stagnated the most.[16]

There are many reasons why the post-1970s economy favored the few over the many. One general reason was technology. By automating a variety of low- and semi-skilled jobs, including everything from manufacturing positions to bank tellers, technology made the labor market more competitive and challenging for low- and semi-skilled workers. At the same time, the growing importance of high-technology increased the rewards for those who could design or operate new technologies. Put differently, late-century technological change was "skill-biased," favoring the highly educated.

At the bottom of the income distribution, there were three additional causes of wage stagnation. One was the government's failure to raise the federal minimum wage from 1981 to 1989 and again from 1997 to 2006, which caused the real (i.e., inflation-adjusted) minimum wage to fall to its lowest level since 1949.[17] Another was mega-retailers' success at resisting wage pressures and unionization.[18] And the third was the mass immigration of low-skilled workers, which provided a huge injection of cheap labor into the economy.

Farther up the income distribution, middle-income manufacturing salaries were held back by deunionization and trade, in addition to automation and immigration. And some middle-income occupations faced unique pressures. For example, wages for one major occupation, truck driving, were set back by late 1970s deregulation and deunionization.[19] Also, public school teachers did not see wage gains from the late 1980s through 2005, which suggests that state-level policymakers were able to resist the demands of teachers' unions, perhaps because teacher supply exceeded demand.[20]

Father up the income distribution are a variety of service-sector professions – like attorneys, financial analysts, health care providers, and software engineers – that require more specialized education and that were not subject to pressure from trade or immigration. For those reasons, and because they were also in fast-growing sectors of the economy, those professions experienced better-than-average wage growth. In fact, a 2012 study by Thomas Philippon of New York University and Ariell Reshef of the University of Virginia estimated that about 15 percent of the growth in income inequality from 1970 to 2005 was driven by wage growth in just one sector: finance. Philippon and Reshef attributed that to the increasing complexity of finance and to deregulation.

More dramatic, however, was the income growth for corporate executives in the top 0.1 percent or top 0.01 percent of the income distribution. Indeed, from the 1970s to 2005, the incomes of the richest 0.01 percent grew sevenfold and the income of the average CEO in a top-100 company grew from about forty average-worker salaries to well over three hundred average-worker salaries.[21] To some extent, those trends can be attributed to the various pressures that kept wages low for average workers. However, Paul Krugman, a Nobel Prize-winning economist, argues that the growth in executive salaries actually had more to do with social and political norms.[22] In particular, he emphasizes the demise of unions, which allowed executives to keep a larger share of corporate profits for themselves, and a shift in public opinion about the "appropriateness" of executive salaries. He notes that in the 1960s a CEO pay package of fifty times the salary of the company's average employee would have generated headlines and public disapproval, but by the 2000s pay packages of many times that amount were shrugged off as normal. People came to tolerate new and extreme levels of inequality, perhaps because they slowly became desensitized to it.

In short, rising income inequality had many causes. There is no clear consensus about which causes were the most important, but a rough ranking might put them in two groups. The first, consisting of lesser causes, would include minimum-wage stagnation, deunionization, inefficiencies in health care financing, changing social and political norms, and deregulation. The second group, of more important causes, would include immigration, skill-biased technological change, and economic globalization, a term that encapsulates both trade and the global expansion of finance.[23] But, whichever causes were actually the most important, it is clear that income inequality was driven by a confluence of factors, including market forces, technological innovations, and public policies.

Immigration

About 20 million immigrants came to the United States between 1980 and 2005, which caused the percent of residents that were foreign born to swell from 6.2 percent to 12.1 percent. Although some of the immigrants were high-skilled workers in the burgeoning tech economy, most were low-skilled migrants from Mexico or Central America, and many of them either came without documents or overstayed their visas. The immigration wave was driven by economic forces – i.e., by the prospect of employment in the United States. Indeed, many employers and sectors came to rely on immigrant labor. Furthermore, Mexican emigration accelerated at times when the Mexican economy contracted, and it slowed or reversed whenever the American economy stagnated.

The immigration wave had many economic consequences. Most significantly, it fueled economic growth, depressed wages in the bottom half of the income distribution, buoyed consumers' purchasing power, and improved the government's budget balance (because most migrants pay more than they receive in taxes and transfers).

The Great Moderation

The Fed's whipping of inflation in the early 1980s was a great achievement. It gave rise to the Great Moderation – the long period of low-inflation growth that stretched until the financial crisis of 2008. It is likely that the Great Moderation was facilitated by the growth in trade and immigration, but, as argued in Chapters 3 and 6, the elected branches deserved credit, too, because the economy's continued success depended on them exercising some measure of fiscal restraint and deference to the Fed. With inflation low and under control, the costs of business fell, labor-management disputes became less frequent, and investment was encouraged. Unfortunately, it also fostered some measure of complacency on the part of investors and financial institutions, which in turn helped to create the crisis of 2008.

The Political Turn: From Great Society to Ronald Reagan

While those economic developments were under way, there were some parallel (and interrelated) developments in the nation's politics. In particular, the Republican Party was becoming more conservative and more competitive in national politics, and its ascent helped pave the way for neoliberal economic reforms.

To contextualize those political developments, it is helpful to recall a string of earlier upheavals, each of which ushered in some type of government expansion. The first began in the late nineteenth century, when industrialization, urbanization, and the rise of large and powerful trusts (corporations) spurred political movements that demanded new regulatory powers for the federal government. By 1920, a variety of agencies and commissions had been established to break industrial monopolies, regulate railroads and interstate transportation, and improve food and worker safety.[24]

The second upheaval was the Great Depression, which prompted a realignment of the party system, characterized by the arrival of an enlarged and more fiscally liberal Democratic Party at the end of a long era of dominance by the Grand Old Party (GOP) – the Republican Party.[25] The response of President Franklin D. Roosevelt and Democratic Congresses to the depression was a sweeping collection of New Deal programs and regulations, including Social Security, jobs programs, agricultural subsidies, banking regulations, deposit insurance, minimum wages, prohibitions on child labor, and rules that empowered trade unions.

Close on the heels of the New Deal was a third upheaval and expansion. Born not of economic change but World War II, the government sharply increased taxes and introduced various controls on the economy, including commodities rationing and wage and price controls. After the war, the controls were removed, but high and steeply progressive tax rates remained, and so did a mighty military.

Thus, the United States had undergone a tremendous transformation over a short period of time, especially over the twelve years from Roosevelt's inauguration until the end of the war. Some people worried about the sustainability and wisdom of a massively enlarged government; however, their ranks were small and getting smaller. Indeed, few could argue that the build-up jeopardized the geopolitical and economic dominance of the United States, which was then being cemented as a global super-power and riding an economic boom that would last through the 1960s. Even so, an unresigned conservative wing of the Republican Party remained, and it succeeded in nominating one of its own, Barry Goldwater, as the party's candidate for president in 1964.[26] There were several reasons why Goldwater was trounced by President Lyndon Johnson in the general election, including the assassination of President John F. Kennedy in 1963 and the fast rate of economic growth in 1964. But another was Goldwater's interest in rolling back liberal-minded social programs. That agenda was insufficiently popular at the time.

After the 1964 elections, which brought extra-large Democratic majorities to Congress, Johnson pursued his ambitious Great Society agenda to combat poverty and reduce economic inequities. Johnson won much of what he wanted, and the flurry of activity – which included new programs to reduce hunger, facilitate access to affordable housing, and provide health care to seniors and low-income citizens – constituted yet another period of rapid government expansionism. Johnson also began an enlargement of the regulatory state, which continued under his Republican successors, Richard Nixon and Gerald Ford. During the three administrations, several dozen major regulatory laws were enacted to do things such as protect endangered species, reduce water and air pollution, improve employee safety in the workplace, ensure the safety of consumer products, reduce racial and gender discrimination, and provide educational support for disabled children.

Significantly, the tail end of that period also featured a good measure of *de*regulation, and it was led by Democrats who recognized that various New Deal era or Progressive Era regulations were outdated and hurting consumers by limiting market innovations and price competition. In other words, the impetus was as much pro-consumer as it was pro-producer, and it culminated in a series of late 1970s laws that deregulated airlines, trucking, railroads, and natural gas.

Regardless of how we choose to interpret those instances of deregulation – as the end of one era or the start of a subsequent, neoliberal era – the 1980 election of Reagan constituted a turn to the right. Reagan argued that the country's problems demanded not more but less government, and he sought to roll back the social programs, taxes, and regulations that had accumulated since the Great Depression. Although Reagan's election was aided by the Fed's tight monetary policy and a sluggish election-year economy, it also reflected a growing conservativism in American politics. Public support for a small-government, pro-market agenda had swelled since the time of Goldwater's failed election bid, sixteen years before.

The conservative turn in the nation's politics continued after Reagan's tenure. Unsurprisingly, some of the developments that contributed to Reagan's victory in 1980 were also responsible for conservativism's momentum in later decades. However, there were also other causes that came into play in the 1990s and later decades. Thus, there is good reason to divide the history into two parts. In the remainder of this section we review developments that explain the turn from 1964 to 1980 – from Johnson's landslide win to Reagan's landslide win. The rest of the chapter reviews policy developments during the Reagan years. Subsequently, Chapter 6 continues the story of the nation's political trajectory through the 1990s and 2000s.

Southern Realignment

The most profound development in the nation's politics over the past half-century was the realignment of the party system that occurred as the South switched from solidly Democratic to overwhelmingly Republican. The shift made the Democratic Party uniformly liberal and the Republican Party more conservative, and it thus spawned the ideological polarization of the parties. Realignment also made the GOP more competitive in national elections, and thus it opened the door to a more conservative policy agenda in Washington, DC.

Although Republicans had achieved some success in the South in presidential elections prior to the mid-1960s, the primary catalyst of southern realignment was the Civil Rights Act of 1964, which moved to end racial segregation in the South. The act, passed with the support of northern Democrats and Republicans and pushed by President Johnson and the Civil Rights Movement, caused (white) southern Democrats to abandon their coalition with northern Democrats.

That rupture occurred after decades of rising tensions within the Democratic Party on issues related to race and racial segregation. For decades after the Civil War, the Democratic Party and southern politics were practically one and the same: the party was rarely competitive outside the South, but there its electoral dominance was virtually uncontested, a privilege that was partly due to the post-war "Jim Crow" laws that whites instituted to disenfranchise blacks and segregate them from whites. The Great Depression changed things by swelling the party's support in the north, and that wing of the party drew its support from the working class, including the large numbers of blacks that were settling down in northern cities after having migrated from the South. The two wings were united in their support for New Deal policies and programs, and as a combined "New Deal coalition" they were able to turn the tables on the GOP and enjoy decades of almost uninterrupted power.[27] However, the coalition was sharply divided on racial issues. The division became more difficult to sustain as momentum for civil rights grew, which itself was largely due to the Civil Rights Movement that was led by figures such as Dr. Martin Luther King, Jr. In July of 1964, a few months after the assassination of JFK, northern Democrats and Republicans were finally able to overcome the opposition of southern Democrats and pass an act to end segregation. The next year, Congress passed the equally consequential Voting Rights Act of 1965, which aimed to dismantle the various laws that southern whites had used to electorally disenfranchise southern blacks. The two pieces of legislation were among the most socially significant acts ever to be passed by Congress, and they ensured that the Democratic coalition would collapse.

Goldwater, the fiscal conservative who secured the Republican nomination in 1964, recognized that the Civil Rights Act created an opening for his party in the South that had not existed before. As an election gambit, he disavowed the Civil Rights Act, and that helped him win several southern states, including Georgia, a state that had never before voted for a Republican. Although Goldwater lost, the election served to illustrate the changing nature of southern politics. And, in time, white southerners would no longer call themselves Democrats or vote with the party that increasingly represented minorities. Instead, they would find a new party label, and their shift to the GOP was amenable to all. In the post-Jim Crow era, the GOP's message of smaller, less-intrusive government was attractive to southern conservatives. And for Republicans outside the South, the appeal of an expanded coalition was obvious: it would improve the party's prospects on the national stage.

In 1968, the Republican presidential nominee Richard Nixon courted southern states by emphasizing "states' rights" and offering private assurances to southerners that as president he would ease up on the enforcement of the Civil Rights Act. Nixon's election victory was aided by the chaos of 1968, which included the assassinations of Dr. King and Bobby Kennedy, urban race riots, anti-war demonstrations, riots at the Democratic Party convention in Chicago, and great discord and disunity in the Democratic Party. However, Nixon's "southern strategy" was also helpful, and he would have won more southern states if not for the segregationist George Wallace, who himself won five southern states in the Electoral College. In subsequent elections, Republican candidates improved on those results, and since at least 1980 no Republican has required much of a southern strategy – the region has greatly favored the party.[28]

Republicans' success in congressional elections developed more slowly. By 1993, the GOP held only 37 percent of southern House seats. That was much higher than the 10 percent or so of the early 1960s, but it did not yet spell the extinction of conservative southern Democrats. Yet, the continued use of the "Democratic" label among conservative southern whites through the 1970s and 1980s did not imply agreement with other Democrats, be they liberals outside the South or newly enfranchised blacks in the South. In most places, they could continue calling themselves Democrats because there was no immediate need for them to change party affiliation. Circumstances were different in presidential elections, where they were given a choice between a "Democratic" candidate who embraced civil rights and a "Republican" candidate who emphasized states' rights. In that context, southern conservatives chose the latter.

Even so, by 2005, the realignment was complete. The GOP's share of southern House seats had risen to 62 percent – a figure that reflected its ability to win nearly every rural or suburban district. The Democratic Party were able to hold on to urban areas, but many of those Democrats were black, and all were liberals.[29]

Naturally, the transformation of the party system was characterized by an upending of public conceptions of the two parties.[30] In their book on party identification, Donald Green, Bradley Palmquist, and Eric Schickler (2002, pp. 163–164) described the realignment as follows:

> In the past, each region perceived the parties in different terms. Southerners associated the Republican Party with the forces of Reconstruction, and non-Southerners associated it with business, farmers, and Protestantism. In the South, the Democratic Party was the party of states' rights and segregation, and in the non-South it was the party of cities, labor, and migrants. For a variety of reasons – economic integration, migration, mass communication, the extension of federal power – the non-South's conception of the parties gradually spread southward.

There were indeed several reasons why the non-southern conception of the GOP took root in the South, but the core reason was the end of Jim Crow via an "extension of federal power." Desegregation was also the primary catalyst for the South's economic integration with the rest of the country. It encouraged in-migration and economic growth.

Southern realignment had far-reaching consequences for the nation's politics. In particular, and as explained more fully in the next chapter, it was the primary catalyst behind the ideological polarization of the parties. And, because it made national elections more competitive, it set the stage for heightened partisan conflict. Realignment also improved the prospects of a conservative like Reagan to win the White House. It did that because it raised the likelihood that the GOP would nominate a bona fide conservative (as opposed to a moderate like Nixon or Ford) and because it increased the GOP's prospects in the Electoral College. To be clear, this argument does not suggest that Reagan could not have won at an earlier time. In fact, he might have won in 1968 if he had been the Republican candidate that year, especially if Wallace had not run. However, one reason why the party did not field a conservative in 1968 was that it was a cowed minority at the time. Another reason was that the party had lost badly with a conservative presidential nominee in 1964. In time, however, as the party made further inroads into southern politics, it would have both cause and opportunity to try again.

Social and Economic Factors

The effect of southern realignment on the partisan balance of power was magnified by the Sun Belt's growing representation in the House and the Electoral College. The GOP's ascendancy was also related to the party's continued success outside of the South. That was mostly just continuity – again, southern realignment was not accompanied by a major shift in non-southern conceptions of the two parties.[31] However, there were also some notable social and economic developments in the 1960s and 1970s that buoyed the GOP in the non-South, and thus at the national level.[32]

First, there was the social and political tumult of the late 1960s, including anti-war protests, countercultural movements with permissive views on drugs and sex, race riots in cities from Los Angeles to Newark, and the arrival of black power groups like the Black Panther Party. Nixon pointed out that the "silent majority" of Americans disapproved of these developments, and indeed public support ebbed from Democratic liberalism and flowed toward a Nixonian law-and-order agenda.

The tumult of the 1960s also eroded the public's trust in government, and the cynicism increased in the 1970s as the Vietnam War festered and Nixon's moral and legal trespassings were exposed in the Watergate scandal.[33] Although the public's new cynicism about government was not confined to one party or the other, it did favor a turn from activist liberalism to Reaganism.

Racial issues also had continued salience, especially on issues like welfare programs, affirmative action policies, and law-and-order topics. Of course, there was nothing necessarily racist about conservative positions on those issues; a purely economic or moral argument can be made against welfare or affirmative action programs. However, those arguments were also attractive to racially prejudiced whites, and thus liberals started talking about "dog whistle politics" – i.e., conservative rhetoric that had no explicit racial bias but which resonated favorably among racially prejudiced whites.[34] The issue at hand is more particular, however, and it is the degree to which a conservative turn in the nation's politics could be attributed to those attitudes in the non-southern electorate. The academic literature makes clear that public support for welfare retrenchment, at least, had some relationship to whites' racial attitudes.[35] And although it does not demonstrate that there was an *increase* in racial animus among non-southern whites that would favor a conservative turn on policy, the notion is plausible because racially charged issues like busing, housing, and affirmative action grew in prominence through the 1970s. Martin Gilens (1999; 2003) points to another possible cause: the mass media's increasing tendency to portray welfare recipients as black. As that occurred, whites' racial attitudes may have become increasingly activated on matters of welfare policy, thus increasing the support for a conservative turn on social spending.

Finally, there were at least two economic developments that favored conservativism in the non-southern electorate. One was deunionization, which eroded a reliable bloc of Democratic support in northern states. The other was the high-inflation economy of the 1970s, which fueled tax bracket creep – an increase in tax bills that occurs when incomes are adjusted upward for inflation while the brackets of the progressive income tax remain fixed. The growing anti-tax sentiment was highlighted by the 1978 property tax "revolt" in California and Reagan's victory in 1980.

Ideological Shift

In the 1950s and 1960s, the minimal-state doctrine of classical liberalism was in general disrepute, the dominant Democratic Party was on a progressive trajectory, and different strains of leftism were ascendant virtually all over the world, from social democratic Sweden to communist Cuba. However, the tide of ideas started to shift in the 1970s. Many economic and political phenomena aided the shift. From a global perspective, the most important were the economic volatility of the 1970s, the fiscal problems in countries with heavy protectionism and extensive government-run industries, and the economic and political collapse that eventually befell the socialist states.[36] It is possible to reject this claim – that troubles for leftist economic ideologies stemmed from economic troubles in the real world – and assert the opposite argument: that economic troubles arose precisely because the ideas of the time were flawed. Actually, both assertions have some claim on the truth, and our analysis must be much more specific if we are to parse their relative explanatory power.

But, regardless, in the 1970s there were three emergent research agendas in economics that offered something of a joint criticism of America's post-war political economy and the idea that government can positively reshape society and manage the economy.[37] One was the public choice school that we reviewed in Chapter 4 and that questioned the government's ability to choose policies that enhance the general welfare. Another was microeconomic work that emphasized the unintended costs of government regulations and programs. And the third was the "monetarist" school of macroeconomics that cast doubt on the Keynesian notions that the government could eradicate unemployment or properly manage the business cycle.

These intellectual schools proved highly influential. Their academic merit was recognized in the form of many Nobel Prizes for the American economists who led their charge, the most preeminent being the intellectual father of monetarism, Milton Friedman. Many of the ideas, along with others of longer standing, like classical trade theory, provided the intellectual foundation for a neoliberal policy agenda focused on trade and deregulation. In varying amounts, that policy agenda was pursued by many countries in the 1980s and 1990s.

As influential as the new economic ideas were, they cannot be credited with being much of a driving force behind the electorate's support for a neoliberal turn on policy. The ideas primarily influenced elites and policymakers, and they percolated very little into public consciousness.

Interest Group Mobilization

One final development deserves mention in this section. At the same time that deunionization was weakening the mobilizing powers of the left, businesses and conservative activists were building the mobilizing powers of the right. The creation and mobilization of pro-business interest groups in the 1970s was a reaction to regulatory expansionism of the late 1960 and early 1970s, which businesses greeted with alarm. With the help of a few wealthy donors, business groups and conservative intellectuals fortified or created organizations like the US Chamber of Commerce, the Business Roundtable, the Heritage Foundation, the American Enterprise Institute, and the CATO Institute.[38] In time, these organizations would enjoy great influence among conservatives and within the Republican Party.[39] But, even by the late 1970s, the mobilization was having an effect. In particular, it helped to kill a landmark bill that would have strengthened labor unions vis-à-vis management. Labor's defeat occurred despite the government being under unified Democratic control, and with a filibuster-proof Democratic majority in the Senate.[40]

Policy in the 1980s

Ronald Reagan not only reflected a growing conservativism in the electorate – he also gave it voice, adherents, and momentum. Additionally, his electoral success illustrated that unabashed conservatism could win at the ballot box.

Reagan's influence on policy was also considerable, especially on policies that he could shape administratively or via appointments. Indeed, to the degree that he can be credited with shifting policies in a neoliberal direction, it was through his appointments to agencies like the Environmental Protection Agency (EPA) and the National Labor Relations Board (NLRB), which on his watch sharply curtailed regulatory enforcement and adopted a more pro-business tilt.[41] Reagan's court appointments were more broadly consequential, especially after the 1986 retirement of Chief Justice Warren Burger, which allowed Reagan to elevate William Rehnquist to Chief Justice and to appoint Antonin Scalia as Associate Justice.

Reagan's legacy on other policies was more modest. Of course, that had much to do with the separation of powers and divided government.[42] But, Reagan's agenda was also, in a sense, a victim of its own success – and of miscalculation and circumstance. Specifically, his first and most emblematic legislative achievement – a package of tax cuts in 1981 – added to a growing budget deficit, so much so that he scaled back the cuts the next year. And, even then, the budget deficit remained the most consuming economic policy issue of his remaining six years in office.

Tax Policy and the Budget Deficit

Reagan's 1980 campaign centered on the issue of tax cuts, and he was able to deliver on his pledge in his first year in office with the Economic Recovery Tax Act. The law, which passed Congress with bipartisan support, was like most tax bills in that it made many changes to the tax code. Some of the most significant were a cut in corporate taxes, an accelerated appreciation schedule for business investments, and a tax deduction (i.e., tax expenditure) for household contributions to individual retirement accounts. However, ERTA's centerpiece was a sharp, across-the-board reduction in individual income tax rates, with the top marginal rate moved to 50 percent from 70 percent. Although the cuts were rather even across tax brackets, there were elements that made the provisions more generous to the rich than to the poor. In particular, the provision that allowed the personal exemption to erode via inflation until 1985 made the rate cut less generous to the working poor.[43]

Perhaps more significant was that all of ERTA's rate cuts were to be inflation-indexed after 1984, which would permanently set (more or less) the government's income tax revenues as a percent of GDP, and thus Congress could no longer "follow the pattern of providing tax reductions that merely offset tax increases driven by inflation."[44] However, ERTA's effect on revenue was not years down the road – it was immediate. The sharp reduction in revenue was significant for multiple reasons. For one, it undermined Reagan's claim that the tax cuts would pay for themselves because they would spur economic activity and thus raise revenues enough to cover the budget shortfall.[45] (ERTA proponents also argued that the tax cuts for businesses and high-income households would benefit the rest of the population via economic investment and expansion; this notion was dubbed "trickle-down economics.") More significantly, the tax cuts caused the budget deficit to balloon. ERTA was not the only reason for that. A sharp economic contraction made a contribution, and so did Reagan's military build-up, which cost more than his cuts to other discretionary programs.[46] But the tax cuts were a major reason why the deficit grew by 66 percent in both 1982 and 1983.

The deficit seemed to raise alarm, in both parties. To constrain it, Reagan embraced several tax increases, including a law in 1982 that canceled or delayed some of ERTA's corporate tax cuts.[47] Those measures only reduced the deficit slightly, and continued worry led Congress to pass the Gramm–Rudman–Hollings Act in 1985. GRH specified that future budgets would need to hit deficit-reduction targets or else the executive branch would have to "sequester" (i.e., cut) congressionally approved expenditures, with equal cuts to defense and non-defense programs. Members of Congress do not like indiscriminate cuts to their budgets, and indeed their intention with GRH was to manufacture a threat that would help them make difficult decisions on the budget. For a couple of years, budgets adhered to GRH targets and the deficit shrank. However, it is difficult to say how much the rules, themselves, mattered. Congress can ignore or change its own budget-making rules, so the rules may tend to *reflect* the institution's budgetary preferences more than they constrain its budget actions. Indeed, when a recession hit in 1990 and it became more difficult to meet GRH targets, Congress replaced GRH with more lenient rules. The new rules also may have helped; but they, too, were scrapped when Congress no longer had much interest in following them.[48]

While post-ERTA budgetary maneuvers displayed unease about the deficit, there are also reasons to question policymakers' real level of concern. For example, and as Alberto Alesina and Geoffrey Carliner (1991) note, there are, besides the possibility that ERTA supporters simply miscalculated the expansionary effects of the tax cuts, other, less-charitable explanations for the discrepancy between their rhetoric and the reality that transpired. One is that Reagan embraced the "starve the beast" strategy that had been hatched by certain movement conservatives (as conservative activist elites were called). The idea, quite simply, was to use tax cuts to grow a debt too large to be ignored, which would then bolster the argument that government spending was out of control and that significant cuts to entitlement programs were necessary. Another possibility is that ERTA defenders simply cared more about the tax cuts than the deficit, and perhaps they anticipated that voters felt the same way. Of course, another possibility is that no one prioritized the deficit, and its growth is to be blamed not just on ERTA supporters but on a bipartisan logroll in a divided government context. That idea, discussed in the previous chapter and elaborated by Mathew McCubbins (1991), derives from the simple proposition that each party prefers to advance its highest priorities – social spending in the case of the Democrats, defense spending and tax cuts in the case of the Republicans – to a set of more modest policies and a more balanced budget.

Arguably, the most landmark tax reform in the Reagan years was not ERTA but the Tax Reform Act of 1986 (TRA). The law made the income tax slightly more progressive via increases in the personal exemption, standard deduction, and the Earned-Income Tax Credit. But the real significance of the TRA – a bipartisan, revenue-neutral reform that was spearheaded by the Reagan administration – was that it provided lower income tax rates and tax-code simplification at the expense of special-interest tax breaks. The law was (and still is) hailed as an illustration that, under the right conditions, Congress can find a way to advance a tax bill that provides particularistic costs and generalized benefits.[49] The achievement was indeed considerable, but the celebrated simplicity did not last long. Congress soon returned to its practice of adding complexity and particularism to the tax code.

Other twists and turns on the budget in the Reagan years need not occupy us here. However, a simple summary of some important budgetary changes is provided in Table 5.2. The table is constructed to mirror Table 5.1, which surveyed economic change from 1980 to 2005. It therefore captures much more than the Reagan years (1981–1989), which it depicts only

Table 5.2 Income taxes, outlays, and debt, 1980–2005

	Individual income tax	*1980*	*1990*	*2000*	*2005*	*Change 1980 to 2005*
1	Average tax rate: family at median income	11.4%	9.3%	8.0%	5.7%	–50.0%
2	Average tax rate: family at twice median income	18.3%	15.1%	15.7%	13.1%	–28.5%
3	Top marginal income tax rate and threshold for married couple filing jointly (2012 $)	70.0% on income >$600k	28.0% on income >$57k	39.6% on income >$384k	35.0% on income >$383k	–50.0%
	Outlays, as percent of GDP					
4	Federal Medicaid	0.90%	1.20%	2.00%	2.40%	+166.0%
5	Medicare	1.30%	1.80%	2.20%	2.60%	+100.0%
6	SNAP	0.29%	0.25%	0.14%	0.23%	cyclical
7	TANF			0.17%	0.13%	
	Aggregates, as percent of GDP					
8	Federal revenues	19.0%	18.0%	20.6%	17.3%	–9.0%
9	Federal net outlays	20.6%	20.9%	17.4%	18.9%	–8.3%
10	US debt	31.0%	56.0%	54.0%	61.0%	+98.0%

Sources: Lines 1–2: Tax Policy Center, via Bartlett, 2012, pp. 255–256. 3. Tax Foundation (https://taxfoundation.org/). 4. Centers for Medicare and Medicaid Services, National Health Expenditure Accounts Historical Tables, Bureau of Economic Analysis (BEA). 5–6. BEA. 7. Congressional Budget Office. 8. Bartlett, 2012, pp. 245–246, Office of Management and Budget (OMB). 9. OMB. 10. OMB, St. Louis Federal Reserve.

roughly. Yet, the data illustrate this about the 1980s: income taxes and federal revenues fell, whereas health care spending and the debt rose. The table also shows that those trends continued in later decades, except that in the 1990s the debt's trajectory reversed and income taxes were made more progressive. Note also that the average individual income tax burden was reduced as much in the Reagan years as it was in George W. Bush's first term (2001–2005), when Republicans enjoyed unified government for the first time in 47 years. A key difference, however, was that the Reagan-era tax cuts were in part a correction for bracket creep in the 1970s and, in the case of the TRA, offset by eliminating tax breaks. Neither was the case with the tax cuts in the 2000s.

Beyond the Budget

We have already taken stock of the major budgetary and tax changes in the Reagan years, and we noted that Reagan's influence was notable where he could shape policy administratively or via appointments. This last section briefly points out four other policy developments of note during the 1980s.

Savings and Loan (S&L) Bailouts

If the 1986 tax reform cast the elected branches in a positive light, the savings and loan (S&L) debacle of the mid-1980s did the opposite. S&Ls were small banks that focused on home mortgages. The government regulated them in various ways, including by capping the interest rates that they could charge, which proved problematic in the inflationary 1970s. In 1982, the government responded with deregulation and oversight reduction. However, because the banks were covered by federal deposit insurance those moves promoted *moral hazard* – i.e., the banks could take excessive risks knowing that their liabilities were insured.[50] The Reagan administration ignored those risks because of its zeal for deregulation, and Congress ignored those risks because members were more eager to help their local banks than to protect the mortgage finance system.[51] Congress changed direction in 1989 with a regulatory overhaul, but the damage had already been done. From the mid-1980s to the mid-1990s, over one thousand S&Ls failed, costing taxpayers well over $100 billion. (The S&L debacle also featured a corruption scandal in which five senators – the "Keating Five" – were alleged to have pressed regulators to help a bank chaired by Charles Keating. The move smacked of a quid pro quo, because Keating had made substantial donations to the senators' campaigns.)

Immigration Reform

The increase in immigration, especially of undocumented workers from Mexico, prompted repeated moves in Congress to enact some sort of reform. In 1986, after years of attempts, a bipartisan coalition finally did so. The legislation did three main things: established a path to legal status for undocumented immigrants who had been in the country since at least 1982, created a system to allow and facilitate seasonal farm labor by immigrants, and established rules and penalties to prevent employers from hiring undocumented immigrants. The first two goals were fulfilled: many migrants came to work as legal farmworkers and at least 1.7 million residents became legal temporary residents, and many of them later became permanent residents or citizens.[52] The third goal was not achieved. In part, that was because the law did nothing to undermine the demand for immigrant labor or the wage gap between the United States and Mexico. Also, the rules and penalties for employers were never really enforced. Illegal immigration not only continued after the reform, it accelerated – no doubt because many future immigrants (correctly) believed that America remained "open for business."

Social Security Adjustments

There was little action on entitlement programs in the 1980s, except for a Social Security reform in 1983. Adjustments were necessary because demographic and economic trends had, by that year, caused the system to switch from cash-flow positive to cash-flow negative. The reform passed with bipartisan support, and it restored solvency mainly by lifting the retirement age and taxing the Social Security benefits of pensioners who had other retirement income. The reforms were phased in over time so that they would not be felt by people in or near retirement.[53]

Trade Policy

Trade policy changed little over the 1980s. The existing framework had been established by legislation and agreements in the 1960s and 1970s, and those moves had lowered trade barriers and strengthened mechanisms by which domestic manufacturers could seek redress from what they considered unfair trading tactics by foreign competitors. During the 1980s, there was a marked increase both in imports and in the number of domestic companies seeking protection from competitors. Those appeals were not all legitimate, but manufacturers did face a serious threat as the dollar rose against other currencies in the early 1980s. That hit exporters hard, and the mounting pressure for protection led the administration to coordinate a devaluation of the dollar. In the 1985 Plaza Accord, America's major trading partners – Britain, France, Japan, and Germany – agreed to intervene in currency markets to bring down the dollar. US exports rebounded, and the boost to manufacturers aided the economy's recovery from the recession of 1981–1982.

Later, as the 1980s drew to a close, the United States and Canada finalized a trade agreement. The agreement became much more significant in 1994, when Mexico was added to the free trade area.

Conclusion

The economic boom in the immediate decades after World War II benefited all income classes. As the decades passed, however, the economy's transformations created more distinct classes of winners and losers. Trade and technology benefited consumers and educated, high-skill workers, whereas much of the domestic manufacturing base felt the pinch. Unskilled and semi-skilled blue-collar workers faced downward wage pressure on account of immigration and competition from states with lower labor costs. In turn, the distribution of income and economic power in the United States became more unequal.

The political system also underwent a great transformation. In particular, southern realignment of the party system made the Republican Party more conservative and the Democratic Party more liberal. It also improved the GOP's prospects in national elections, so politics became more competitive at the same time that the parties were becoming ideologically polarized. Those trends helped Reagan become president, but they would really make their mark on politics in the 1990s and later decades.

Reagan brought a new brand of conservativism to Washington, DC, and over his two terms he was able to tilt the federal judiciary to the right. The most significant economic policy developments during his presidency were tax cuts and tax reform, and the budget deficit was an issue that consumed much attention. Other significant – but also easy to overstate – policy developments included a measure of deregulation, some steps toward freer trade, and an immigration reform. Those policy changes went hand in glove with the decade's economic trends, and they contributed to those trends to some extent. In the 1980s, the nation's policies and economy embarked on a joint and intertwined neoliberal trajectory. That trajectory would continue in the decade to come.

Notes

1 Boudette, 2016.
2 Over the 1980s, real auto manufacturing wages in Michigan fell (Block and Belman, 2003).
3 McCully, 2011.
4 China initially started to embrace trade and foreign investment in the late 1970s. With a large and extremely impoverished population, China was able to attract investment to build export-oriented manufacturing. That brought the country tremendous economic growth through the 1980s, 1990s, and 2000s. Eventually, labor costs started to rise, which made the country less competitive vis-à-vis Mexico.

5 Studies focused on the North American Free Trade Agreement (NAFTA) find that its effects on the nation's employment was minimal, but that does not mean that it did not have localized effects. Studies of Chinese import competition show employment and wage effects on various local communities in the United States (Autor et al., 2014). While trade grew, the government continued providing a measure of trade adjustment assistance (TAA) to workers who could demonstrate that their jobs were displaced by foreign imports. But TAA programs and income assistance programs did not create new employment opportunities.

6 Greenwood and Scharfstein, 2013, p. 5. See also Philippon and Reshef, 2012.

7 Blinder, 2013, p. 60.

8 See Grant and Wallace, 1994 and Grant, 1996.

9 States that gained House seats from 1980 to 2010 are the following (number gained in parentheses): AZ(4), CA(10), CO(2), FL(10), GA(3), NC (2), NV(2), TN(1), TX(10), UT(1), VA(1), WA(2). States that lost seats over the same period were: CT(1), IL(5), IA(1), KS(1), KY(1), LA (1), MA(2), MI(4), MO(1), MT(1), NJ (6), NY (10), OH(5), PA(6), SD(1), WI(1), WV (1).

10 Hacker and Pierson (2010, p. 59) summarize the connections between Reagan's pro-management NLRB and deunionization.

11 Largely for that reason, Krugman (2007) argues that the economy's deunionization should be understood as a mostly political phenomenon.

12 See Freeman, 2003 and Feigenbaum, Hertel-Fernandez, and Williamson, 2018.

13 Interestingly, growth in real GDP per capita was the same (70%) over both quarter-centuries, 1955–1980 and 1980–2005.

14 Data from Piketty, Saez, and Zucman, 2016. Their figures for the share of the national income that was collected by the richest 10% are: 36.5% in 1955, 34.2% in 1980, and 45% in 1980.

15 Health cost estimate from Schoen and How, 2006.

16 Krugman (2007, p. 127) notes that men aged 34 to 44 made 12% *less* in 2005 than in 1973.

17 The longest period in history without a federal minimum wage increase was 1981–1989 until the period from 1997 to 2006 set a new record. See Lee, 1999 for its effects on income inequality in the 1980s.

18 In the 1990s, Walmart became the nation's largest private sector employer. Its effect on wages was significant. In 2005, the average Walmart salary was about $18,000, which was less than half of what a GM worker received in the 1970s (Krugman, 2007, p. 139).

19 Belman and Monaco, 2001. See also Belzer, 2002.

20 National Center for Education Statistics, 2007.

21 Krugman, 2007, pp. 129 and 142. Krugman's statistics about CEO pay are from Frydman and Saks, 2007.

22 Krugman, 2007.

23 Many would argue against this categorization, and especially its depiction of immigration and skill-biased technological change (SBTC). Indeed, estimates of the effect of 1980s and 1990s immigration on low-wage incomes have generally been rather modest. However, it is a basic law of economics that more supply means lower prices. And any attempt to estimate the wage effects of immigration is complicated by several issues, including the possibility that immigrants are attracted to localities with more robust economies (see Borjas, 2003 and Krugman, 2008). On SBTC, Krugman (2007, pp. 132–136) notes there is a paucity of "direct evidence for the proposition that technological change has caused rising inequality." And, he notes, the SBTC argument fails to explain why the growth of inequality has been so concentrated at the very top of the income distribution.

24 During the Progressive Era there were also many changes to the political system, including civil service reform and women's suffrage. For more on Progressive Era economic regulations, see Eisner, 2013 and Glaeser and Schleifer, 2003. See also Law and Kim (2011), which argues that the Civil War was also a major contributor to the rise of the regulatory state.

25 The GOP nickname dates to the Reconstruction Era.

26 Neither President Eisenhower nor congressional Republicans, who were the majority in 1946–1948 and 1952–1954, sought to dismantle New Deal programs. However, they did enact the Taft Hartley Act of 1947, which weakened labor vis-à-vis management and passed, with considerable Democratic support, over Truman's veto.

27 Yet, the party's liberal social programs were tempered by southern Democrats who were less enthusiastic about using public monies to help blacks (Glenn, 2014, pp. 7–9; Katznelson, 2013). Drawing on that and subsequent history, Alesina and Glaeser (2004) argue that racial prejudice explains why American welfare programs are not as generous as those of European countries.

28 In 1978, a Republican won a Senate seat in Mississippi for the first time in a century. Two years later, Republicans won four more Senate seats in southern states, and along with them majority control of the Senate for the first time in twenty-eight years.

29 The Voting Rights Act of 1965 (VRA) greatly increased voting among blacks by dismantling literacy tests and other barriers to voting in southern states. The VRA, which generated strong opposition from southern whites, allowed the federal government to oversee election laws in southern states, and it empowered the federal government to register voters.

30 Regarding the slow change in southern voters' partisan identities, Green, Palmquist and Schickler (2002) estimate that about half of the Republican Party's post-1960s gains among southern white identifiers was due to switching party loyalties; the remainder came via cohort replacement – i.e., from generational change and the in-migration of northerners.

31 As the decades passed, the GOP did lose some support outside of the South, as measured by House seats, presidential voting, or party identification. But the dip was modest, especially compared to the party's gains in the South.

32 This section does not emphasize the Christian conservative movement that swelled in the 1970s and later decades and that came to be a significant faction of the Republican Party. The reason is that it was largely a southern phenomenon, so it went hand-in-hand with southern realignment.

33 See Flanigan et al., 2015, p. 38 for data on trust in government.

34 Perhaps the most oft-cited instance of the tactic was the "Willie Horton" ad that aired in the 1988 elections. The ad, run by a group that sought to help Vice President Bush, alleged that the Democratic nominee, Governor Michael Dukakis, was soft on crime for supporting a weekend furlough program for inmates in his state, Massachusetts. The ad stoked controversy because rather than focusing on the program's overall results it focused on the gruesome crimes of one inmate, William Horton, whose mugshot featured prominently in the ad.

35 See Dyck and Hussey, 2008 and Gilens, 1999.

36 Yergin and Stanislaw (2002) provide a sweeping overview of the global turn toward neoliberalism.

37 A broader analysis of conservative thought would also emphasize the social commentators Irving Kristol and William F. Buckley Jr. and the novelist Ayn Rand, whose anti-government moral philosophy influenced many, including Alan Greenspan, the future Federal Reserve Chair.

38 See Mayer, 2016; Hacker and Pierson, 2010; Krugman, 2007; and Vogel, 1989. It is significant that these various groups received most of their new funding

from a very small group of donors because that helps to explain why the groups mobilized so successfully in the face of potential free-rider problems.

39 Like neoliberal ideology, the mobilization of interest groups had more of a direct effect on lawmakers than it did on the electorate. However, groups like Heritage and CATO did seek to shift public opinion, and to some degree they were aided by the mainstream press, which often cited their analyses when they wanted to report conservative positions on policy issues.

40 Hacker and Pierson, 2010.

41 See Vogel, 1989; Baker, 2007; and McCartin, 2011.

42 Republicans won control of the Senate in 1980 for the first time in nearly three decades. Nationwide, the GOP picked up twelve Senate seats in those elections, four of which were in the South and had long been in Democratic hands.

43 The personal exemption is a flat sum that individuals can deduct from their gross income. Steuerle (2008, p. 84) notes that whereas all of the rates were allowed to erode until 1985, the erosion of the personal exemption was poised to make the greatest contribution to after-tax inequality.

44 Steuerle (2008) also notes that the rate cuts – as substantial as they were – could be interpreted as mostly just an adjustment for bracket creep.

45 The idea was often associated with Arthur Laffer, an economist who argued that tax cuts would often pay for themselves by spurring growth. But most other economists rejected that idea. So did George H. W. Bush, who had criticized Reagan's claim as "voodoo economics" in the 1980 presidential primary.

46 Social programs that faced spending cuts in the 1982 budget included SNAP, Medicaid, AFDC, and rental housing assistance. Those cuts won bipartisan support, and they largely stuck in the years to come, even though Democrats would pick up House seats in 1982 and 1984 and retake the Senate in 1986. The budget deficit was perhaps the main reason why. By contrast, defense spending fell slightly after its peak in 1984 (Austin, 2014).

47 The 1982 law, the Tax Equity and Fiscal Responsibility Act, was one of eleven tax increases approved by Reagan (Bartlett, 2012, p. 45).

48 See Miller, 1989; Poterba, 1996; and Auerbach, 2008.

49 Birnbaum and Murray (1988) tell the making of the TRA, with all of its drama. The reform is also much discussed in Arnold, 1992; Patashnik, 2014; Bartlett, 2012; and Steuerle, 2008.

50 The 1982 legislation was the Garn-St. Germain Depository Institutions Act.

51 Litan, 1991 and Romer and Weingast, 1991.

52 Daniels, 1990, pp. 391–397.

53 After the reform, the trustees projected that Social Security would be solvent for at least seventy-five years. However, with longer lifespans and other demographic developments, the trust funds are expected to be depleted sooner.

References

Alesina, Alberto, and Geoffrey Carliner. (1991). *Politics and economics in the eighties*. Chicago, IL: University of Chicago Press.

Alesina, Alberto, and Edward Ludwig Glaeser. (2004). *Fighting poverty in the US and Europe: A world of difference*. Oxford, UK: Oxford University Press.

Arnold, R. Douglas. (1992). *The logic of congressional action*. New Haven, CT: Yale University Press.

Auerbach, Alan J. (2008). Federal budget rules: The US experience. NBER Working Paper No. 14288. *National Bureau of Economic Research, Inc.* 55.

Austin, Andrew. (2014, November 26). The Budget Control Act and trends in discretionary spending. Washington, DC: Congressional Research Service. 7-5700.

Autor, David H., David Dorn, Gordon H. Hanson, and Jae Song. (2014). Trade adjustment: Worker-level evidence. *The Quarterly Journal of Economics*, 129(4), 1799–1860.

Baker, Dean. (2007). *The United States since 1980*. Cambridge, UK: Cambridge University Press.

Bartlett, Bruce. (2012). *The benefit and the burden*. New York, NY: Simon & Schuster.

Belman, Dale L., and Kristen A. Monaco. (2001). The effects of deregulation, de-unionization, technology, and human capital on the work and work lives of truck drivers. *ILR Review*, 54(2), 502–524.

Belzer, Michael H. (2002). Trucking: Collective bargaining takes a rocky road. In Paul F. Clark, John T. Delaney, and Ann C. Frost (Eds.), *Collective bargaining in the private sector*. (pp. 311–342). Champaign, IL: Industrial Relations Research Association Series.

Birnbaum, Jeffrey H., and Alan S. Murray. (1988). *Showdown at Gucci gulch: Lawmakers, lobbyists, and the unlikely triumph of tax reform*. New York, NY: Vintage.

Blinder, Alan S. (2013). *After the music stopped*. New York, NY: Penguin.

Block, Richard N., and Dale Belman. (2003). Automotive and other manufacturing industries in Michigan: Output, employment, earnings, and collective bargaining, 1980–2001. In Charles L. Ballard, Paul N. Courant, Douglas C. Drake, Ronald C. Fisher, and Elisabeth R. Gerber (Eds.), *Michigan at the millennium: A benchmark and analysis of its fiscal and economic structure*. (pp. 145–168). East Lansing, MI: Michigan State University Press.

Borjas, George J. (2003). The labor demand curve is downward sloping: Reexamining the impact of immigration on the labor market. *The Quarterly Journal of Economics*, 118(4), 1335–1374.

Boudette, Neal E. (2016, November 18). Ford move, cited as victory by Trump, has no effect on US jobs. *The New York Times*.

Camarota, Steven A. (2005, December 1). Immigrants at mid-decade [Web log comment]. Retrieved from: https://cis.org/Immigrants-MidDecade (accessed January 14, 2018).

Daniels, Roger. (1990). *Coming to America*. New York, NY: HarperCollins.

Dyck, Joshua J., and Laura S. Hussey. (2008). The end of welfare as we know it? Durable attitudes in a changing information environment. *Public Opinion Quarterly*, 72(4), 589–618.

Eisner, Marc Allen. (2013). *The American political economy: Institutional evolution of market and state* (2nd ed.). New York, NY: Routledge.

Feigenbaum, James, Alexander Hertel-Fernandez, and Vanessa Williamson. (2018). From the bargaining table to the ballot box: Political effects of right to work laws. NBER Working Paper No. 24259.

Flanigan, William H., Nancy H. Zingale, Elizabeth A. Theiss-Morse, and Michael W. Wagner. (2015). *Political behavior of the American electorate* (13th ed.). Washington, DC: CQ Press.

Freeman, Richard B. (2003). What do unions do ... to voting? NBER Working Paper No. 9992.

Frydman, Carola, and Raven Saks. (2007). Historical trends in executive compensation. *Federal Reserve Bank of* New York.

Gilens, Martin. (1999). *Why Americans hate welfare: Race, media, and the politics of antipoverty policy.* Chicago, IL: University of Chicago Press.

Gilens, Martin. (2003). How the poor became black. In Sanford F. Schram, Joe Brian Soss, and Richard Carl Fording (Eds.), *Race and the politics of welfare reform.* (pp. 101–130). Ann Arbor, MI: University of Michigan Press.

Glaeser, Edward L., and Andrei Shleifer. (2003). The rise of the regulatory state. *Journal of Economic Literature,* 41(2), 401–425.

Glenn, Brian J. (2014). *The American welfare state: A practical guide.* New York, NY: Routledge.

Grant, Don Sherman. (1996). The political economy of new business formation across the American states, 1970–1985. *Social Science Quarterly,* 77, 28–42.

Grant, Don Sherman, and Michael Wallace. (1994). The political economy of manufacturing growth and decline across the American states, 1970–1985. *Social Forces,* 73(1), 33–63.

Green, Donald, Bradley Palmquist, and Eric Schickler. (2002). *Partisan hearts and minds: Political parties and the social identities of voters.* New Haven, CT: Yale University Press.

Greenwood, Robin, and David Scharfstein. (2013). The growth of finance. *The Journal of Economic Perspectives,* 27(2), 3–28.

Hacker, Jacob S., and Paul Pierson. (2010). *Winner-take-all politics.* New York, NY: Simon & Schuster.

Katznelson, Ira. (2013). *Fear itself: The New Deal and the origins of our time.* New York, NY: W.W. Norton & Company.

Krugman, Paul. (2007). *The conscience of a liberal.* New York, NY: W.W. Norton & Company.

Krugman, Paul. (2008). Trade and wages, reconsidered. *Brookings Papers on Economic Activity,* 103–154.

Law, Marc T., and Sukkoo Kim. (2011). The rise of the American regulatory state: A view from the progressive era. In David Levi-Faur (Ed.), *Handbook on the politics of regulation* (pp. 113–128). Northampton, MA: Edward Elgar.

Lee, David S. (1999). Wage inequality in the United States during the 1980s: Rising dispersion or falling minimum wage? *The Quarterly Journal of Economics,* 114(3), 977–1023.

Litan, Robert E. (1991). Comment. In Alberto Alesina and Geoffrey Carliner (Eds.), *Politics and economics in the eighties* (pp. 209–214). Chicago, IL: University of Chicago Press.

McCartin, Joseph A. (2011). *Collision course: Ronald Reagan, the air traffic controllers, and the strike that changed America.* Oxford, UK: Oxford University Press.

McCubbins, Mathew D. (1991). Government on lay-away: Federal spending and deficits under divided party control. In Gary W. Cox and Samuel Kernell (Eds.), *The politics of divided government.* (pp. 113–153). Boulder, CO: Westview Press.

McCully, Clinton P. (2011). Trends in consumer spending and personal saving, 1959–2009. *Survey of Current Business,* 91(6), 14–23.

Mayer, Jane. (2016). *Dark money: The hidden history of the billionaires behind the rise of the radical right.* New York, NY: Doubleday.

Miller, Preston J. (1989). Gramm–Rudman–Hollings' hold on budget policy: Losing its grip? *Quarterly Review*, Winter, 11–21.

National Center for Education Statistics. (2007). Table 75. Estimated average annual salary of teachers in public elementary and secondary schools: Selected years, 1959–1960 through 2005–2006. *Digest of Education Statistics*. Washington, DC: US Government Printing Office.

Patashnik, Eric M. (2014). *Reforms at risk: What happens after major policy changes are enacted.* Princeton, NJ: Princeton University Press.

Philippon, Thomas, and Ariell Reshef. (2012). Wages and human capital in the US finance industry: 1909–2006. *The Quarterly Journal of Economics*, 127(4), 1551–1609.

Piketty, Thomas, Emmanuel Saez, and Gabriel Zucman. (2016). Distributional national accounts: methods and estimates for the United States. NBER Working Paper No. 22945. Data retrieved from World Wealth and Income Database, http://wid.world/ (accessed January 14, 2018).

Poterba, James M. (1996). Do budget rules work? NBER Working Paper No. 5550. *National Bureau of Economic Research Inc.*

Romer, Thomas, and Barry R. Weingast. (1991). Political foundations of the thrift debacle. In Alberto Alesina and Geoffrey Carliner (Eds.), *Politics and economics in the eighties*. (pp. 175–214). Chicago, IL: University of Chicago Press.

Schoen, Cathy, and Sabrina K. H. How. (2006). National scorecard on US health system performance: Technical report. *The Commonwealth Fund.*

Steuerle, C. Eugene. (2008). *Contemporary US tax policy*. Washington, DC: The Urban Institute Press.

Visser, Jelle. (2015 October). ICTWSS Database. Version 5.0. Amsterdam: Amsterdam Institute for Advanced Labour Studies (AIAS). Retrieved from: www.uva-aias.net/en/ictwss (accessed October 1, 2018).

Vogel, David. (1989). *Fluctuating fortunes: The political power of business in America*. Washington, DC: Beard Books.

Yergin, Daniel, and Joseph Stanislaw. (2002). *The commanding heights: The battle for the world economy*. New York, NY: Simon & Schuster.

6 High-Stakes Politics, 1990–2008

The 1992 presidential election vividly illustrated many trends in the nation's political economy.[1] One was the Federal Reserve's independence from the elected branches, and the license it gave the Fed to tighten policy as it deemed necessary, even if doing so might jeopardize the president's reelection. Indeed, like President Carter twelve years before, President Bush became a victim of that policy. Even though the mild, Fed-induced recession of 1990 was over well before November 1992, the turnaround was too little too late for Bush.[2] Clinton's charge that he was ignoring the economy resonated with voters.

The budget deficit also loomed large in the 1992 campaign, and it hurt Bush in more ways than one. Public concern about the deficit, which had swelled during the Reagan years, gave a boost to Ross Perot, an independent candidate who focused his campaign on the nation's debt. Perot went on to win 19 percent of the vote, which made him the most successful third-party presidential candidate in eighty years. But perhaps more troublesome for Bush was the 1990 budget and deficit-reduction deal, the Budget Enforcement Act. The legislation introduced new budget-making rules that were designed to limit the deficit, and it included modest spending cuts and tax increases. It was the latter that troubled Bush. He had pledged in his 1988 campaign that he would reject all new taxes – "read my lips: no new taxes," he had said. Yet, the Democratic Congress included the tax increase as part of the Budget Enforcement Act, so Bush could only reject it by risking a government shutdown. Bush signed the budget bill, and he got hammered for it. Clinton labeled him untrustworthy for reneging on his pledge, and conservatives abandoned him for accepting a tax hike.

In a way, the southern realignment of the party system was also highlighted by the 1992 election. The three previous presidential elections had all been Republican victories, and in each case the Republican candidate had swept the South, with the sole exception of Georgia in 1980, which had voted for Carter, its former governor. Clinton, however, won several southern states, in part because he had been a governor of one (Arkansas), and perhaps because southern votes for Perot came more at Bush's expense than Clinton's. Either way, Clinton's win underscored that Democratic success in presidential elections was more likely if the party could pierce the Republican South.

Still more prominently, the 1992 elections underscored the expansion of trade. The presidential campaigns focused heavily on the North American Free Trade Agreement (NAFTA), which had been negotiated by Bush and was pending ratification by Congress at the time of the election. Although Mexico had already taken steps in the 1980s to liberalize trade and open its economy to American investment, NAFTA promised to accelerate those trends, especially the emigration of American manufacturing. Most telling about the debate was Clinton's embrace of the trade deal. His position underscored both the neoliberal turn in American politics and the decline of union power in the Democratic Party.[3]

Of course, Clinton's economic centrism and the Democratic Party's partial embrace of certain neoliberal policies did not herald the arrival of a new era of bipartisan consensus on economic policies. Rather, on Clinton's watch the Republican Party tacked further to the right. A watershed moment came in the 1994 midterm elections, when a surge of conservatives were elected to Congress – so many that the GOP won control of the House for the first time in forty years. It was expected that Democrats would lose seats in the midterms, because the president's party almost always suffers *midterm losses.*[4] That occurs for two reasons. One is that presidents and their parties tend to be less popular at midterms than two years prior, when their victories were propelled by the candidate's popularity and perhaps a partisan "tide." The other is that voter turnout in midterms tends to favor the president's opponents – they are simply more motivated to vote than the president's defenders, even if the president's popularity has remained steady.

Still, Republican gains in 1994 were unusually large. That was partly because the midterm dynamic helped flip many southern districts that had not yet realigned. The "Republican Revolution" was also a product of the party's effort to nationalize the elections. Unlike previous midterms, which tended to focus more on the local concerns of each congressional district, the 1994 elections were given a common purpose by the GOP's manifesto – dubbed the Contract with America – which the party promised to pursue if it were to become the majority. Among other things, the Contract proposed to cut welfare and taxes and to amend the Constitution to include a balanced budget requirement. It demonstrated the GOP's interest in moving economic policies to the right, even though Republicans had controlled the White House for twelve of the previous fourteen years.

As the 1990s gave way to the 2000s, then, many already existing trends maintained course: the Republican Party's takeover of the South was completed, the parties became more polarized, and partisan politics became more competitive and combative. In addition, neoliberalism advanced as NAFTA was implemented and banks and telecoms were deregulated. This chapter takes stock of these and other developments that laid the foundation for the nation's political economy in the early twenty-first century.

Party Polarization

The advance of party polarization through the 1990s and later decades was one of the most significant political developments of the past half-century. The emergence of parties that were highly ideologically polarized – along with the emergence of a more evenly matched party system – raised the stakes of elections, intensified partisan conflict and obstructionism, and led the parties to place partisan political objectives ahead of policy objectives, workable bipartisan compromises, and sound governance.[5] Those consequences are given some attention in later chapters. First, we review why, how, and when the parties became so ideologically polarized.

At the outset, note that polarization was both a mass phenomenon and an elite phenomenon, and that each fueled the other. At the mass level, polarization consisted of ideological divergence between the two party bases – the Republican base became more conservative and the Democratic base became more liberal. Similarly, one can describe mass polarization as the ideological intensification and homogenization of Republican and Democratic "identifiers." That is, people who say that they identify with the Republican Party became more conservative, and those who identify with the Democratic Party became more liberal. This trend, which is illustrated by Figure 6.1, occurred at the same time that the proportion of non-ideologues and non-identifiers (i.e., independents) remained steady or grew.[6] As such, it is not exactly the case that the citizenry as a whole became more ideological or partisan.[7] Instead, polarization was confined to the voting electorate and especially partisan identifiers.

The polarization of the bases contributed to polarization in Congress, for two reasons. First, voters in party primaries increasingly favored conservatives or liberals over moderates. Second, it became less common for voters to cross the partisan divide in any general election, so electoral districts became more strongly and reliably Republican red or Democratic blue.[8] That development also had much to do with the sharpening geographical divide between the party coalitions – i.e., urban areas and certain coastal states became more reliably Democratic, whereas other areas became more reliably Republican. (Note that this was not due to *gerrymandering* – the practice of drawing House districts to "pack" or "crack" the opposing party's voters so as to win more House seats for your party. Perhaps the best evidence against the gerrymandering hypothesis is the fact that the Senate became as polarized as the House, even though Senate districts are whole states, which cannot be gerrymandered.[9] Senate polarization occurred because the party bases polarized and because voters' partisanship became a more reliable guide to election outcomes. So, red states became more reliably Republican and amenable to conservative Republicans, and blue states became more reliably Democratic and amenable to liberal Democrats. The same thing occurred within states. The urban–rural divide was real, so the polarization of House members was likely under any districting scheme.

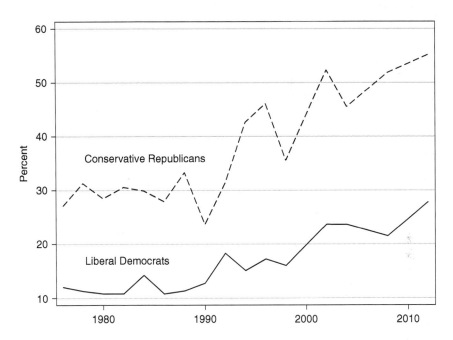

Figure 6.1 Ideologies of partisan identifiers, 1975–2012.

Notes: Data are the percent of "strong" or "weak" Democrats (Republicans) saying that they are "liberal" or "extremely liberal" ("conservative" or "extremely conservative").

Source: American National Election Studies. Data for 2000 excluded because survey was conducted differently that year.

This does not mean gerrymandering made no contribution to polarization in Congress. On the contrary, each map that eliminated swing districts was important in that respect. However, the more fundamental causes of polarization lay elsewhere.)

As districts became more reliably partisan, members of Congress faced less pressure to work with members of the other party and more pressure to hew to the demands of their base, lest they draw a challenger in a primary election who would accuse them of compromising the party's principles and accommodating the opposition. As such, the party-polarized electorate actually created two obstacles to legislative productivity and compromise. First, it made the parties in Congress more ideologically polarized. Second, it gave members strong incentives to reject any attempt to bridge the wide ideological divide.[10] For office-holders who wanted to remain in Congress, obstructionism became the safer political strategy.

The polarization of elites – or, more narrowly, House members – is illustrated by Figure 6.2. The figure shows the ideological placement (on a left–right scale that appears on the vertical axis) of the average member of each

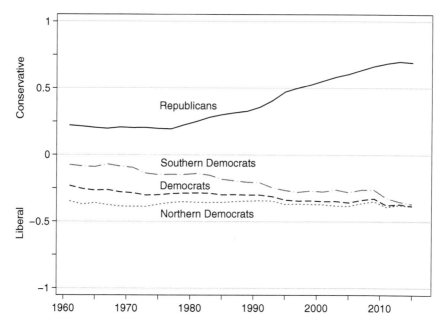

Figure 6.2 Party polarization in the House of Representatives, 1960–2016.

Notes: The figure shows the left–right placement of the mean ideological member of each House caucus. The data are first dimension DW-NOMINATE scores of Poole and Rosenthal (2007) and available at VoteView.com.

party group in the House from 1960 to 2016.[11] The figure illustrates several important facts about polarization in Congress. First, its timing: it began in the late 1970s and has been steady ever since, such that each of the past four decades has ended with greater polarization than existed at its start. Second, the change in the Democratic caucus was essentially a southern phenomenon. Outside the South, there was little ideological shift to speak of, whereas in the South the party's delegation became increasingly liberal on account of southern realignment. And, third, the ideological drift was more pronounced in the Republican caucus – it moved much farther to the right than the Democrats did to the left. (Note that the Republican shift was also national. Although many of the party's most conservative members in recent decades have been southerners, many others have hailed from states like Minnesota, Wisconsin, and Colorado.[12])

The parties' contrasting trajectories reflected their evolving positions on economic policies. Again, whereas Democratic politicians embraced a good measure of centrist measures – including deregulation, welfare reform, and trade expansionism – Republican politicians expressed ever-greater frustration about the status quo, and that was despite the many policy successes that they had accumulated after Reagan's wins in 1980 and 1984, the Republican take-over of Congress in 1994, and the party's sweep in the 2000 elections, which gave it control of both legislative chambers and the White House.[13]

Of course, the ideological rift was not confined to economic issues. In particular, there was also a growing partisan divide on "cultural issues" like gun control, abortion, gay marriage, and prayer in schools. Such issues were poised for heightened salience and contestation precisely because they rather neatly divided the GOP's increasingly rural, southern, socially conservative, and Christian coalition from the Democratic Party's increasingly urban, liberal, and secular coalition. They also made partisan politics more combustible and contentious, because they relate to different lifestyles and moral views and do not admit easy compromises. By contrast, differences on economic issues like budget allocations and tax rates can be settled relatively easily – the parties can simply pick numbers that are somewhere in between their preferences.

Issues related to race also increasingly divided the parties, and thus the nation's politics became unidimensional. Recall that, prior to realignment, the country's most divisive social issues – on race and civil rights – internally divided one of the parties. Thus, politics operated rather differently on racial issues (dimension #2) than they did on economic issues (dimension #1). On the former, northern Democrats and Republicans agreed more with each other than either did with southern Democrats, whereas, on the latter, the partisan divide was activated. That changed as segregation was relegated to history, southern realignment progressed, and the new politics of race focused on questions of redistribution, especially social programs like welfare, Medicaid, and subsidized housing.[14] To some degree, the grafting of racial issues onto the economic policy divide may have widened the ideological gap between the parties. Or it may have simply added an additional layer of contestation to the increasingly charged debates about economic policy.

Each of these aspects of the evolving partisan–ideological divide was clearly connected to southern realignment. However, there were two other primary causes of polarization in the 1990s and later decades. One was the continued efforts of "movement conservatives" to pull the GOP to the right.[15] Reagan had only begun the government-slimming project – indeed, he had abolished no major program and federal spending as a percent of GDP was essentially unchanged over the 1980s.[16] Furthermore, the opportunity for a more ambitious overhaul of government presented itself as the Republican Party became more competitive in congressional elections. To hasten that, and to shift the party's agenda farther to the right, conservatives founded and fortified various activist institutions. Two of note were Americans for Tax Reform and the Club for Growth. The former, founded by Grover Norquist in 1985, became a powerful force in DC, largely because its anti-tax pledge proved a very effective way to hold Republican representatives to a firm, no-compromise position on tax policy. The Club for Growth was founded in 1999 to provide financial support to conservative Republicans who would challenge – and increasingly defeat – the party's moderates.[17]

The second cause was the fragmentation of the media and, more specifically, the arrival of non-centrist radio and television. The innovation came first to radio, and it was enabled by the government's repeal of the so-called fairness doctrine in 1987. The regulation, put in place in the late 1940s, had required radio and television programs to provide opposing views on political issues. The government repealed it because it was said to have a "chilling effect" on political speech, as media outlets might prefer to avoid an issue rather than cover how it might be received by both liberals and conservatives. The shift coincided with the emergence of many highly partisan radio shows. The most notable was Rush Limbaugh's, which was first broadcast nationally in 1988 and soon reached tens of millions of people per day. And it was not long before the same model came to cable television, itself an innovation of the 1980s. *Fox News* would prove the most consequential. It was launched in 1996 as a conservative take on national news, and it quickly became the nation's most popular cable news network and a very powerful shaper of public opinion. Of course, the Internet then emerged, and along with it came an explosion of ideologically focused news sites, including conservative pages like *The Drudge Report* and liberal pages like *The Huffington Post* (now *HuffPost*). With this new media environment, liberals and conservatives were drawn farther into alternate realities, and each was fed a steady stream of information that reinforced their views and disparaged the motives and opinions of the other side.

These two observations return us to our original point: that the forces of polarization operated on both elites and the masses. The media helped to polarize the party bases, which in turn helped to polarize the parties in Congress. And, the polarization of party elites, which was spurred by interest group pressure, fueled the polarization of the electorate.[18] To some degree, perhaps, the elite-to-masses pathway could be attributed to voters' perceptions that the parties were polarizing, which encouraged them to choose sides. But, again, mass polarization was predominantly between partisan identifiers. Therefore, the more important means by which party elites caused mass polarization was to be found in the basic nature of partisanship – specifically, the fact that partisanship is more social and psychological than analytical. More succinctly, partisans follow their parties.

To summarize, the polarization of the parties was first and foremost a consequence of southern realignment, which made the Democratic Party more liberal and the Republican Party more conservative. A variety of secondary causes, which we have just reviewed, are depicted in Figure 6.3. They include media fragmentation, pressure from interest groups and campaign financiers, and partisan electoral geography, which itself had much to do with the strengthening of partisan attachments among partisan voters. The whole ideology machine was more powerful on the right, which

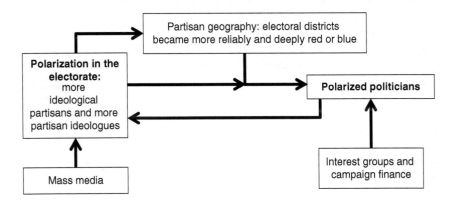

Figure 6.3 Elite and mass polarization.

Source: Author.

is why the Republican Party traveled farther than the Democratic Party.[19] That asymmetry had several causes, including the GOP's electoral ascendancy, the starker and more deliberate contrast between new media that had a conservative bent and the established ("mainstream") media, and the more concerted and coordinated effort of conservative interest groups to effect change in federal policy. By contrast, the Democratic Party's move to the left was only mildly related to those factors, and it was mostly due to just one development: southern realignment.

Income Inequality and Polarization

Could rising income inequality also have contributed to the polarization of the parties? The notion is plausible because inequality may polarize the rich and the poor on issues of redistribution. Indeed, that is the assumption in the redistributive taxation models that we reviewed in Chapter 4. However, those models predict not polarization but convergence to the median voter, and they also predict movement that is opposite to what occurred. The Democratic Party did not move left to court an increased demand for redistribution, and the redistribution models predict that Republican ideology would be constrained – not radicalized – when inequality is on the rise.

In fact, to the extent that polarization and income inequality were related, the relationship mostly ran in the other direction. There are two reasons why. First, the Republican Party's move to the right was partially responsible for changes in policy – on trade, taxes, and regulations – that increased inequality. Second, the gridlock and party wars that accompanied polarization foreclosed policy changes, like minimum wage increases and other labor policy reforms, that could have slowed the pace at which inequality was rising.[20]

But, if income inequality did not pull the parties to the left, why was that? And, why, in an era of rising inequality, did the Republican Party move to the right and remain electorally competitive?

One simple answer is that the forces pulling the parties to the right were stronger than the counter-force of wage stagnation and income inequality, and perhaps that was because the electorate was slow to recognize and appreciate wage stagnation and rising inequality. Or, Democrats may have shunned economic populism because of the electoral rise of the GOP, the waning influence of unions, and its leaders' embrace of neoliberalism and reliance on corporate campaign donations.[21] A third and more basic possibility is suggested by Nolan McCarty, Keith Poole, and Howard Rosenthal in their 2006 book, *Polarized America*. Their argument retains the theoretical framework of a spatial model of redistributive taxation and emphasizes the difference that large-scale immigration makes. Specifically, they emphasize that when non-citizens make up a large and growing share of the bottom of the income distribution rising inequality will not be accompanied by a leftward shift by the median *voter*.

While each of these answers focuses on why the Democratic Party did not have a more leftward trajectory, it is also common to hear a different line of argument that focuses on the primacy of cultural issues on the right. The most well-known thesis of this sort appears in Thomas Frank's 2004 book, *What's the matter with Kansas?* The title of Frank's book was recycled from an 1896 editorial by William Allen White, which sought to explain why Kansas was then a bastion of left-wing progressivism. Frank's question was about how things had changed, and specifically why economic conservatism had become so popular in the late twentieth century in places like Kansas, where incomes are modest by national standards. More precisely, he wondered, why did so many Kansans support a party that focused its legislative agenda on the interests of the elite, including policies like financial sector deregulation and estate tax repeal? Frank's answer was that they had become "values voters" who placed cultural values ahead of their economic interests. That is, Kansans ignored economic policies and focused their political attention on fighting gun control laws, pro-choice regulations, and other social policy laws that were advanced by liberals in coastal states.

Frank's argument can be twisted and broadened into a more general claim about post-material politics as follows: in a wealthy society, voters shift their attention from bread-and-butter economic policies to values issues, like social norms and environmental sustainability. Both arguments may have some truth to them, and some Republican voters may have placed values ahead of economics. On the whole, however, that depiction is a distortion, since most Republican voters fully embraced the party's economic policy agenda.[22] They did not ignore economic issues; they wanted deregulation, tax cuts, and smaller government. So, to explain why the party's economic policy agenda moved to the right in an era of rising inequality, the main answer is to be found elsewhere, like in southern realignment, the mass media, and movement conservativism.

Campaigns and Lobbying

The ideological polarization of the parties, the increasingly ambitious pro-market agenda of movement conservatives and the Republican Party, and the heightened competitiveness of national elections contributed to another trend in the nation's politics: campaign spending. The rate of change was dramatic and sustained. Over the past half-century, spending on House and Senate campaigns increased by about 10 percent per two-year election cycle.[23] That amounted to a doubling of campaign expenditures every fifteen years, and it meant that by the 2010s major-party candidates in competitive House districts spent nearly $2 million on their campaigns, whereas candidates in competitive Senate races spent many times more. But that was just the half of it. Parties and interest groups also upped their campaign spending, and at a clip that was perhaps even faster. (See Box 6.1 for a brief explanation of federal campaign finance laws.)

Although partisan competition and movement conservativism were important drivers of campaign spending, they were not the only ones. Another, more fundamental, cause was the professionalization and technological advancement of campaigns, which came to incorporate television ads, individualized polling, and professional campaign consultants. Additionally, money flowed into politics because corporate interests found political spending to be a worthwhile investment.[24] That investment also came in the form of lobbying. In fact, according to the calculations of the political scientist Lee Drutman, corporate lobbying grew at a pace that was similar to the growth in campaign finance. In particular, Drutman found that the number of corporate lobbyists doubled from 1980 to 2004, and that corporate lobbying expenditures doubled in the decade after 1998, when lobbying expenditures began to be tracked by the government.[25] By 2008, annual lobbying expenditures by corporations had surpassed $2 billion. That was nearly $4 million per member of Congress.

In his 2015 book, *The business of America is lobbying*, Drutman traces the growth in corporate lobbying to the 1970s, when businesses started to mobilize against regulations. The success of those initial efforts suggested that lobbying investments could provide a favorable return on investment, and lobbyists found ways to maintain that profitably, especially by broadening their services to include attempts to secure grants, tax breaks, and favorable regulatory decisions. Put another way, the spectacular growth in corporate political expenditures meant that Congress increasingly catered to corporate interests and that federal policy and policymaking became increasingly tilted against consumers and taxpayers. Parties remained the vehicles by which general-interest policies could be advanced, but that became more difficult – and perhaps less frequent – as corporate money flooded campaign coffers and K Street (the street in Washington, DC, where many lobby shops have their offices). Those developments are difficult to demonstrate with any sort of data analysis, but it is equally difficult to argue that federal policymaking was unchanged by corporate America's large investments. And, in fact, many veteran legislators argued that Congress changed in that way.[26]

That said, it is important to keep other parts of the equation in focus. In particular, the influence of corporate cash was closely tied to – or contingent upon – parties' and politicians' demand for campaign funds. Indeed, if that had not been the case, parties would not have tried so hard to extract campaign contributions from lobbyists and their clients. Those efforts took many forms, the most famous being the Republicans' "K Street Project." The 1995 project, led by House Majority Whip Tom DeLay, was a threat to snub all lobby shops that did not hire more Republicans and donate more money to Republican campaigns. The initiative was notable because it implied a *quid pro quo* and because it highlighted the two-way power dynamic between officeholders and pressure groups. In other words, as much as interest groups, corporations, and their lobbyists seek to pressure policymakers, officeholders are in a position to apply similar pressure in return.[27]

Furthermore, it is a mistake to think that corporate and interest group success in the policymaking arena is due only to lobbying expenditures and campaign donations. On a more basic level, interest group success stems from the disparity in political pressure that accompanies policies that have concentrated benefits and diffuse costs (see Chapter 4). Recall also that there are groups, such as the NRA, which derive their power not from campaign contributions but from their large and active memberships.

And, finally, it is important to note that at the same time that politicians were pressured to fill ever-larger campaign war chests, they were also becoming increasingly tethered to their political parties. Of course, many partisan objectives can be pursued without clashing with deep-pocketed industries, and such conflicts are most unlikely for Republicans. But there was at least one situation in which corporate interests and Republican interests came into some degree of conflict and the latter prevailed: in 2002, in the wake of the Enron scandal, the GOP enacted a bill known as Sarbanes-Oxley that tightened regulations on corporate accounting practices.

Box 6.1: Federal campaign finance regulations and practices

Under federal campaign finance law, businesses and groups that wish to donate to candidates or parties must establish a specific entity for that purpose, and candidates must do the same to accept donations and finance their campaigns. The entities – called political action committees or PACs – are regulated by the Federal Election Commission for transparency and compliance with statutory contribution limits. The limits include caps on the size of donations that can be made to PACs and caps on the size of the donations that PACs can make to candidates and parties.

There are no limits on how much candidates, parties, or others may spend on political campaigns. Congress attempted to introduce campaign spending limits in 1974, but the Supreme Court ruled them unconstitutional in *Buckley v. Valeo* (1976). The Court held that spending limits violated the First Amendment's protections of free speech, because the ability to spread a political message depends on being able to finance its transmission. Put another way, limits on spending could effectively limit the ability of individuals and groups to spread their political ideas, so they run afoul of the First Amendment. At the same time, the Court upheld the donation limits in the 1974 law because they did not pose a similar constitutional conflict. The Court argued that contribution limits were justifiable because they can prevent corruption or the appearance of corruption.

It can be difficult to enforce contribution limits because donors can funnel money through intermediaries or find other ways to spend money to influence specific elections. The latter practice has been especially pronounced. In the 1980s and 1990s, big-money donors exploited the "soft money" loophole by which they would donate large sums to political parties for initiatives that were dubbed "party-building activities" but which were actually intended to help specific candidates. A 2002 law closed that loophole, but then donors started doing something similar with 527 and 501(c) organizations. These non-profit entities can accept donations of unlimited size and run political advertisements. Their ads cannot advocate the *explicit* election or defeat of a candidate, because to do so would violate the spirit of the contribution limits in campaign finance law. However, 527s and 501(c)s can run campaign ads that are otherwise indistinguishable from candidates' ads, so they can be just as influential. So, the loophole remains, and the contribution limits do not prevent big-money donors and groups from spending as much as they want to influence particular elections. After a change in campaign finance law in 2010, "super PACs" emerged as another means for big money to influence elections. That development is discussed in Chapter 7.

Politics and Policy in the New Century

As noted in the previous chapter, the growth of trade and the service sector in the late twentieth century had much to do with economic growth, new technologies, and economic reforms in other countries. To a lesser extent, the neoliberal economy was forged by changes in domestic economic policies, and many of those advanced with Democratic support. In fact, some of the most notable reforms in the 1990s, including NAFTA and a reform to deregulate banks, occurred while Democrats enjoyed unified government in 1993–1994. After Republicans won control of Congress in the 1994 elections, and continuing through George W. Bush's presidency, a host of other pro-market and pro-business policies were enacted, including a telecoms deregulation and reforms to shareholder lawsuits and personal bankruptcy laws.[28]

While neoliberalism advanced, so did the party wars. A sharp escalation occurred after the Republican Revolution and Newt Gingrich's selection as Speaker of the House. The first big fight concerned the budget for 1996. Gingrich overplayed his hand in that episode, and he did so again in his attempt to impeach Clinton in late 1998. Yet, while those and other partisan dramas unfolded, there was also a decent amount of bipartisan collaboration. Most notably, the parties demonstrated a shared interest in eliminating the budget deficit, and after years of attention to the issue they succeeded in generating a budget surplus throughout Clinton's second term.

After the 2000 elections, when the conservative majority on the Supreme Court waded into the disputed vote count in Florida and effectively decided the presidential contest in favor of George W. Bush, Republicans enjoyed unified government for the first time since the 1950s. That enabled large tax cuts in 2001, which brought the return of budget deficits. In the same year, an unexpected change in the Senate handed Democrats control of the chamber for a short period. (The shift occurred in May, when Senator Jim Jeffords of Vermont left the GOP to caucus with the Democrats. For the previous five months, the Senate had been split fifty-fifty between the two parties, though Republicans had the edge because tie votes could be broken by the vice president. Jeffords' switch handed majority control to the Democrats until the end of 2002, when Republicans bucked the midterm losses trend and retook control of the chamber.[29]) So, both Clinton and Bush II experienced divided government as well as unified government, and it is instructive to study how legislative politics and policies differed between the two settings. The following review of Clinton- and Bush-era economic policies provides such an analysis, after it first tells the story of the disappearing and reappearing budget deficit.

Taxes and Deficits

The elimination of the budget deficit in the 1990s was greatly eased by the decade's long stretch of economic growth, but politicians also made it happen. From 1990 to 1997, four budget deals were instrumental. The first was the Budget Enforcement Act of 1990, which was described at the beginning of this chapter and which replaced the deficit-reduction targets of Gramm–Rudman–Hollings with a pay-as-you-go (PAYGO) rule. The new rule specified that all changes to entitlement programs or tax policies should be offset by other budgetary changes so that there was no increase in the deficit over a five-year period. The rule was not necessarily any more effective than the procedures in Gramm–Rudman–Hollings, and for the same reason: budget rules are binding only as long as Congress chooses to follow them. However, the rule was followed for several years.

The second step was the 1993 budget, which included tax hikes on high-income households and sizable cuts to defense spending. The defense cuts were justified on account of the 1991 collapse of the Soviet Union, but they and the tax cuts reflected a Democratic approach to deficit reduction, and indeed the bill was enacted by a unified Democratic government with all congressional Republicans voting in opposition.[30] The legislation also included an increase in the Earned-Income Tax Credit for the working poor, but it did not include several of Clinton's campaign pledges, like a middle-class tax cut, more infrastructure spending, or more social spending. Clinton's decision to focus on the deficit instead of broad-based social policies and other campaign pledges was unusual for a first-term president, but Clinton was worried about the Federal Reserve, which was poised to raise interest rates if deficit spending increased.[31]

The third step was the budget deal for 1996. It was the first budget deal after Republicans' historic takeover of Congress, and it was reached only after the long government shutdown of late 1995. The impasse occurred because Clinton objected to the scale of Republicans' proposed cuts to domestic spending and hikes in Medicare premiums. The battle ended when Speaker Gingrich agreed to pare the spending cuts, though Clinton allowed them to be restored if the government collected more revenues than Congress was anticipating. Although the spending cuts were more modest than what Gingrich had sought, they built on the deficit-reduction measures of the previous couple of years.

The final step was the Balanced Budget Act of 1997. The bill's headline items were new tax expenditures, including the Child Tax Credit, two tax credits for higher education, and the Roth IRA, which provides a tax break on retirement savings. However, those tax cuts were offset by measures that were meant to provide significant Medicare savings.[32] And, on balance, the changes were projected to eliminate the deficit in five years. However, faster-than-expected economic growth delivered a budget surplus the following year.

As the budget went into surplus, Congress started ignoring its PAYGO rules. But, the real change came in 2001, when Republicans enacted large tax cuts. The "Bush tax cuts" of 2001, as the Economic Growth and Tax Relief Reconciliation Act of 2001 (EGTRRA) was known, were deep and broad and skewed in favor of the wealthy. They included an across-the-board cut in income tax rates, a phase-out of the estate tax, and an increase in the Child Tax Credit. The Child Tax Credit was also made partially refundable, which benefited lower-income households. EGTRRA was estimated to reduce revenues by $1.5 trillion over ten years.[33]

As EGTRRA was being finalized, the economy slipped into recession. Then, in September, terrorists hijacked planes and flew them into the Pentagon and the World Trade Center towers. The Bush administration began the war in Afghanistan, and the budget for 2002 upped defense spending by almost one-quarter. That budget also increased spending on many other items, especially education spending, which was necessary to implement a newly passed education reform, the No Child Left Behind Act. At the same time, Congress passed another round of tax cuts that were intended to buoy investment and employment (via extended employment and investment tax breaks for employers). Then, at the end of 2002, Congress let the PAYGO rule expire, and Bush prepared for war in Iraq, a Medicare expansion, and another round of tax cuts, most of which were accelerations of the 2001 tax cuts.[34] The budgetary effect of all these moves was straightforward: large deficits were back. In 2004, the deficit was 3.3 percent of GDP, which was about as large as the deficit in 1993. One-fourth of the 2004 deficit could be attributed to war spending, which amounted to $96 billion that year. War spending increased over subsequent years, peaking in 2008 at $195 billion.[35]

Clearly, the attitudes of the White House and Congress toward the budget deficit were very different in 2001–2003 than they had been over the previous twenty years. As many as four reasons explain the shift. First, policymakers inherited a surplus. Second, the attack on American soil was shocking and the first major incident of that kind since World War II. Third, the economic downturn in 2001 warranted deficit spending. And, fourth, the GOP was enjoying its first stint of unified government in half a century, and as such it was unlikely to pass on the opportunity to pass tax cuts. That was especially true in 2001, when the surplus existed. In 2003, when it was gone, the tax cuts were more difficult to sell, and opponents included the Secretary of the Treasury, Paul O'Neill, and the Fed Chair, Alan Greenspan.[36] Yet, there was just enough support to get the tax cuts through Congress – in the Senate the vote was split fifty-fifty, so vice president Dick Cheney cast the tie-breaking vote. And Cheney led the charge in the administration, reportedly rebuking O'Neill's worries with the claim that "Reagan proved deficits don't matter." Presumably, Cheney meant that deficits do not matter to voters or to a president's reelection chances. And, indeed, in the 2004 elections, voters were less focused on the deficit than they were on the Medicare expansion, the economic rebound, and the war on terrorism.[37]

The tax reforms of the Clinton and Bush II years were asymmetric – the hikes were narrow and modest, whereas the cuts were broad and deep. The reasons are straightforward. Tax hikes have opponents, and if the opponents are too numerous the reform will be defeated. Tax cuts are much easier, especially when they come in the form of tax expenditures that advance social ends that solicit Democratic support.[38] Tax cuts are difficult to enact if they only benefit the wealthy, so they are usually packaged with tax cuts for households of all income levels.

After the various tax cuts of the late 1990s and early 2000s, income tax revenues and rates were at their lowest levels in decades, and the tax code included more large tax expenditures. The progressivity of the income tax was not dramatically altered one way or the other, but the decrease in the top marginal rate was a significant benefit for wealthy households, and the full tax system was made less progressive via the repeal of the estate tax.[39]

Divided Governments

Democrats' tax hikes in 1993 and Republicans' tax cuts in 2003 were both possible because of unified government, and in each case budget reconciliation was used to avoid minority party interference. However, each period of unified government also included major economic reforms that drew some bipartisan support. For example, the Bush tax cuts of 2001 won the votes of many congressional Democrats.[40] And the Democrats' Family and Medical Leave Act (FMLA) of 1993, which required employers to allow their workers to take up to twelve weeks of unpaid leave from work without fear of losing their jobs to attend to family medical needs, enjoyed enough support from Republicans to reach the Senate's cloture threshold. More noteworthy in this respect were NAFTA, the 1994 banking deregulation bill, and a 2005 reform of bankruptcy laws, as each passed with a large amount of support from the minority party.

To a degree, then, unified governments can and do advance legislation with coalitions that resemble those that emerge during divided governments. Indeed, their contrast with divided governments lies not in the absence of bipartisan legislation but in the presence of partisan reforms. In addition, the two configurations differ in terms of vetoes and veto overrides. For example, neither Clinton nor Bush vetoed any legislation during unified government, but both issued vetoes during divided government, and both had at least one of their vetoes overridden by Congress.

These and other differences between unified and divided governments are highlighted by Table 6.1, which also summarizes the major economic policy reforms of the Clinton and Bush II presidencies. The table highlights coalitions and processes that are common or noteworthy under each government type.[41] The top half of the chart, covering unified governments, contains four categories. The first includes major presidential initiatives that met with defeat, each of which could be blamed on party disunity. One was Clinton's attempt to provide universal health care coverage. The reform was strongly opposed by the insurance industry and doctors' associations – and congressional Democrats who represented competitive districts wavered. The other two failures were Bush's calls to partially privatize Social Security and to enact comprehensive immigration reform. Congressional Republicans avoided discussion of the first idea, and they divided sharply on the second, with the battle line drawn between those who adopted a pro-business stance and those who adopted a nativist, anti-immigration stance.

From top to bottom, the next three rows in the unified government section list legislation that passed with increasing amounts of minority party support. The first includes reforms that were passed on (nearly) party-line votes, and in each case budget reconciliation rules were in place. The two examples have already been noted: the 1993 budget and the 2003 tax cuts. The next row lists three reforms that were passed with barely enough minority party support to invoke cloture (and could perhaps be labeled

Table 6.1 Unified government, divided government, and major economic policy initiatives, 1993–2008

Outcome and coalition	Unified governments	
	Democratic (1993–1994)	*Republican (2001, 2003–2006)*
1 Failure of major reform pushed by the president	Health care expansion (1994)	Social Security partial privatization (2005) Immigration reform (2006)
2 Passage on (nearly) party-line vote	*1993 budget and tax increase*	*2003 tax cuts*
3 Passage with barely enough minority party votes to invoke cloture	Family and Medical Leave Act (1993)	*Economic Growth and Tax Relief Reconciliation Act tax cuts* (2001) Medicare Modernization Act (2003)
4 Bipartisan reform	NAFTA (1993) Riegle–Neal Interstate Banking and Branching Efficiency Act (1994)	Bankruptcy reform (2005)

	Divided governments	
	Republican Congress, President Clinton (1995–2000)	*Democratic Congress, President Bush (2002, 2007–2008)*
5 Legislation approved by president	1996 budget (deal reached only after a prolonged government shutdown) Welfare reform and cuts (1996) Minimum wage increase and tax breaks for businesses (1996) Telecoms deregulation and reform (1996) Budget deficit deal, with new tax expenditures (1997) Gramm–Leach–Bliley Act banking reform (1999)	Sarbanes–Oxley corporate accounting regulations (2002) Various economic stimulus and bailout bills (2008)
6 Vetoes sustained	*Various tax cuts* (1999, 2000) Bankruptcy reform (2000)	CHIP expansion (2007)
7 Vetoes overridden	Limits on shareholder lawsuits (1995) Defense construction projects (1997)	Water projects (2007) Farm bill (2008) Medicare part D reforms and temporary "doc fix" (2008)

Note: The table lists economy-focused legislation that the author deemed to be notable. The pre-2003 measures were identified by Mayhew (2005). Items in italics were passed via budget reconciliation.

"bipartisan"). Besides FMLA and the Bush tax cuts of 2001, one piece of legislation is listed: Republicans' Medicare expansion. Although it passed with some bipartisan support, members in both parties objected to its budgetary implications and its provision that prevented the government from being able to negotiate drug prices with pharmaceutical companies.[42] In fact, when Republican leaders brought the bill up for a vote in the House, the initial tally showed that it would be defeated. In response, they kept the vote open for hours – until they successfully pressured some members to switch their votes.

The final row in the unified government section lists three reforms that were passed with considerable bipartisan support: NAFTA, which passed with the support of 40 percent of House Democrats and 75 percent of House Republicans,[43] the Riegle–Neal Interstate Banking and Branching Efficiency Act of 1994, which liberalized banking so that banks could operate across state lines, and the 2005 bankruptcy reform that was favored by banks and credit card companies and that made it more difficult for individuals to file bankruptcy. Clinton had vetoed a similar measure five years earlier, though not all in his party shared his position. In 2005, Republicans passed the reform with the support of 40 percent of congressional Democrats.

The second half of Table 6.1 turns to divided governments. The first section includes items that were approved by the president and thus enacted into law. Some featured high levels of ideological and partisan conflict and some did not. In the first case, there was usually a political impasse that was surmounted by a moderation of the original proposal or by some other accommodation of the president's party. As noted above, the budget for 1996 followed that legislative trajectory. The welfare reform of 1996 and the Gramm–Leach–Bliley Act of 1999 were similar in that respect. As noted in Chapter 2, the welfare reform converted AFDC into TANF and led to a reduction in welfare spending. Twice, Clinton had vetoed a version of that proposal before congressional Republicans advanced a more moderate reform that the president and some congressional Democrats found acceptable. Clinton also threatened to veto the Gramm–Leach–Bliley Act, which deregulated the financial sector, and famously eliminated the Depression Era rule that separated retail banks from investment banks (put in place by the Glass–Steagall Act of 1933). Some Democrats supported the measure as is, but Republicans could not overcome a Democratic filibuster or Clinton's veto threat until they added provisions that aimed to help minorities in the mortgage market and to penalize banks that had poor records of lending to minorities.[44]

Other reforms featured more bipartisan agreement for one reason or another. In the case of the 1997 budget, it was because Congress did not want a repeat of the previous year's budget battle, and it was because the bill paired a 60 cent increase in the minimum wage with tax cuts for businesses – a clear example of a bipartisan logroll. In the case of the 1996 telecommunications reform, it was because both parties felt that the changing media landscape required new federal policies and a good amount of deregulation. In the case of the tax cuts in the 1997 budget deal, which introduced education credits and the Child Tax Credit, it was because the package was designed to benefit middle-class parents. And, in the other cases, bipartisan collaboration owed something to a scandal or crisis that demanded attention from lawmakers, either because voters demanded action or because the economy required assistance. One example was the Sarbanes–Oxley corporate accounting reform, which Congress swiftly passed in the wake of the Enron and WorldCom accounting scandals. Other examples were the various economic stimulus and bank bailout bills of 2008, which are discussed in Chapter 7.

The second-to-last row in Table 6.1 lists measures that were killed by veto. Each was a core partisan objective – like the children's health care expansion or tax cuts that would have favored high-income households. And each was motivated as much by politics as policy, because congressional leaders sent them to the president even though they expected them to fail.

Finally, the bottom row lists veto overrides, all of which required some support from the president's party. Three of the five bills – one for defense projects, another for water projects, and the third being a farm bill – were laden with particularistic projects that congressional super-majorities wanted to enact.[45] The override of the shareholder-lawsuit bill was more ideologically rooted. The proposal had been a component of the GOP's Contract with America, and defenders argued that it would protect companies from frivolous and excessive lawsuits by opportunistic shareholders. Clinton and some in his party worried that the change would weaken a means to control corporate fraud, but others in the party shared the Republican view and voted to override Clinton's veto. The politics of the 2008 Medicare bill were similar. The legislation, advanced by a Democratic Congress, expanded Medicare's drug coverage, increased the subsidies for that program, and passed a temporary "doc fix" that prevented cuts to providers' pay for Medicare provision. President Bush argued that it was all too costly, but some in his party joined Democrats in the override vote.

In full, Table 6.1 illustrates several things simultaneously. First and foremost, it illustrates the differences between unified and divided governments, and it brings to life some of the theories from Chapter 4, especially the spatial and partisan models of inter-branch bargaining, which emphasized ideological compromises and logrolls, respectively.[46] Second, it illustrates that even during a period of rising partisan conflict and polarization, there was room for bipartisanship. Indeed, all but two of the reforms were passed with some bipartisan support under normal Senate rules. Third, the table shows that two key proposals – immigration reform and universal health care – were killed not by partisan conflict but by insufficient resolve or unity within the majority party. Finally, the table illustrates that most major economic legislation in the 1990s and 2000s was of the neoliberal or conservative variety.

Conclusion

This chapter continued the story of the nation's economic and political change in the neoliberal era. It explained why campaign and lobbying expenditures rose so quickly throughout the period and why party polarization accelerated in the 1990s. It also reviewed legislative politics and economic policy reforms in the 1990s and 2000s, and it illustrated how coalitions and policy outcomes differ between unified and divided governments.

The multiple narratives highlighted something paradoxical about the period: party polarization and conflict intensified at a time when a Democratic president (Clinton) was busy embracing a fair number of conservative and neoliberal policies, including free trade, welfare reform, and deregulation. But the nation's politics is sufficiently complex to allow crisscrossed storylines. And, indeed, the party wars in the capitol were not just about ideological polarization; they were also about political strategy and gamesmanship in a more competitive party system. Likewise, the polarization of the parties was not just about economic policy, for it had much to do with an emerging partisan–cultural divide on issues of race, religion, and social values. So, the inter-party conflict that commanded so much attention could mask a measure of inter-party agreement on economic policies. And, perhaps more significantly, the parties remained willing to bridge some of their differences through moderation or logrolling.

While the general thrust of policy reforms in the 1990s and 2000s was conservative and neoliberal, there were some exceptions to the trend, especially the Medicare expansion, the Family Medical Leave Act, and the Sarbanes–Oxley accounting reform. However, those reforms were not the reason why government was not fundamentally transformed in the neoliberal era. Rather, it was because the Bush tax cuts were paired not with spending cuts but spending hikes, so both the government and the debt grew. And it was because deregulation and trade agreements did little to change the size and scope of government.

But to focus on the size of government is to miss the importance of those reforms, which had an economic focus. Indeed, they contributed to the major economic trends of the day, including trade flows, business maneuverability, investment, and economic growth. Of course, those developments benefited some regions, sectors, and professions more than others. In general, they benefited high-skilled workers and service-sector corporations. By contrast, trade pressures, along with mass migration and the erosion of the minimum wage, caused wage stagnation for low-skilled workers.

Income inequality and the economic challenges in rural and Rust Belt America were easy to overlook while the Great Moderation continued. And few policymakers foresaw its end and the growing dangers in the financial and housing sectors. When the financial crisis hit, however, a number of problems with the economy and economic policy quickly came into focus. Yet, the government was hamstrung in its ability to respond. The forces that drove partisan conflict did disappear after the crash. If anything, they gathered pace, and congressional gridlock intensified.

Notes

1 These trends are also discussed in Chapters 3 and 5.
2 The causes of the recession were various, but foremost among them was the Fed's rate-tightening in the late 1980s (Walsh, 1993). Another cause was the spike in oil prices that followed Iraq's invasion of Kuwait, which led Bush to launch Operation Desert Storm. Other possible causes (or perhaps consequences) were the on-going savings and loan (S&L) crisis and the bursting of the regional housing bubbles in New England, California, and Texas.
3 Clinton argued that NAFTA should be amended to provide greater protections for Mexico's environment and workers, in part so that production costs in Mexico could not be so low relative to those in the United States.
4 Prior to 1994, the last time that the president's party did *not* lose seats in a midterm election was 1934. Before that, the last time was 1866. The average loss in the House for the president's party in midterms between 1946 and 2006 was thirty-three seats.
5 The effects of polarization on congressional activity are discussed in Sinclair, 2006; Theriault, 2008; and Lee, 2015.
6 See Flanigan et al., 2015, pp. 116, 169.
7 Fiorina et al. (2006) emphasize this point.
8 See Jacobson, 2013. Bishop (2009, p. 10) provides a complementary illustration by tracking the percent of voters living in counties that mirror the national divide in close presidential elections, in which a small difference in the popular vote separated the Republican from the Democrat. Prior to the 1980s, about two-thirds of the public lived in such counties. In the competitive elections of the 2000s, however, only about 55% did, which meant that 45% of the public lived in highly partisan, landslide counties.
9 McCarty, Poole, and Rosenthal, 2006.
10 Jacobson, 2013.
11 The numbers on the scale are meaningless, but the methodology that produced them is designed to accurately capture ideological change over time. Poole and Rosenthal, 2007.
12 Chapter 5 noted that the party system did not change much outside the South post-realignment. That is accurate: the demographics of each party were steady, and so was aggregate partisanship. Still, the GOP became more conservative over time.
13 See also Gerring, 1998 and Fuller, 2014. The former illustrates that, over time, the Democratic Party put less emphasis on social welfare issues. The latter tracks the GOP's rightward move on issues of environmental policy.
14 Poole (2016) makes this point. See also Chapter 5 in this volume for some reasons why debates about welfare programs became increasingly also about race.
15 Chapter 5 discussed the beginnings of this fortification in the 1970s. And see Sinclair, 2006 for a more extensive analysis.
16 See Table 5.3.
17 Many other interest groups and individual donors pursued this strategy of financing primary challengers. And, in line with that development, McCarty, Poole, and Rosenthal (2006) document that campaign contributions increasingly favored more ideological members of Congress, and that that occurred on both the left and the right.

18 Several analyses (e.g., Bartels, 2000) suggest that the elite-to-masses polariza-
    tion was the initial and more powerful cause of party polarization. Mass-to-elite
    polarization only reinforced that process.

19 See Sinclair, 2006.

20 This two-pronged argument is made by McCarty, Poole, and Rosenthal (2006),
    who also document that contemporary polarization has been accompanied by
    growing party-income stratification among voters, with ever fewer high-income
    voters voting Democratic and ever fewer low-income voters voting Republican.
    And still, they point out, that does not suggest that inequality drove polarization.
    On the contrary, it was largely an artifact of southern realignment, as conserva-
    tive southerners, and especially those in the top portions of the income distribu-
    tion, switched parties. In another study, Poole and Rosenthal (1991) analyze
    minimum wage proposals in Congress in the 1970s and 1980s and calculate that
    Democratic proposals became less liberal over time.

21 Frank (2004) argues that corporate campaign contributions had that effect.

22 Bartels (2006) illustrates this point, and it shows that the GOP's growth among
    the white working class was confined to the South, suggesting that the rise of cul-
    tural issues was a consequence – not a cause – of the party's growth. In another
    study, Bartels (2009) demonstrates that many voters did not understand that
    policies like tax cuts would be adverse to their economic interests and would
    increase inequality. That claim is more compatible with Frank's argument, but it
    is quite different. While Frank emphasizes cultural values, Bartels points to vot-
    ers' ignorance about policies.

23 Kernell et al., 2018, p. 467.

24 Another, related point is that the amount of money in politics was arguably low
    to begin with. See Ansolabehere, de Figueiredo, and Snyder, 2003, which argues
    that most political contributions are a form of consumption, rather than "a mar-
    ket for buying political benefits."

25 Drutman, 2015.

26 See, for example, Kaiser 2009, p. 19. In addition to Drutman, 2015 and Kaiser,
    2009, both of which chronicle the growth of money in politics and its effects,
    Citizens against Government Waste, a conservative watchdog group, documents
    (2016) that the number and value of earmarks increased sharply through the
    1980s, 1990s, and early 2000s. Another consequence of the growth of corpo-
    rate lobbying was the "revolving door" phenomenon, whereby members of
    Congress, congressional staff, and government bureaucrats fled public service
    for more lucrative jobs on K-street. That reduced expertise in government fell
    and caused the legislature to become more reliant on lobbyists for information
    and expertise.

27 As easy as the money came in, it was not without considerable work. Indeed, as
    the demand for funds grew, politicians spent more and more of their time attend-
    ing fundraisers and dialing for dollars.

28 As noted already, this change in power allowed Republicans to restructure the
    lobbying industry, and it allowed the party to reorganize Congress. On those
    changes in congressional procedure, see Sinclair, 2006; Theriault, 2008; and Lee,
    2015.

29 Republicans avoided midterm losses because of the terrorist attacks of September
    11, 2001, and the subsequent war in Afghanistan, which swelled President Bush's
    public-approval ratings.

30 Republicans were spurred by Grover Norquist's anti-tax pledge and the fresh
    memories of the problems that befell Bush I for approving the 1990 budget and
    tax hikes.

31 Steuerle (2008, p. 163) notes the unusual nature of Clinton's priorities, and Mallaby (2016) reports that Clinton was concerned about the Federal Reserve.

32 The Medicare reforms contained a mistake that would have cut doctors' payments more than planned, and over the next two decades Congress repeatedly passed a temporary "doc fix" to prevent the steep cuts from taking place. Congress kept enacting short-term fixes because a long-term fix was expensive and politically difficult. A long-term solution was finally passed in 2015.

33 Estimate is from Congressional Budget Office, 2012. EGTRRA ignored the PAYGO rule, but it did have a "sunset clause," which meant that the tax cuts would expire at a specific date (specially, in ten years). The sunset clause was to satisfy the Senate's Byrd rule, which specifies that any policy change considered via budget reconciliation that would add to the deficit for more than ten years may be subject to a point of order. In other words, the sunset clause allowed the legislation to pass via the Senate's budget reconciliation rules, which allows the bill to pass on only a simple majority. When the tax cuts were about to sunset, in 2011, circumstances did not favor their expiration. The economy was weak after the deep recession and Republicans controlled Congress. At first, the tax cuts were extended for two more years. Then, in 2013, most of the tax cuts were made permanent.

34 The 2003 tax cuts were in the Jobs and Growth Tax Relief Reconciliation Act of 2003 (JGTRRA). Its three costliest elements were: (1) an increase in the Alternative Minimum Tax, which benefited high-income households, (2) higher depreciation markdowns for corporate investments, and (3) lower dividend and capital gains tax rates. More modest tax cuts were offered to middle-income and lower-income families (Steuerle 2008, pp. 223–224).

35 Belasco, 2014.

36 Mallaby, 2016.

37 Carroll, 2003.

38 Steuerle (2008, p. 194) notes that many Democrats supported the 1997 tax cuts for that reason.

39 See Table 5.2 and Steuerle, 2008. It is worth recalling that at the same time that the wealthy received these tax cuts, economic growth was skewed in their favor and the minimum wage and TANF were eroded away. The erosion of the minimum wage and TANF are discussed in Chapters 5 and 2, respectively. The growth of income inequality was discussed in Chapter 5.

40 The 2001 tax cuts advanced under budget reconciliation rules, so Senate Republicans did not need sixty votes to defeat a filibuster. However, the Senate's vote was 62–38, which might imply that the legislation would have passed if normal rules had been in effect. Then again, maybe not. Perhaps many Senate Democrats figured that because they could not stop the tax cuts they might as well vote in favor.

41 The identification of May 2001 through 2002 as a period of divided government follows Mayhew, 2005, which is also the primary source of the entries in the table. Other noteworthy economic reforms of the Clinton and Bush II years (most of which are identified by Mayhew 2005) include a reform to college loan financing (1993), the Brady bill waiting period for gun purchases (1993), ratification of the World Trade Organization (1994), lobbying reform (1995), line item veto authority (1996), agriculture deregulation (1996), immigration reform (1996), health insurance portability act (1996), FDA reform (1997), transportation construction (1998), public housing (1998), trade with China normalization (2000), development in poor communities (2000), the Patriot Act (2001), airline bailout (2001), No Child Left Behind (2001), campaign finance reform (2002), agriculture subsidies (2002), subsidies for first-time homebuyers (2003), class action lawsuits (2005), energy regulations, grants, and tax

incentives (2005 and 2007), transportation projects (2005), extending the fence at the Mexican border (2006), pension regulations reform (2006), science and education initiatives (2007), and consumer product safety (2008).

42 This provision, and its estimated cost to taxpayers, is discussed in Chapter 2.

43 Although the Constitution requires that treaties like NAFTA only be passed by the Senate, the NAFTA votes were structured differently, and both the House and the Senate voted on the implementing legislation. That approach is typical of contemporary trade agreements.

44 Labaton, 1999.

45 The defense bill (and Clinton's line-item veto thereof) is discussed in Chapter 4.

46 Chapter 4 also drew attention to the debate about divided government and legislative productivity, and it offered a hypothesis about divided government and particularism. Both subjects are interesting, but they are difficult to evaluate, so this chapter does not dwell on them.

References

Ansolabehere, Stephen, John M. de Figueiredo, and James M. Snyder Jr. (2003). Why is there so little money in US politics? *Journal of Economic Perspectives*, 17(1), 105–130.

Bartels, Larry M. (2000). Partisanship and voting behavior, 1952–1996. *American Journal of Political Science*, 44(1), 35–50.

Bartels, Larry M. (2006). What's the matter with what's the matter with Kansas? *Quarterly Journal of Political Science*, 1(2), 201–226.

Bartels, Larry M. (2009). *Unequal democracy: The political economy of the new gilded age*. Princeton, NJ: Princeton University Press.

Belasco, Amy. (2014). *The Cost of Iraq, Afghanistan, and other global war on terror operations since 9/11*. Washington, DC: Congressional Research Service.

Bishop, Bill. (2009). *The big sort*. New York, NY: Houghton Mifflin Harcourt.

Carroll, Joseph. (2003, September 25). Economy, terrorism top issues in 2004 election vote. *Gallup News*. Retrieved from: //news.gallup.com/poll/9337/economy-terrorism-top-issues-2004-election-vote.aspx (accessed June 15, 2018).

Citizens Against Government Waste. (2016). Pig book and historical trends. Retrieved from: www.cagw.org/reporting/pig-book#historical_trends (accessed October 9, 2017).

Congressional Budget Office. (2012). Changes in CBO's baseline projections since January 2001. Retrieved from: www.cbo.gov/sites/default/files/cbofiles/attachments/06–07-ChangesSince2001Baseline.pdf (accessed February 17, 2018).

Drutman, Lee. (2015). *The business of America is lobbying*. Oxford, UK: Oxford University Press.

Fiorina, Morris P., Samuel J. Adams, and Jeremy C. Pope. (2006). *Culture war? The myth of a polarized America*. New York, NY: Longman.

Flanigan, William H., Nancy H. Zingale, Elizabeth A. Theiss-Morse, and Michael W. Wagner. (2015). *Political behavior of the American electorate* (13th ed.). Washington, DC: CQ Press.

Frank, Thomas. (2004). *What's the matter with Kansas?* New York, NY: Henry Holt.

Fuller, Jaime. (2014, June 2), Environmental policy is partisan. It wasn't always. [Web log comment]. Retrieved from: www.washingtonpost.com/news/the-fix/wp/

2014/06/02/support-for-the-clean-air-act-has-changed-a-lot-since-1970/?utm_
term=.4da686369d89 (accessed February 17, 2018).

Gerring, John. (1998). *Party ideologies in America, 1828–1996.* Cambridge, UK:
Cambridge University Press.

Jacobson, Gary C. (2013). Partisan polarization in American politics: A background
paper. *Presidential Studies Quarterly,* 43(4), 688–708.

Kaiser, Robert G. (2009). *So damn much money.* New York, NY: Alfred A. Knopf.

Kernell, Samuel, Gary C. Jacobson, Thad Kousser, and Lynn Vavreck. (2018). *The
logic of American politics* (8th ed.). Washington, DC: CQ Press.

Labaton, Stephen. (1999, October 23). A new financial era – the overview: Accord
reached on lifting of depression era barriers among financial industries. *The New
York Times.*

Lee, Frances E. (2015). How party polarization affects governance. *Annual Review
of Political Science,* 18, 261–282.

McCarty, Nolan, Keith T. Poole, and Howard Rosenthal. (2006). *Polarized America.*
Cambridge, MA: MIT Press.

Mallaby, Sebastian. (2016) *The man who knew.* New York, NY: Penguin.

Mayhew, David R. (2005). *Divided we govern* (2nd ed.). New Haven, CT: Yale
University Press.

Poole, Keith T. (2016). The polarization of the Congressional parties. [Web log
comment]. Retrieved from: https://legacy.voteview.com/political_polarization_
2015.htm (accessed February 17, 2018).

Poole, Keith T., and Howard Rosenthal. (1991). The spatial mapping of minimum
wage legislation. In Alberto Alesina and Geoffrey Carliner (Eds.), *Politics and
economics in the eighties.* (pp. 215–250). Chicago, IL: University of Chicago
Press.

Poole, Keith T., and Howard Rosenthal. (2007). *Ideology and congress.* New York,
NY: Transaction Publishers.

Sinclair, Barbara. (2006). *Party wars.* Norman, OK: University of Oklahoma Press.

Steuerle, C. Eugene. (2008). *Contemporary US tax policy.* Washington, DC: The
Urban Institute Press.

Theriault, Sean M. (2008). *Party polarization in Congress.* Cambridge, UK:
Cambridge University Press.

Walsh, Carl E. (1993). What caused the 1990–1991 Recession? *Federal Reserve
Bank of San Francisco Economic Review,* 2, 33.

7 Financial Crisis and the Obama Years

In early 2007, a long-building bubble in the housing sector began to deflate, and at year's end the economy slipped into recession. Although the downturn was mild, some large and long-standing financial institutions found themselves under severe stress. In March, the Federal Reserve rescued Bear Stearns, a venerable Wall Street institution that had weathered every turn in the economy for the previous eighty-five years, including the Great Depression, but had suddenly found itself on the brink of collapse. The Fed was worried that Bear's collapse would trigger panic throughout the financial sector, so it extended a $30 billion loan to encourage J.P. Morgan Chase, another investment bank, to buy the stressed firm.[1] Critics said that this "bailout" would encourage moral hazard – i.e., other banks might behave recklessly out of the belief that they, too, would be rescued if they got into trouble. Others worried that the Fed's action overstepped its authority; and still others said that Bear was too small to merit a bailout. However, Fed officials believed that a meltdown in the financial sector was imminent, and that swift, bold action was required to prevent that from happening.

A few months later, in September, the Fed failed in its attempt to rescue a larger firm, Lehman Brothers. Many people had encouraged the Fed to let Lehman fail to avoid the moral hazard problem, but when the firm declared bankruptcy the Fed's fears of a financial crisis came true: panic engulfed the financial system and the stock market plunged. Worse, the broader economy slipped from downturn to free fall. GDP growth was –8 percent in the fourth quarter of 2008 and –4 percent in the first quarter of 2009. From September through March, the economy lost 700,000 jobs per month. By mid-2010, nearly nine million Americans had lost their jobs.[2] The Great Recession, as it was dubbed, was the economy's deepest contraction since the Great Depression.

Financial sector crises tend to bring sharp contractions in the economy that elevate the unemployment rate for a long time. In their 2009 book, *This time is different*, economists Carmen Reinhart and Kenneth Rogoff found that the average modern banking crisis causes a 9 percent drop in a country's GDP, a 7 percent increase in its unemployment rate, and a period of elevated unemployment that lasts five years. The 2008 crisis in the

United States reaped similar havoc: real GDP fell by almost 5 percent and the unemployment rate increased by 6.5 percent, peaking at 10 percent in 2010, a year after the contraction was officially over. And the recovery was slow. It was not until early 2017 – the very end of Obama's presidency and nearly a decade after the crisis struck – that employment returned to 2006 levels.

In the meantime, tremendous pain had been inflicted. Millions of Americans suffered from long-term joblessness and the loss of their homes or savings. Although the government softened the blow with increased safety-net spending, its measures were modest given the scale of the crisis. Furthermore, many Americans felt wronged by the fact that the government did much more to help the banks and bankers who were so instrumental in causing the financial crisis than to help ordinary Americans who suffered great distress through no fault of their own.

Overall, the government's record in the tragedy was mixed. On the one hand, its responses to the crisis and recession worked, in the sense that both were less severe than they would have been without those responses. In particular, there is broad agreement among economists that Congress's bank bailout, though unpopular, prevented a meltdown of the financial sector, and that its stimulus bill softened the recession and quickened the recovery. On the other hand, the government was blameworthy in three main respects. First, policymakers could have prevented the financial crisis if they had not been so blasé about the risks of deregulation and non-regulation. Second, as explained below, some government policies fueled the housing bubble that precipitated the financial crisis. And, third, the government's responses to the financial crisis and recession were undermined by party wars and ideological polarization. Most notably, they made the government's fiscal response smaller and less effective than it could have been.

The crisis had many consequences for the nation's political economy. Firms went bust; savings and investments were lost; financial sector regulations were overhauled; government debt ballooned; macroeconomic policy was reinvented; and confidence in America's political economy was replaced by deep anxieties about slow growth and income inequality.[3] Yet, as significant as these and other developments were, much remained as it was. There was no party system realignment or major new jobs programs, as occurred after the Great Depression. And many trends continued on their pre-crisis trajectories. In particular, trade expanded (after a short lull); income inequality grew; and the ideological gap between the parties widened.

The advance of polarization was most evident in the Tea Party movement of 2010, which pulled the Republican Party to the right and was the animating force behind the party's wave in the 2010 midterms. The elections reintroduced divided government, and Congress was immediately overtaken by gridlock and partisan warfare. Equally noteworthy was the simultaneous and related conflict within the Republican Party. It was marked by the Tea Party's refusal to compromise on policy and its persistent challenges to the party's leader, House Speaker John Boehner. Although Boehner survived the challenges, he eventually tired of them and resigned the speakership.[4] With his abrupt resignation, Boehner also intended to bring a cessation in the party's internal conflict, and it succeeded for a period. However, deep fissures in the Republican Party remained, and they continued to shape national politics and policy.

The Financial Crisis

The bursting of the housing bubble set the financial crisis and Great Recession in motion. But why was that? Why was the financial sector so exposed to housing? And how did government policy contribute to the housing bubble and to financial sector fragility? This section answers those questions. It also describes the government's responses to the crises.[5]

The Bubble and Housing Finance

The housing bubble was a decade or so in the making. While it was inflating, few people understood that it was a bubble – an unsustainable rise in prices that is fueled by speculation and optimism rather than a change in economic "fundamentals" like supply costs. That is generally the case with asset bubbles – they are difficult to spot until they pop. That is because the economy is complex and always changing, and there is always some development that seems to justify rising asset prices. For example, in the early 2000s, people could point to the tech economy or population growth as causes of rising house prices.[6] In addition, bubbles are inflated by *accurate* perceptions of financial rewards. As asset prices rise, people make money, which attracts more money and buyers into the market, and the trend continues. Indeed, to rent during the housing bubble was to sit back and watch everyone else make money as their homes appreciated.

To put these points another way, the housing bubble of the early 2000s can be understood as any other asset bubble – as the product of widespread assumptions and incentives in the market. Yet, there were also specific policies and market developments to blame. One was low interest rates. After the bursting of the dot-com bubble in 2000, in which investors suddenly unloaded their (wildly overvalued) stocks in Internet technology companies, a mild recession occurred, and the Federal Reserve lowered rates. That was a standard monetary response, but it was maintained for too long, especially as household indebtedness and the housing bubble grew.

Another important cause was the dramatic growth in subprime lending. Traditional, "prime" mortgages are those given to homebuyers who have a stable income and a good credit rating and can make a considerable down payment, typically 20 percent of the purchase price. Subprime loans, by contrast, are those given to homebuyers who are less financially secure. The subprime market was virtually non-existent in the early 1990s, but it grew rapidly over the late 1990s and early 2000s. That growth went hand-in-hand with the housing bubble. As subprime grew, demand for housing grew, and prices increased. Also, as bubble mentality took root, borrowers and lenders grew complacent, and lending standards fell. In fact, at the height of the housing craze, standards had fallen so low that people could obtain huge mortgages with no proof of a job and no money down.[7] (Those borrowers were highly exposed to market fluctuations. Any dip in house prices would cause them to be "under water" on their mortgages – owing more than their homes are worth. Not surprisingly, subprime borrowers were more likely to default on their mortgages after the bubble burst.)

The subprime market was also spurred by federal policy. In the 1990s and 2000s, both Democrats and Republicans encouraged subprime lending in order to expand homeownership and help lower-income families build assets and ownership stakes in neighborhoods. The push was applied to both banks and underwriters. Banks were encouraged to expand subprime under the terms of the Community Reinvestment Act of 1977 (CRA), a bill that sought to increase mortgage offerings to lower-income and minority households that had been underserved by mortgage lenders. That initiative became increasingly important in the late 1990s, when deregulation under the Riegle–Neal Act allowed bank mergers and the creation of national mega-banks. The reason: bank mergers were more likely to face government resistance if they were not in compliance with the CRA. Thus, banks found it worthwhile to offer more loans to lower-income and minority households.[8]

Simultaneously, the government pressed Fannie Mae and Freddie Mac, two government-sponsored underwriters, to expand subprime. Fannie and Freddie underwrote most of the housing market, so when they embraced subprime the market was made. Although the government had long ago privatized both institutions, the president still appointed some members to their boards.[9] Also, the firms operated with the implicit backing of the government, which gave the government some influence over their operations. After all, the implicit backing had allowed Fannie and Freddie to borrow money cheaply, which allowed them to become highly profitable financial giants. That, in turn, strengthened the belief in a government backstop, because the firms' sizes made them "too big to fail."[10]

A less significant but still noteworthy boost to the housing market came in 2003, when Congress increased the subsidies that were available to first-time homebuyers. The initiative, which was sponsored by Republicans and signed by President Bush, authorized $200 million in down-payment assistance to encourage more families to take the plunge into homeownership.

And on top of all of those policies was one other relevant market development: securitization in housing finance. Starting in the 1980s and accelerating in the 1990s and 2000s, lenders and intermediaries began combining mortgages into large pools and selling securities that were backed by those pools to investors. The innovation appealed to all parties, and it had some economic merits. Mortgage lenders could cash in on their mortgages immediately and turn their attention from servicing mortgages to finding new lenders.[11] Investment banks and Fannie and Freddie made money by packaging mortgages and selling them as securities to investors. And investors were pleased to buy a profitable and marketable asset that was assumed to be safe because it was immune to most housing downturns, which tend to be localized. The trouble was that the housing bubble was not local. It was national, and when it popped the mortgage-backed securities plummeted in value. That prompted the crisis in the financial sector. But, before that occurred, securitization fueled the housing bubble because it increased investment in the market.

Fragility in the Financial Sector

As mortgage-backed securities lost value, crisis mounted in the financial sector. One reason was that financial firms owned hundreds of billions of dollars' worth of mortgage-backed securities and other complex and inter-related financial products that were difficult to value in a fast-changing market.[12] With no one to buy those "toxic" assets, troubled firms could not sell them to cover their short-term debts, so they could not borrow money to ride out the market downturn. Put differently, firms like Lehman Brothers faced a liquidity crisis – i.e., their assets were not quickly salable (liquid), so they could not adjust to the changing market.

Another reason for the financial crisis was that firms were very highly leveraged. That is, they had borrowed huge sums of money in order to magnify their investment profits. With leverage comes risk, because even a small drop in asset values can quickly generate huge investment losses. So, as asset prices nose-dived, some firms careened toward insolvency and bankruptcy, with debts that exceeded their own assets and capital.

Why had financial firms assumed so much risk? There were three main reasons.[13] The first was the combination of optimistic market perceptions and inter-firm competition. Firms believed the economy was on a stable growth trajectory, which was justifiable given the economy's performance over the previous two decades; and as some firms increased their leverage and risk, it was copied by their competitors throughout the sector.[14] Second, the government did not regulate most of the firms and products that were at the heart of the crisis, and it did not prevent firms from operating with dangerously high levels of leverage.[15] And the third reason was moral hazard. In particular, large firms like Lehman and Fannie may have assumed that they would receive a bailout from taxpayers if they got into trouble.

The "too big to fail" issue received much attention after the crisis, and so did the idea that a long period of economic growth can foster complacency and excessive risk-taking, which in turn sows the seeds of a financial crisis. That dynamic was explained and anticipated by the economist Hyman Minsky (1919–1996), although his "instability hypothesis" was ignored by economists until the 2008 crisis. Minksy's idea was that long expansions create booms and bubbles because people start to discount the chance of a bust and assume ever-greater risks and debts. The boom continues until something startling happens to shake confidence. Then, suddenly, everyone wants to sell, and the crash causes a crisis in a highly leveraged financial sector.

As noted already, the debt-fueled boom-and-bust story was not confined to the financial sector. Households also assumed large debts during the bubble years.[16] Indeed, from the late 1980s until 2000, total household mortgage debt as a percent of GDP increased from about 50 percent to 70 percent, and it accelerated further in the early 2000s, hitting 100 percent in 2007.[17] Then, once the financial crisis triggered a deep recession in the wider economy, households were hit, and they needed to cut back on spending in order to service their hefty debt burdens. The deep and sustained drop in demand made for a sluggish economic recovery.

This review has already noted how both market and government were to blame for the crises in the housing and financial sectors. Market participants in both sectors were highly leveraged, and they failed to anticipate a housing crash and to understand the dangers of complex financial products. As for policy, it was noted that the government's housing push and low interest rates contributed to the housing bubble. It was also noted that the government's approach to financial-sector regulation was insufficient, in two key respects. First, the government could have prevented excessive leverage in big firms like Lehman, Bear, Fannie, and Freddie. Second, the government could have regulated products like mortgage-backed securities and firms like hedge funds and insurance companies that had become significant players in the financial sector but remained unregulated because they were outside of the sector's core. If government regulators had limited the growth of leverage and introduced transparency into product markets, then the housing downturn would have been less likely to precipitate a financial sector crisis.

To some extent, the government's regulatory approach can be explained by special-interest politics. Banks, mortgage lenders, and other financial firms fought regulations and lobbied for deregulation.[18] However, the bigger culprit was ideology.[19] The common assumption among policymakers was that the financial sector could regulate itself and that government regulations would be ineffective, distortionary, and costly. Of course, there were some voices in favor of regulation, but theirs was the minority view, and it was rejected by the chorus of policymakers who favored a neoliberal approach.[20]

The government's regulatory failures can also be linked to the short-termism of elected officials.[21] Regardless of their party and ideology, elected representatives are not very inclined to put the brakes on a boom economy. Instead, their inclination is to let the good times roll. The solution – albeit not a foolproof one – is to have independent regulators who have the mandate, disposition, and power to slow an overheating economy and to prevent the build-up of systemic risks in the financial sector.

The Government's Response

The government took many steps to prevent the crisis that eventually came. Its first major steps were a series of very aggressive interest rate cuts in late 2007 and early 2008, which the Fed took as the economy dipped into recession and the full magnitude of the housing crash was becoming clear. Then, in February 2008, Congress tried to stimulate the economy with a tax cut. In March, the Fed again lowered rates, and it offered its $30 billion loan to save Bear Stearns, a firm that was not even under its regulatory authority. In July, Congress acted on the Treasury Department's request to capitalize Fannie and Freddie and backstop the housing market. A few months later, the government went further and took Fannie and Freddie into conservatorship.

Each of those steps was remarkable by itself, but they remained insufficient to the task. A week after Fannie and Freddie were taken under government control, Lehman collapsed, and then events became really extraordinary. The day after Lehman's bankruptcy, the Fed nationalized the insurance giant AIG, which was not under the Fed's purview but was systemically important because it had trillions of dollars of exposure to troubled firms and toxic financial products.[22] Two days later, the Fed and four other central banks announced an internationally coordinated move – an unprecedented action – to provide liquidity to financial markets. The day after that, Treasury and the Fed took steps to prop up the market in "commercial paper" and backstop an array of non-financial corporations that were exposed to the crisis. Two days after that, the nation's two biggest investment banks, Morgan Stanley and Goldman Sachs, applied to become "bank holding companies," which gave them some protection from the crisis via their new regulator, the Federal Reserve.[23] And, as this whirlwind of events was transpiring, the Fed continued to lower interest rates. Within a few months, the federal funds rate had been moved to 0.25 percent – which was very far from the 5.25 percent of mid-2007.[24]

Another major action in September and October of 2008 was Congress's Troubled Asset Relief Program (or TARP), a $700 billion program to save banks by buying their toxic assets. The initiative began three days after Lehman declared bankruptcy, when the Fed Chair Ben Bernanke and Treasury Secretary Henry ("Hank") Paulson met with leaders in Congress and told them that the financial system was on the brink of failure and that the legislature needed to immediately pass a large rescue plan. Most members understood the need to save the financial sector, but they did not savor the idea of a huge taxpayer-funded bailout of investment banks whose troubles were born of poor and reckless investment decisions, and especially because federal elections were less than two months away.

So, many members chose to vote against the proposal even while they hoped a majority of their colleagues would vote to pass it. The trouble was that too many members chose that strategy when the House first voted on the bill.[25] After it was defeated, the stock market plummeted. Facing intense criticism and pressure, the House held another vote two days later, and two to three dozen "no" voters in each party switched to a more politically courageous "yes," passing the measure.

TARP was indeed unpopular with voters. It struck many Americans as unfair, not only because it bailed out banks for their poor decisions but also because it did nothing for ordinary Americans who were facing foreclosure or unemployment on account of the recession and housing crash. As a matter of policy, however, the program was a success. The government ended up purchasing about $426 billion of troubled assets in order to help banks weather the storm, and years later it sold those holdings for a profit.[26]

The government's responses to the crisis and recession continued through 2009 and 2010. The two most significant actions of the 111th Congress, which began in January 2009, were the stimulus bill, passed February 2009, and the Dodd–Frank financial sector reform of 2010. The former authorized $800 billion in deficit spending, mostly for road improvements, transfers to state governments, and tax breaks. As noted in Chapter 3, the transfers to states and tax cuts made the stimulus smaller and less significant than its budgetary impact suggested, and partisan and ideological fights hindered the government's ability to do any more. Indeed, the stimulus bill was Congress's only significant fiscal policy response to the recession, and it mostly left the recovery effort to the Federal Reserve. But the regulator found that it could do little once it had already dropped the federal funds rate to (near) zero. Although it did experiment with new types of monetary policies to further stimulate the economy, its main policy tools had already been exhausted. The economy seemed to suffer from too much debt-over-hang from the bubble, so low interest rates did little to spur borrowing, investment, and spending.

The Dodd–Frank Wall Street Reform and Consumer Protection Act, known simply as Dodd–Frank after its two main legislative pilots, Senator Chris Dodd (D-CT) and Representative Barney Frank (D-MA), introduced several regulatory reforms that were intended to prevent a similar financial crisis in the future. Key components included the creation of a new "systemic risk council" to bring different regulatory agencies together in order to spot problems in the entire financial sector, new regulations on the issuance and sale of complex derivatives like mortgage-backed securities, a new requirement that banks with more than $10 billion in assets conduct annual "stress tests" that simulate their ability to withstand various types of economic shocks, and two measures to address the "too big to fail" problem.[27] Another notable component, and the one that solicited the greatest partisan conflict, was the creation of the Consumer Financial Protection Bureau (CFPB) to protect and empower consumers in markets for mortgages, auto loans, and credit cards. The partisan controversy is on-going and ideologically rooted – Democrats want the agency to be a strong advocate for consumers and a check against predatory lending whereas Republicans think that the regulator overly burdens financial businesses and consumer product markets.[28] During its first years of operation, the CFPB took action against mortgage providers, credit card companies, and pay-day lenders that the Bureau said directly or indirectly harmed consumers.

Although TARP, Dodd–Frank, and the stimulus bill were three most significant legislative responses to the crisis, the 111th Congress also passed the following: (1) the Credit Card Accountability Responsibility and Disclosure (CARD) Act, which gave credit card holders greater protection from bank fees and more information about their payoff schedules; (2) the Fraud Enforcement and Recovery Act (FERA), which increased criminal sanctions for mortgage fraud and other types of financial fraud and improved the government's tools for recouping tax dollars lost to fraud; (3) the short-lived "cash for clunkers" program, which sought to help the auto industry and the environment by giving consumers a $4,000 subsidy to sell their old cars (twenty-five years old or older) for new, more efficient cars; (4) the Worker, Homeownership, and Business Assistance (WHBA) Act, which extended by twenty the number of weeks that people could draw on unemployment benefits and which created a temporary tax credit for first-time homebuyers; (5) the Helping Families Save Their Homes (HFSH) Act, which sought to help homeowners avoid foreclosure with a few changes to bankruptcy law and an expansion of federal mortgage insurance; and (6) the Hiring Incentives to Restore Employment (HIRE) Act, which created a one-year payroll tax credit for employers who hired people who were unemployed or underemployed at the time of hire.

The Recovering Economy

It is impossible to identify how much the government's various actions affected the economic recovery that began in 2010. Certainly, low interest rates and other measures by the Fed were helpful, as was Congress's stimulus. Subsequently, Congress's spending cuts in 2011 probably slowed the rebound a little. Beyond that, it is difficult to conclude anything. There were no major changes in monetary or fiscal policies after 2010, and the economy's trajectory was influenced by many developments that had almost nothing to do with federal policy, including the crisis in the Eurozone that began in 2010 and America's oil fracking boom, which caused gasoline prices to fall by a third after the summer of 2014.[29]

It is clear, however, that the recovery was slow and uneven. The sluggishness made for some stark figures. For example, average annual growth in real GDP per capita was only 1.4 percent from 2009 through 2017, whereas it had averaged 2.1 percent from 1991 through 2007. Thus, the nation's unemployment rate did not return to 2007 levels until 2016, seven years after the recovery began. In contrast, the stock market had then long since rebounded. In 2016, the Dow Jones Industrial Index was 30 percent higher than where it had been before the crash.

That was one way in which the recovery was uneven. Another was the difference across states. Naturally, states that were particularly hard hit by the housing bust, such as Nevada and Arizona, were slower to rebound than others. Also, states that had been suffering relative economic decline before the crisis, such as West Virginia, Illinois, and Pennsylvania, were slow to recover.[30] By contrast, states on the west coast and states that benefited from the fracking boom, like Oklahoma and North Dakota, enjoyed faster growth in the recovery years.

The unevenness in wage growth was also striking. After a brief decline during 2007–2010, wages in the top half of the income distribution increased, to the point that, in 2015, they were 4 percent to 5 percent higher than where they had been in 2005. That growth was not enough to keep up with certain costs borne by those households, especially fast-rising health care premiums and college tuitions, but it was much better than what befell the bottom quintile of the income distribution, where wages in 2015 were 5 percent *lower* than where they had been in 2005.[31] Put another way, the 2010–2016 recovery was similar to three decades that preceded the crash in that income inequality increased (see Figure 5.1). The fundamental cause had not changed: the economy continued to reward certain categories of high-skill jobs, whereas other forces kept wages stagnant in other parts of the economy.[32]

Politics and Policy in the Obama Years

During 2009 and 2010, when Democrats enjoyed unified government, Congress enacted the stimulus bill, a number of minor, crisis-related reforms, and two major pieces of legislation: the Dodd–Frank overhaul of financial sector regulations and the Affordable Care Act, which was the largest expansion of the federal safety net in decades. Then, after divided government returned following the Republican wave in the 2010 midterms, Congress became gridlocked, and few economically significant reforms were enacted during the remainder of the Obama years. The most significant changes after 2010 were fiscal, including spending cuts in 2011 and 2013 and the permanent extension of most of the Bush income tax cuts. Other economically significant policies were initiated by Obama but ceased by Trump in 2017, including Obama's executive orders to create a Clean Power Plan, increase overtime pay, and expand student loan forgiveness.[33] A similar fate befell the Trans-Pacific Partnership (TPP) trade deal with a dozen Asian-Pacific countries. The groundwork for the TPP had begun under George W. Bush and had been pursued by the Obama administration, but Trump pulled the United States out of the agreement soon after his inauguration.

Therefore, Dodd–Frank and Obamacare loom large in a retrospective of Obama-era policies. Although both reforms were substantial, they were not evidence that the neoliberal era was being replaced by something wholly different. On the contrary, Obama's willingness to expand trade deals, make the Bush tax cuts permanent, and consider deficit-reduction deals that included cuts to entitlement programs illustrated his party's centrism and incrementalism on economic policy.

Meanwhile, the Republican Party became more conservative and embold-ened, with positions and strategies that were dictated by the burgeoning Tea Party movement and the donors, groups, and media that supported it. Tea Party members of Congress adopted a no-compromise approach on policy, which was at times focused on immigration or other social policies but was more consistently and squarely focused on government spending and debt. The no-compromise approach routinely brought Tea Partyers into conflict with other Republicans.

The Tea Party movement was said to have been born after Obama's February 2009 call for legislation to help homeowners avoid foreclosure. Congress's response in May of that year was not very strong – the most gen-erous and forceful provisions had been removed from the Helping Families Save Their Homes Act while the bill was being considered by the Senate, and the features that remained offered only modest and indirect support to homeowners in distress. However, Obama's call did receive a very forceful rebuttal (or "rant," it was called) from political commentator Rick Santelli on CNBC. Santelli complained that taxpayers should not have to pay for "losers'" mortgages, and he said he would organize a Tea Party to protest Obama's initiative. The rant was said to ignite a huge grassroots movement that started calling itself the Tea Party. The movement was somewhat less grassroots than it appeared, and it received a great deal of financial backing from the Koch brothers, the libertarian-minded billionaires who own the oil and gas conglomerate Koch Industries.[34] Regardless, the Tea Party enjoyed a good measure of popular support. Surveys by Gallup News indicated that 32 percent of Americans supported the movement in November of 2010.[35]

It was predictable that there would be a large Republican wave in the midterm elections of that month.[36] The Democratic majorities in Congress were unsustainably large artifacts of the party's wave in 2008, and the economy was in miserable shape, with millions of Americans suffering from long-term unemployment. Additionally, Republicans could use Obamacare as a rallying cry. The Tea Party movement was propelled by all of those fac-tors, and the funding and energy behind the movement added to the GOP's midterm success.

That success was not just at the federal level. The Republican Party net-ted six governorships in 2010, allowing it to control almost three-fifths of the nation's statehouses. That gave the party unprecedented control over state policies, with some notable consequences. One was a smaller Medicaid expansion. The Supreme Court's Obamacare ruling in the spring of 2010 allowed states the option of skipping the law's Medicaid expansion, and more states that flipped to GOP control in 2010 skipped the Medicaid expansion than states that flipped to Democratic control and pursued the expansion. The Republican wave also affected labor law, especially in Wisconsin and Michigan, where new Republican governors enacted right-to-work laws.

A third consequence was an enhanced advantage in the redistricting that was due after the 2010 census. Most notably, the elections gave Republicans control over redistricting in several states with large congressional delegations, including Pennsylvania, Florida, Ohio, and North Carolina. Those states – particularly Pennsylvania and North Carolina – subsequently engaged in aggressive partisan gerrymandering that gave the GOP huge wins in 2012 and beyond.[37] For example, the new map in Pennsylvania handed Republicans victories in thirteen of the state's eighteen House districts in the 2012 elections, even though Democrats won more votes statewide (50 percent versus the GOP's 49 percent). That was a considerable improvement over the 2010 elections, when the GOP won a majority of votes statewide but secured only twelve of nineteen seats. North Carolina's new map had a similar effect. Although Republicans won 49 percent of the votes for House candidates in the 2012 elections – compared to the Democrats' 51 percent – they won 69 percent of the districts, or nine of thirteen seats.[38] Collectively, the two states handed the GOP about five or six seats to its House majority that would not have been won under a more neutral districting scheme.[39] Later, in 2016 and 2018, federal courts ruled the two maps unconstitutional.

Although the Tea Party wave in the 2010 elections heightened partisan gridlock on Capitol Hill, an escalation was already under way in early 2009. It was most evident in Senate Republicans' new filibuster strategy, which was to filibuster every piece of legislation, including those that the party supported. An example was the Worker, Homeownership, and Business Assistance Act, which extended unemployment benefits for up to thirteen extra weeks for people facing long-term unemployment.[40] The bill passed the Senate unanimously after the cloture vote, but the filibuster was effective as a delay tactic, because chamber rules require that a filibuster be followed by two days before the cloture vote and then thirty hours of debate and that the floor can consider no other business during those periods. In other words, each filibuster can consume an entire work week for the Senate. Starting in 2009, the minority party began filibustering for that purpose alone.

The politics surrounding Obamacare were also extraordinary, especially Republicans' flip-flop on the three-legged-stool system to expand the health insurance market.[41] The system – consisting of the individual mandate, subsidies, and prohibitions on discrimination by insurance companies (see Chapter 2) – was the brainchild of the Heritage Foundation, a conservative think tank, and it had been praised by many Republicans and enacted in Massachusetts by Republican Governor Mitt Romney. The system appealed to conservatives because it was a market-oriented approach to reducing the number of uninsured and because it advanced individual responsibility – people had to carry their own insurance so their bills were covered in the event that they needed medical care. Yet, when Obama pushed the plan, Republicans decried it as an unconstitutional, job-killing, government takeover of health care. The flip was partly just party strategy: regardless of the system's merits, it had become Obama's plan, so Republicans opposed it, at least in public.[42] Indeed, it was revealing that Republican members of Congress failed to repeal the legislation in 2017, when they enjoyed unified government (see Chapter 8). However, there was also some genuine opposition to the system within the Republican caucus, and that reflected the party's move to the right since the 1990s, when Heritage proposed the system, and since 2006, when Romneycare was enacted.

As much as the Tea Party pulled the Republican Party to the right, it also opened a rift within the Republican Party. The conflict was evident in the 2010 elections, when there were some pitched primary battles between Tea Party challengers and more established Republicans.[43] Over the next few years, the Tea Party lost its novelty and popularity, and the name was used less and less frequently. However, the conflict between Republican factions remained and made the party's congressional caucuses ungovernable.[44] The conflict was also the animating force behind the cascading fiscal crises that occurred between 2011 and 2015.

Fiscal Fights

The fiscal fights between late 2010 and 2016 were highly dramatic, especially the near default on the US debt in the summer of 2011 and the two-week government shutdown of 2013. Along the way, there were several other near-shutdowns and intense battles over tax cuts and spending cuts. They took a toll. Public opinion of Congress, which was never high, fell to a historical low.[45] The US credit rating was downgraded by Standard & Poor's for the first time ever. And Congress failed to pass any full-year budgets.

With respect to policy, the main sequence of events between 2010 and 2015 was as follows. First, at the end of 2010, the Bush income tax cuts were extended for two years. Then, in 2011, each of two deals, one to avert a government shutdown and one to avert a debt default, cut annual spending (by $38 billion and $90 billion, respectively).[46] In 2013, the extended Bush tax cuts were made permanent for households with incomes up to $400,000. (Put differently, the income tax cuts for wealthier households were allowed to expire, causing them to revert to 2001 levels.) A few months later, spending was cut again (via sequestration[47]) when the parties could not reach a deal to resolve their self-imposed "fiscal cliff."

Twice over the next several months the sequestration cuts were eased a little, and in October 2013 there was a two-week government shutdown that centered over Tea Party demands to cut spending again – specifically, to defund Obamacare. The shutdown ended with that demand unfulfilled. The budget deals for fiscal year 2014 kept spending at late 2013 levels. Then, in 2015, after the GOP had taken control of both chambers of Congress in the 2014 midterms, Congress increased spending, reversing some of the spending cuts of the previous four years.

In terms of politics, a noteworthy step along the way was the House majority's threat in 2011 to refuse a debt-ceiling increase unless the Democratic Senate and White House agreed to its fiscal agenda. While it had long been the practice of whatever party was in the minority to object to debt-ceiling increases, never had a majority threatened a default on the national debt if the other branches of government refused to give it what it wanted on budget policy. The brinksmanship prompted the most serious crisis of the period, and the near default is what prompted Standard and Poor's to downgrade the creditworthiness of US debt.

The deal that broke the impasse, the Budget Control Act of 2011, introduced the larger of the two spending cuts in 2011 ($900 billion over ten years). It also staged a plan for an additional, larger deficit-reduction bill. A special bipartisan committee was to be created to present a deficit-reduction plan to Congress, and if it failed to pass there would be an automatic "fiscal cliff" in the form of a tax increase and across-the-board cuts in discretionary spending, half of which would be in defense.[48] The plan was supposed to work because no member of Congress wants indiscriminate cuts to discretionary programs. Nevertheless, the committee failed. Although it was created as a bipartisan committee – which implied it would produce a plan that included both tax hikes and spending cuts – the committee's Republicans refused to consider tax hikes and insisted that deficit reduction occur via spending cuts alone.

The committee's demise meant that the fiscal cliff was pending on January 1, 2013. On the issue of taxes, which mostly had to do with the pending expiration of the Bush income tax cuts, Obama proposed that the cuts expire for households with incomes over $250,000.[49] House Speaker John Boehner countered with an income threshold of $1 million, which he thought would be acceptable to both Democrats and his caucus. However, it was rejected by the latter, especially its Tea Party wing, which wanted all of the tax cuts to be made permanent.[50] The impasse continued until the early hours of January 1, at which point the Senate took the lead. The Senate voted to make the tax cuts permanent for all households with incomes below $400,000. House Republicans allowed that bill to come to the floor, where it passed with bipartisan support, with Tea Partyers in opposition.[51] That was noteworthy because Tea Partyers had a better deal with Boehner's proposal, and because it underscored that conservatives might have just allowed the deficit-reduction committee to consider tax hikes, which would have prevented the fiscal cliff and perhaps yielded a larger deficit-reduction plan. Yet, those steps would have required conservatives to express approval for a deal that included tax hikes, and at a moment when a tax cliff was not pending. In the process that unfolded, by contrast, Tea Partyers were able to stick to their anti-tax pledges, even though that meant that more households saw higher taxes as a result.[52] In other words, they put political posturing ahead of policy.

Subsequent fiscal dramas shared the three main political features of the debt-ceiling and fiscal-cliff sagas of 2011–2013 that we just reviewed: (1) Tea Partyers used a fiscal deadline to demand a policy change, (2) they placed politics ahead of policy and refused any compromise on their policy positions, and (3) government shutdowns were averted or ended by bipartisan coalitions, as is necessary under divided government. The first such episode was the government shutdown in October 2013. The shutdown was precipitated by the demand of Republican Senator Ted Cruz and other Tea Partyers to cut spending on top of the budget sequester and previous years' cuts. Specifically, they sought to defund Obamacare, a proposal that the Senate majority and the president were certain to reject. The two-week-long government shutdown was brought to an end when many Republicans broke with their Tea Party colleagues to pass a continuing resolution that kept spending at existing levels.

Twice in 2015, a similar process unfolded. First, in the spring, Republican Senators Cruz and Jeff Sessions demanded cuts to the Department of Homeland Security in order to prevent the implementation of an Obama executive order that would defer the deportation of some undocumented immigrants. Although the GOP had won enough Senate seats in the 2014 midterms to take majority control, the measure was unable to get through the chamber. Eventually, a "clean" Department of Homeland Security (DHS) budget (i.e., without the immigration provision) was passed by a coalition of Democrats and moderate Republicans. Then, in October, Tea Partyers demanded that Planned Parenthood be defunded. In the midst of that battle, Republican Speaker of the House John Boehner abruptly resigned, becoming the first Speaker in more than three decades to step down from the position before the end of a two-year Congress.[53] Boehner had tired of the Tea Party's routine threats to his leadership and its "hostage-taking politics" – as Thomas Mann and Norman Ornstein, two veteran scholars of Congress, dubbed the group's strategy of exploiting fiscal deadlines for unilateral changes in policy.[54] When announcing his resignation, Boehner demanded that the House Freedom Caucus, as the House Tea Party wing had named itself, drop their demand so that political clashes over a very minor budget item were not responsible for a sweeping government shutdown. A clean budget bill was passed by a bipartisan coalition, with Tea Partyers in opposition.

With Boehner's departure, Paul Ryan was picked as the new Speaker, and he demanded that his caucus pass a budget that covered the remainder of the fiscal year so that there would be no hard fiscal deadlines that could be exploited by the Tea Party wing. Congress delivered, producing its first "normal" budget since 2010. Republican majorities logrolled with Democrats, passing a budget that both increased spending (in part by easing sequestration caps) and cut taxes.[55] The Tea Party wing voted against the deficit-increasing deal.

Citizens United

In addition to the passage of Obamacare and the GOP's electoral wave, there was another event in 2010 that had lasting political significance: the Supreme Court's decision in *Citizens United* v. *Federal Election Commission*. The ruling, supported by five of the Court's nine members, struck down limits on political spending by corporations and unions. The limits under consideration originated in a 2002 law, the Bipartisan Campaign Reform Act (BCRA), also known as McCain–Feingold for its two Senate sponsors. Among other things, BCRA prevented corporations and unions from broadcasting political communications within thirty days of a primary election or sixty days of a general election. In a 2003 case, the Court held that the law only barred ads that contained a message to vote for or against a particular candidate, and that it did not prevent the funding of ads that focused on political issues. But the *Citizens United* decision went further and held that all limits on corporate political spending – except those regarding direct contributions to candidates – were an unconstitutional abridgment of corporations' rights to free speech, which the Court said are established by the First Amendment.[56]

The ruling allowed for the creation of "super PACs" that can run campaigns for or against particular candidates and accept donations of any size, including from corporations.[57] The chief limit on super PACs is that they must be operationally independent of candidates' campaigns, and that is to maintain the integrity of the candidate donation limits that have been upheld since *Buckley* v. *Valeo* (1976) (see Box 6.1). In practice, however, the separation means little. A candidate may be no less grateful for campaign ads that are financed by a super PAC that is separate from her campaign than she is for ads that are financed by her own PAC and its donors. Put differently, *Citizens United* undermines the effectiveness and purpose of the law that limits donations to candidates. It also encourages corporations to get involved in specific elections, thus making members of Congress more reluctant to pursue policies that burden specific companies or sectors.

Not surprisingly, super PACs quickly became popular. According to the Center for Responsive Politics, there were 247 single-candidate super PACs in the 2016 elections which collectively spent more than $500 million. Although that was only one-third as much as was spent by congressional candidates during that cycle, super PAC spending is concentrated on close races. CRP calculated that super PAC and other non-candidate spending exceeded candidate spending in as many as twenty-six key congressional races.

While these developments are meaningful, it is also important to recognize that before *Citizens United* there were already means by which corporations and wealthy individuals could spend unlimited amounts in order to influence particular elections. Specifically, they could donate to non-profit organizations that are chartered as 527s or 501(c)s under the tax code, both of which can engage in political activities and can accept donations of any size. As noted in Chapter 6, both types of non-profits must focus their ads on political issues, and they cannot produce material that explicitly asks voters to support or oppose a specific candidate. However, that restriction means little in practice, because issue ads can still praise or attack specific candidates, and they may be just as effective at influencing candidates' electoral prospects as direct, candidate-oriented ads.[58] Therefore, like super PACs, 527s and 501(c)s undermine the purpose of legal limits on donations to candidates. There is no easy fix to the issue, except perhaps to drop candidate donation limits from campaign finance law.

One final point is worthwhile. Unlike 527s and all types of PACs, 501(c)s need not disclose their donors, which helps explain their popularity, especially as a vehicle for negative campaign ads. Among those who think that transparency in political finance is an issue of utmost importance, "dark money" 501(c)s are of greater concern than super PACs and *Citizens United*.

Special-Interest Politics

According to the Center for Responsive Politics, lobbying expenditures hit a historical high in 2009 and 2010, when Democrats were working Obamacare and Dodd–Frank through Congress. Both pieces of legislation were still able to provide generalized benefit at the expense of industry, but the circumstances and limits of those reforms were instructive. In the case of Dodd–Frank, Congress's ability to impose new regulations on Wall Street was attributable to the magnitude of the financial crisis and big banks' need for taxpayer-funded bailouts. In addition, the bill succeeded because it was careful to shield small banks and auto dealers – both of which exist in every congressional district – from most of the new regulations.[59] In the case of Obamacare, success was related to the fact that the new regulations on health insurers were also part of a system that sought to *expand* their customer bases (via subsidies and the individual mandate). In addition, the architects of Obamacare avoided doing anything about the problem of health care costs because to do otherwise would have meant sparring with well-financed interests like pharmaceutical companies.[60] In other words, Obamacare made it through Congress because it did not impose large costs on industry.

After 2010, lobbying expenditures dipped a little. The main reason for that was the arrival of divided government. The dip probably had nothing to do with Republicans' new ban on earmarks, which was put in place as the party retook the House majority after the Tea Party wave of 2010. However, the earmark ban was a noteworthy development. According to Citizens Against Government Waste (2016), a conservative interest group that opposes earmarks, pork projects fell sharply after the ban. However, the group also documented that earmarks in appropriations bills began a steady climb in the years after 2012, while the ban was still in place. In addition, a new and different type of earmark seemed to emerge. Research by Russell Mills, Nicole Kalaf-Hughes, and Jason MacDonald suggests that with the demise of earmarks in legislation, members of Congress pursued "letter-marks" – i.e., letters written to agencies requesting that they consider specific district-level needs when they use appropriations dollars for programs.[61]

Conclusion

The financial crisis and Great Recession brought an end to the Great Moderation, but not to the neoliberal era. While Congress did enact new financial sector regulations in response to the crash, there was otherwise no change in the overall structure of economic policy. The government did not enact a major jobs program, as it did during the Great Depression; and it did not seek to roll back free trade agreements or right-to-work labor laws. On the contrary, both advanced in the Obama years – the former by Obama, himself, the latter by Republican politicians in state governments. Similarly, many trends of the neoliberal era, like rising trade and income inequality, maintained course.

The financial crisis was avoidable, and the policy decisions of the 1990s and 2000s that fueled the housing bubble and allowed the financial sector to construct a fragile house of cards were responsible for the crash. The deep recession and slow-paced recovery that followed meant great pain for households, and the attendant frustration infused the nation's politics, especially in the momentum it gave to the Tea Party movement.

After the Republican wave in the 2010 elections, the party wars escalated to a level that had not been witnessed in modern times. Partisan gerrymandering was pursued with vigor, and obstructionism and hostage-taking in Congress produced great drama and dysfunction. In the fiscal and debt ceiling fights, the Republican House was able to win a series of spending cuts, but the policy outcomes were much less dramatic than the politics that produced them. The deals reflected divided government and the need for bipartisan compromise, and in each case the Republican caucus had to split in two in order to keep the government running. Aside from the fiscal deals that Congress was compelled to pass, the legislature accomplished little. The gridlock was much more pronounced than it had been during the divided governments of the 1990s and 2000s, and it prevented Congress from addressing issues like immigration, the rising costs of health care, and the opioid crisis that arose during the 2000s and 2010s.[62]

As in prior decades, the party wars in the 2010s were driven by partisan media, partisan electoral geography, and the deep partisan–cultural divide in the electorate. But the arrival of the "no compromise" caucus added a salient new fissure to Congress. Boehner exaggerated it when he remarked that his speakership would be remembered as the "end of the two-party system."[63] That end has not yet occurred, and it is somewhat unlikely to happen given the strength of party attachments, the competitiveness of the party system, and America's plurality rule electoral systems. But Boehner's remark underscored the degree to which his party's politics frustrated the nation's governance. And those politics received a remarkably fast and profound transformation in 2016, when Donald Trump took the Republican Party by storm.

Notes

1 The Fed helped negotiate the sale of Bear to J.P. Morgan Chase, and to do so it extended a $30 billion loan. Because the loan was for assets that had lost most of their value, there was no telling how much of that money would be repaid. By mid-2012, however, the money had been repaid with interest.

2 Because during 2008–2010 jobs were disappearing instead of being created to accommodate population growth, the "jobs deficit" was larger – some twelve million by 2010 (Blinder, 2013, p. 11).

3 Government debt increased 50% from mid-2008 to mid-2011 – less than the 86% that Reinhart and Rogoff (2009) found was typical after a financial crisis.

4 Boehner was the first Speaker to resign since Newt Gingrich in 1999, who had lost the support of his caucus after his attempt to impeach Clinton backfired and caused the GOP to lose seats in the 1998 midterms.

5 For a more thorough review of these topics, see Blinder, 2013 and Geithner, 2014.

6 Fed governors were attuned to the housing bubble as it was expanding, but no one anticipated it would crash the financial system and cause so deep a recession.

7 Some lenders were predatory, offering loans that they knew would fail. Many loans were complex, with adjustable interest rates and other elements that made it difficult for borrowers to keep up with payments. Subprime borrowers were generally first-time homebuyers and unsophisticated in matters of mortgage finance. One may fault them for taking on complex loans that they could not afford, but one can also blame unscrupulous lenders (Blinder, 2013).

8 Calomiris and Haber, 2014.

9 Fannie Mae, a colloquial short-hand for the Federal National Mortgage Association, had been created in the 1930s to support the housing market. It was privatized in 1968 and made a publicly traded company. The Federal Home Loan Mortgage Corporation, dubbed Freddie Mac, was created in 1971 to compete with Fannie.

10 Calomiris and Haber (2014, pp. 209–210) note that, in exchange for supporting subprime, Fannie and Freddie were allowed to operate with greater leverage, which meant greater profit potential and greater exposure to risk.

11 Put another way, mortgage lenders could focus on volume, not quality. And that was another problem with the housing market. Many lenders extended loans to

people who could not afford them. When those loans failed, they were someone else's problem.

12 On the complexity of the financial products at the heart of the crisis, see Blinder, 2013.

13 A fourth reason was that independent ratings agencies deemed mortgage-backed securities and other derivatives to be safe investments. Those agencies had made the same assumption about mortgage-backed securities – that they were safe because they were based on large pools. Also, they often had a conflict of interest – most were paid not by the buyers of securities but by the firms that created and sold them, so they were inclined to underestimate the products' riskiness. See Blinder, 2013.

14 In July 2007, more than a year before the financial crash, Charles "Chuck" Prince, the CEO of Citigroup, famously remarked that: "when the music stops, in terms of liquidity, things will be complicated." Yet, Prince continued, "as long as the music is playing, you've got to get up and dance. We're still dancing" (Nakamoto and Wighton, 2007).

15 On the topic of banking regulations and the crisis, see Admati and Hellwig, 2013.

16 The growth in mortgage debt, like the rise of leverage in the financial sector, was related to broader developments in the global economy. In particular, high levels of debt in the United States and some European countries were facilitated by high levels of savings in other parts of the world, including China. The "global savings glut" kept the price of credit in the United States low and facilitated the boom. See King, 2016 and Mian and Sufi, 2014.

17 Statistics from Beim, 2009. Another illustration of household debt growth is this: the debt-to-income ratio of the average American increased from about 1.25 to 1.5 from the mid-1980s until 2000; and by 2007, it exceeded 2.0 (Admati and Hellwig, 2013).

18 Interestingly, a study by Igan, Mishra, and Tressel (2011) found that the firms that had been profiting the most from the lax subprime lending rules had engaged in significant lobbying to keep the rules.

19 McCarty, Poole, and Rosenthal (2013) thoroughly defend this claim.

20 One who called for derivatives regulation was Brooksley Born, who was then Chair of the CFTC. Her call was rejected by top officials at the Treasury and the Federal Reserve.

21 McCarty, Poole, and Rosenthal, 2013.

22 AIG had been insuring mortgage-backed securities and other derivatives. See Blinder, 2013.

23 As all of this was occurring, Merrill Lynch, Washington Mutual, and Wachovia quickly sold themselves to other firms in order to avoid bankruptcy.

24 At the end of 2008, the Fed also began the first of its three unprecedented "quantitative easing" programs, which were designed to lower long-term interest rates.

25 On that first vote, 40% of Democrats, the majority party, voted against the measure. Despite the request coming from the Bush administration, 75% of Republicans voted against the measure.

26 Tracy, Steinberg, and Demos, 2014.

27 The first of these two measures requires that large banks – specifically, those with assets over $50 billion – craft "living wills" that explain how they would, in the event that they become insolvent, liquidate themselves in a way that is orderly and non-disruptive to financial markets. The FDIC and Federal Reserve review those plans, and they have the ability to sanction banks that produce non-credible plans. The second measure, which is meant as a backstop to the living will system, is a system for regulators to liquidate large, systemically important

firms. The process seeks to liquidate firms in a way that is orderly and minimally disruptive to the financial sector.

28 Dodd–Frank placed the CFPB in the Federal Reserve instead of making it an independent agency. It did so because it lowered the agency's profile (which Republicans liked) and because it protected the agency's budget into the future because it would be funded by the Fed, which has its own revenue stream, and is not dependent on a line item in a budget bill. See Kaiser, 2013, p. 251.

29 Economists disagree about whether the drop in oil prices helped or hurt the economy's growth rate. See *The Wall Street Journal*, 2016.

30 See Rosewicz, Mantell, and Fleming, 2016 on income growth by state; and see Moretti, 2012 for more about the geography of growth.

31 A related statistic was the share of households receiving food stamps that had at least one income earner increased year after year during the recovery (Department of Agriculture, 2017). That trend pre-dated the crisis, however, underscoring the decades-long wage stagnation for low-income earners.

32 Immigration did not add to the downward pressure on wages, since it fell sharply after the recession and did not rebound (Gonzalez-Barrera, 2015).

33 These executive orders are discussed in Chapter 4.

34 Mayer, 2016. Charles and David Koch had long been active in politics, but in the Obama years they greatly fortified and expanded their array of political organizations. The brothers' network spent hundreds of millions of dollars on political campaigns and donations, and it became a powerful force in the nation's conservative politics.

35 Gallup News Service, 2015.

36 Chapter 6 discusses why "midterm losses" are typical for the president's party.

37 There were also changes to voter-ID laws that sparked intense partisan controversy. In short, Republican-controlled states started enacting more-stringent photo identification requirements for voting. The expressed rationale was to limit fraud in elections. However, the real purpose was partisan – the laws were expected to depress votes for Democrats, since urban, poor, and minority citizens were less likely to have the required type of state identification cards. A compromise would have been easy to reach if the controversy were not about electoral advantage: Republicans could have blunted Democratic criticism by making it easier for voters to obtain the required types of identification. But those types of deals did not occur, precisely because the laws had an electoral purpose.

38 The 2012 results in Pennsylvania and North Carolina were mirrored nationwide: Democrats won more votes, but Republicans retained their House majority.

39 The redistrictings were not necessarily *the* reason for the GOP's majorities in 2012, 2014, and 2016. One analysis, by John Sides and Eric McGhee (2013), suggested that the gerrymandering accounted for perhaps seven seats in the GOP's seventeen-seat spread over the Democrats in 2012. Jacobson's (2013) analysis was similar: "The Republicans' sweeping national victory in 2010 gave them control of the redistricting process in 18 states with a total of 202 House seats, whereas Democrats controlled the process in only 6 states with a total of 47 seats. Republicans exploited this opportunity to shore up some of their marginal districts ... creating about 11 net additional Republican-leaning seats."

40 See Mann and Ornstein, 2012. Two other bills that were filibustered before they passed almost unanimously were the Credit Cardholders Bill of Rights Act and the Fraud Enforcement and Recovery Act. Senate Republicans also become more obstructionist on judicial nominations. After 2010, they took to blocking all of Obama's nominees to the federal courts. Democrats responded in 2013 by changing Senate rules so that nominees to district courts and circuit courts require only fifty votes, not the sixty-vote supermajority.

41 Obamacare politics was extraordinary in many other ways, including the Senate's passage of the bill in the short period of 2009 when Senate Democrats had sixty votes, the GOP's shocking Obamacare-propelled victory in the Massachusetts special election to fill the late Ted Kennedy's senate seat in January 2010, and the subsequent loss of a sixty-member caucus that meant that Congress's passage of the legislation only occurred because House Democrats could pass the Senate bill as-is, leaving out elements that the House majority wanted. Also extraordinary was the Supreme Court's expedited consideration of Obamacare. Its decision was discussed in Chapter 2: the individual mandate was upheld, but the Court allowed states to skip the Medicaid expansion. Many Republican-controlled states chose that option, and the Medicaid expansion was smaller by 2.6 million people as a result (Garfield and Damico, 2016).

42 See Klein (2012a), who also notes that in addition to Romney's distancing from his own Romneycare, Senators Bob Bennet and Orrin Hatch retracted their prior support for the Heritage plan. In 2012, Stuart Butler, author of the Heritage Foundation's proposal in the 1990s, wrote that he changed his mind on the individual mandate component of the system. For his reasoning and some skeptical commentary, see Butler, 2012; Klein, 2012b; and Taylor, 2012.

43 For a while, it even seemed like the Tea Party might break away from the GOP. That did not occur because of the pressures of the winner-take-all electoral system (see Chapter 1). Indeed, in-fighting among conservatives in 2010 created some unexpected openings for Democrats. Most notably, Republicans lost a winnable Senate seat in Delaware in 2010 after the party nominated the Tea Party candidate and political neophyte Christine O'Donnell instead of the incumbent representative and former governor Michael Castle.

44 The most dramatic Tea Party challenge to the GOP occurred in 2014, when Eric Cantor, a staunch conservative who was then the House Majority Leader, lost his primary election to a Tea Party candidate.

45 Gallup News Service, 2017.

46 The spending cuts were demanded despite the fact that the economy was still weak, with an unemployment rate hovering around 9%.

47 Sequestration refers to the cancellation of funds that have already been appropriated by Congress.

48 The sequestration part of the cliff was set to be $1.2 trillion over several years.

49 This was a repeat of the battle in late 2010. Obama sought to let the tax cuts expire for households with incomes over $250,000, but Republicans rejected that plan and succeeded in getting all tax cuts extended.

50 A similar fate befell several other budget proposals by Boehner between late 2010 and 2015.

51 The tax deal also reduced the size of the impending budget cuts by 20% and delayed them until March 1. When the deadline came, the parties could not negotiate a deal and sequestration began, triggering cuts that included $42 billion to defense and $11 billion to Medicare. Democrats' desire to avoid tax hikes was greater than Republicans' desire to avoid indiscriminate cuts.

52 Karol and Lee, 2013.

53 Steinhauer, 2015.

54 See Mann and Ornstein, 2012.

55 The tax breaks were poised to cut revenues by $700 billion over ten years. Many of them already existed but were temporary cuts that were due to sunset. Those the budget bill made permanent. The bill also postponed two Obamacare taxes: one on medical devices and the other on premium ("Cadillac") employer-subsidized health insurance plans. The bill also ended a long-standing ban on US oil exports, thus opening a revenue stream for US oil companies.

56 The Court had long maintained that corporations were protected by the First Amendment.
57 "PAC" stands for political action committee. It is a campaign finance account for political contributions and spending that is monitored by the Federal Election Commission.
58 A famous example was the Swift Boat ads that attacked John Kerry in the 2004 elections.
59 Kaiser, 2013.
60 Brill, 2015, p. 58.
61 Mills, Kalaf-Hughes, and MacDonald, 2016 and Mills and Kalaf-Hughes, 2016.
62 According to the Centers for Disease Control, annual deaths from overdoses of opioid prescriptions tripled from 2001 to 2014. Simultaneously, there was a sharp increase in overdose deaths from non-prescription use and from heroin. In 2009, drug overdoses overtook car accidents as the leading cause of injury death (Rocheleau, 2015).
63 Alberta , 2017.

References

Admati, Anat, and Martin Hellwig. (2013). *The bankers' new clothes: What's wrong with banking and what to do about it.* Princeton, NJ: Princeton University Press.
Alberta, Tim. (2017, November/December). John Boehner unchained. *Politico Magazine.*
Beim, David O. (2009, March 19). It's all about debt. *Forbes.* Retrieved from: www. forbes.com/2009/03/19/household-debt-gdp-markets-beim.html (accessed April 5, 2018).
Blinder, Alan S. (2013). *After the music stopped.* New York, NY: Penguin.
Brill, Steven. (2015). *America's bitter pill: Money, politics, backroom deals, and the fight to fix our broken health care system.* New York, NY: Random House.
Butler, Stuart. (2012, February 6). Don't blame heritage for ObamaCare mandate. *USA Today.* Retrieved from: https://usatoday30.usatoday.com/news/opinion/forum/story/2012-02-03/health-individual-mandate-reform-heritage/52951140/1 (accessed August 28, 2017).
Calomiris, Charles W., and Stephen H. Haber. (2014). *Fragile by design: The political origins of banking crises and scarce credit.* Princeton, NJ: Princeton University Press.
Citizens Against Government Waste. (2016). Pig book and historical trends. Retrieved from: www.cagw.org/reporting/pig-book#historical_trends (accessed October 9, 2017).
Department of Agriculture. (2017). SNAP increasingly serves the working poor. Retrieved from: www.ers.usda.gov/data-products/chart-gallery/gallery/chart-detail/?chartId=82672 (accessed April 5, 2018).
Gallup News Service. (2015). In US, support for Tea Party drops to new low. Retrieved from: http://news.gallup.com/poll/186338/support-tea-party-drops-new-low.aspx (accessed April 5, 2018).
Gallup News Service. (2017). Congress and the public. Retrieved from: www.gallup.com/poll/1600/congress-public.aspx (accessed April 5, 2018).
Garfield, Rachel, and Anthony Damico. (2016). The coverage gap: Uninsured poor adults in states that do not expand Medicaid. *Kaiser Family Foundation.* Retrieved from: www.kff.org/uninsured/issue-brief/the-coverage-gap-

uninsured-poor-adults-in-states-that-do-not-expand-medicaid/ (accessed June 28, 2017).

Geithner, Timothy F. (2014). *Stress test: Reflections on financial crises.* New York, NY: Crown.

Gonzalez-Barrera, Ana. (2015). More Mexicans leaving than coming to the US. (Chapter 1: Migration flows between the US and Mexico have slowed – and turned toward Mexico). *Pew Research Center.* Retrieved from: www. pewhispanic.org/2015/11/19/chapter-1-migration-flows-between-the-u-s-and-mexico-have-slowed-and-turned-toward-mexico/ (accessed April 5, 2018).

Igan, Deniz, Prachi Mishra, and Thierry Tressel. (2011). A fistful of dollars: Lobbying and the financial crisis. In Daron Acemoglu and Michael Woodford (Eds.), *NBER Macroeconomics Annual, 26.* (pp. 195–230). Chicago, IL: University of Chicago Press.

Jacobson, Gary C. (2013). Partisan polarization in American politics: A background paper. *Presidential Studies Quarterly,* 43(4), 688–708.

Kaiser, Robert G. (2013). *Act of Congress: How America's essential institution works, and how it doesn't.* New York, NY: Alfred A. Knopf.

Karol, David, and Francis Lee. (2013, January 3). The house GOP and the fiscal cliff: Position-taking vs. policy-making. *The Monkey Cage* [Web log comment]. Retrieved from: http://themonkeycage.org/2013/01/03/the-house-gop-and-the-fiscal-cliff-position-taking-vs-policy-making/ (accessed September 8, 2017).

King, Mervyn. (2016). *The end of alchemy: Money, banking, and the future of the global economy.* New York, NY: W.W. Norton & Company.

Klein, Ezra. (2012a, June 25). Unpopular mandate: Why do politicians reverse their positions? *The New Yorker.*

Klein, Ezra. (2012b, February 6). Stuart Butler explains his change of heart on the individual mandate. *The Washington Post* [Web log comment]. Retrieved from: www.washingtonpost.com/blogs/ezra-klein/post/stuart-butler-explains-his-change-of-heart-on-the-individual-mandate/2011/08/25/gIQAnEDptQ_blog.html?utm_term=.92cdbe54e760 (accessed August 28, 2017).

McCarty, Nolan, Keith T. Poole, and Howard Rosenthal. (2013). *Political bubbles: Financial crises and the failure of American democracy.* Princeton, NJ: Princeton University Press.

Mann, Thomas E., and Norman J. Ornstein. (2012). *It's even worse than it looks: How the American constitutional system collided with the new politics of extremism.* New York, NY: Basic Books.

Mayer, Jane. (2016). *Dark money: The hidden history of the billionaires behind the rise of the radical right.* New York, NY: Doubleday.

Mian, Atif, and Amir Sufi. (2014). *House of debt: How they (and you) caused the great recession, and how we can prevent it from happening again.* Chicago, IL: University of Chicago Press.

Mills, Russell W., and Nicole Kalaf-Hughes. (2016). Exit earmarks, enter letter-marks. Legislative, branch capacity working group [Web log comment]. Retrieved from: www.legbranch.com/theblog/2016/12/9/exit-earmarks-enter-letter-marks (accessed April 5, 2018).

Mills, Russell W., Nicole Kalaf-Hughes, and Jason A. MacDonald. (2016). Agency policy preferences: Congressional letter-marking and the allocation of distributive policy benefits. *Journal of Public Policy,* 36(4), 547–571.

Moretti, Enrico. (2012). *The new geography of jobs.* New York, NY: Houghton Mifflin Harcourt.

Nakamoto, Michiyo, and David Wighton. (2007, July 9). Citigroup chief stays bullish on buy-outs. *Financial Times.*

Reinhart, Carmen M., and Kenneth S. Rogoff. (2009). *This time is different: Eight centuries of financial folly.* Princeton, NJ: Princeton University Press.

Rocheleau, Matt. (2015, October 22). Opioid overdoses far outpace car-crash deaths in Mass[achusetts]. *Boston Globe.*

Rosewicz, Barb, Ruth Mantell, and Joe Fleming. (2016). States' personal income shows uneven economic recovery. *Pew Charitable Trust.* Retrieved from: www.pewtrusts.org/en/research-and-analysis/analysis/2016/11/01/states-personal-income-shows-uneven-economic-recovery (accessed April 5, 2018).

Sides, John, and Eric McGhee. (2013, February 17). Redistricting didn't win Republicans the House. *The Washington Post* [Web log comment]. Retrieved from: www.washingtonpost.com/news/wonk/wp/2013/02/17/redistricting-didnt-win-republicans-the-house/?utm_term=.184cfe56cdf9 (accessed August 28, 2017).

Steinhauer, Jennifer. (2015, September 25). John Boehner, House Speaker, will resign from Congress. *The New York Times.*

Taylor, Don. (2012, February 6). Stuart Butler's change of mind. *The Incidental Economist* [Web log comment]. Retrieved from: http://theincidentaleconomist.com/wordpress/stuart-butlers-change-of-mind/ (accessed August 28, 2017).

Tracy, Ryan, Julie Steinberg, and Telis Demos. (2014, December 19). Bank bailouts approach a final reckoning. *The Wall Street Journal.*

The Wall Street Journal. (2016, November 13). Are low oil prices good for the economy?

8   The Trump Turn

The 2016 presidential election was the most dramatic and surprising election in modern history. Donald Trump, a real estate mogul and reality-TV star who had never served in government, defied both norms and expectations in his march to the Republican nomination. His general election victory over Hillary Clinton surprised nearly everyone, because almost every poll pointed to a Clinton win. The drama of the election escalated even further after the election, when it was revealed that Russia had undertaken social media campaigns to manipulate voters, sow discord, and elect Trump.

The most notable of Trump's norm violations during his campaign and the early part of his presidency were his regular attacks on all news media outlets that criticized him, his insistence that the election would be rigged against him, his baseless claim that millions of people voted illegally for Clinton, his refusal to say (when asked at one of the presidential debates) that he would recognize the result of the election if he were to lose, his extra-judicial pronouncement on Clinton's behaviors and promise to "lock her up," and his denigration of federal judges and the Justice Department. Those actions were violations of democratic norms that have been respected by American politicians in both parties for generations, and with good reason. For democracy and the rule of law to survive, both parties must respect the electoral process, the free press, and the due process of law and other legal institutions.[1]

Many Republicans greeted Trump's statements with alarm and sought to defeat him.[2] Trump received almost no endorsements from Republican politicians or conservative newspapers during his campaign, and scores of conservative elites announced that they would cast their votes not for him but for Clinton.[3] Yet, as Trump withstood those challenges and maintained a committed electoral base, those detractors dropped their challenges. In time, the only vocal Republican opponents to Trump were those who had retired from electoral politics. Republicans in Congress kept their criticisms to themselves, fearing that public rebukes of their new leader would cost them their next primary election. In stunning speed, Trump – a political outsider who was neither socially nor fiscally conservative – had taken control of the Republican Party.

Trump's popularity with the Republican base had much to do with his populist attacks on politicians and his willingness to defy "political correctness." Yet, his economic platform, especially his full-throated critiques of America's free trade agreements, also contributed to his success in the presidential primaries, especially in Rust Belt states. The success of Trump's economic nationalism was a remarkable development given that free trade had long been a pillar in the party's platform. In fact, many Republican voters disliked the agenda, but they still found good reason to vote for Trump, especially because Clinton's campaign also had a protectionist bent. Indeed, she, too, criticized the then-pending Trans-Pacific Partnership (TPP), a multilateral Asian trade deal that had been initiated by George W. Bush and finalized under Obama. But Trump's protectionism was much stronger, and it was aimed more at NAFTA, a trade agreement that Clinton did not criticize.

Other Republican voters embraced Trump's anti-trade agenda. Some may have long been ambivalent on free trade, and others may have veered toward protectionism in the later Obama years, as the TPP became an Obama initiative.[4] The populist ring of Trump's protectionism was also significant. Trump's charge against NAFTA was part of a broader argument that America had fallen from greatness and been taken advantage of by other countries and that out-of-touch politicians had struck the trade deals that let that happen. The charge was as much against the GOP establishment as it was against Democrats, and it thus bore a resemblance to the Tea Party surge of a few years before, which also targeted Republican politicians and reshaped the GOP's agenda.

Trump's protectionism resonated most strongly in the Rust Belt, and that is where he did particularly well – in both the primary and the general election. Not since the 1980s had Pennsylvania, Michigan, or Wisconsin voted for the Republican presidential candidate, but in 2016 all three narrowly chose Trump over Clinton. Of course, those states were not the only reason why Trump won the Electoral College. He also won major swing states like Florida and Ohio, and he held the Republican South. However, Trump's success (and Clinton's failure) in Pennsylvania, Michigan, and Wisconsin tilted the Electoral College from Blue to Red.[5]

Other factors that explained the election outcome were the public's lack of enthusiasm for both candidates, the slow-paced rebound since the Great Recession, and the unimpressive rate of economic growth in 2016 – it was only 0.9 percent. On that statistic alone, history would suggest that the incumbent party would lose control of the White House, as it did.[6]

Policy Moves

Republicans struggled to notch legislative achievements in 2017, despite their control of the House, Senate, and White House. Most dramatically, the Senate majority failed on multiple roll call votes to repeal Obamacare, even though they used budget reconciliation so that no Democratic votes were required. It was a remarkable failure for a party that had campaigned on "repeal" for seven years. It both underscored the party's internal divisions and, more significantly, illuminated that many in the party thought that repeal was actually bad politics or bad policy.

Nevertheless, by mid-2018, when this book was being finalized, Trump and congressional Republicans had made a number of very considerable changes to economic policies, including Obamacare. The four most significant legislative moves were a major tax reform, a large deficit-financed fiscal boost, a reform of Dodd–Frank, and the Senate's confirmation of Neil Gorsuch and Brett Kavanaugh to the Supreme Court, which will help maintain a conservative majority on the Court for years to come. Gorsuch's confirmation vote was also politically significant in and of itself, because it was the first time a Senate majority had suspended the filibuster rule for a Supreme Court confirmation vote, thus enabling it to appoint a justice without any votes from the minority party.[7] That procedure may become the new normal for Supreme Court confirmation votes.

Tax Reform

At the end of 2017, Republicans passed a major tax reform, dubbed the Tax Cuts and Jobs Act (TCJA). Congress used budget reconciliation to advance the legislation and passed it on a party-line vote. The law's most significant changes to the tax code were a major restructuring of the corporate tax system, a temporary regressive cut in the individual income tax, and a repeal of Obamacare's individual mandate. The law also made hundreds of finer alterations to the tax code, many of which would not fully be understood until they are administratively clarified by the Treasury Department. That type of uncertainty comes with all major legislative reforms, but it was especially pitched with the TCJA, because it was compiled and passed with atypical speed and without normal, open hearings and independent evaluations. Republican leaders did that in order to shield the law's provisions from criticism, avoid internecine battles, and pass a major bill before the end of 2017.[8]

The corporate tax overhaul had two marquee elements. One was a switch from a progressive tax, with a top marginal rate of 35 percent, to a flat tax of 21 percent. The second was a move to a "territorial" tax system for multinational corporations. In essence, foreign income was made tax exempt in order to eliminate the tax incentive for corporations to hold assets and income in foreign jurisdictions. That and other, lesser provisions were intended to increase corporate investment in the United States. A third component of the corporate overhaul sought to reduce a tax code preference for debt finance as opposed to equity finance. It and other changes to the corporate tax system are poised to significantly alter corporate behavior.

Naturally, the changes in the individual income tax were less tied to investment and economic objectives and more about distribution. The core changes were a cut in marginal rates and a reduction in the tax brackets. Both were concentrated on the higher end of the tax schedule, so their effect was to reduce tax progressivity and increase post-tax income inequality.[9] Other changes included an increase in the Child Tax Credit and a limit on the deductibility of state and local taxes, which made headlines because it will disproportionately hit taxpayers in high-tax states, which tend to be controlled by Democrats.[10] That provision caused several blue-state House Republicans to vote against the tax cuts. All of the changes to the individual income tax were set to expire in 2025, the year after the next presidential term ends.

After Republicans failed at repealing Obamacare, they included in the TCJA a repeal of the Obamacare individual mandate, which had been the least popular component of the law since its inception. The repeal eliminates one of the legs of the three-legged stool. It is expected to increase the uninsured rate, because the absence of the tax penalty will cause some healthy people to forgo the purchase of insurance. It is thus also expected to increase premiums for full insurance plans in the individual market.

Deficit Spending

On the heels of the TCJA, which was estimated to increase the deficit by $1.9 trillion over ten years, Congress passed a budget with a $1.5 trillion deficit – the largest deficit since the depths of the Great Recession, and another great fiscal boost to an already strong economy.[11] Unlike the tax cuts, the budget was a bipartisan logroll. Republican leaders might have been able to pass a more partisan budget, but they wanted to avoid a government shutdown at a time when they enjoyed unified government, and, as in previous congresses, they could not rely on their right wing to vote for a budget, so they needed Democratic votes. The budget increased spending on social programs, election security, and the military, but it did not include monies for Trump's desired wall on the United States–Mexico border. That upset the president and illustrated that Trump had not fully remade the GOP in his image.

Financial Sector Regulatory Reform

In mid-2018, Congress passed a bill to loosen banking regulations that had been put in place by Dodd–Frank.[12] The bill was passed under normal Senate rules, with enough Democratic support to invoke cloture. Most of the provisions focused on small banks, and they included looser capital requirements, reporting requirements, and trading restrictions. The bill also allowed auto loan companies to offer more subprime loans, repealed a consumer right to sue banks, and delivered a couple of benefits to larger banks – in particular, a higher permissible leverage ratio and a higher threshold for qualifying as a systematically important institution, a designation which subjects banks to greater oversight and regulation.[13] Although the various provisions were significant, they left most of Dodd–Frank intact. Republicans and the financial industry found most of Dodd–Frank agreeable or tolerable.

The Administration's regulatory reforms

More bold and sweeping than Congress's reforms was the administrative action on regulations. Trump's White House and cabinet sought to quickly and dramatically reverse a wide range of Obama-era regulations and to make federal policy more conservative and business friendly. For example, Trump issued executive orders to cease Obama's Clean Power Plan, reopen offshore sites for oil and gas drilling, reduce the burden of environmental impact reviews on infrastructure projects, revoke three Obama executive orders on federal contracting, and study the addition of work requirements to all safety-net programs. Subsequently, HHS issued a rule that allowed states to add work requirements to receive Medicaid benefits, and several states began to put such rules in place. Meanwhile, Trump cut Obamacare subsidies and relaxed Obamacare rules on insurance plans; his EPA and Interior Departments approved oil pipelines, eased regulations on river pollution and methane emissions, and loosened rules on federal land use, commercial fishing, and mining companies;[14] his Education Secretary changed rules regarding for-profit colleges and financial aid lenders for higher education; and his head of the Consumer Financial Protection Bureau sought to weaken the agency, reduce its budget, and make it less threatening and burdensome to lenders. Other significant moves were spearheaded by his appointees at the Federal Reserve, who led the charge in easing up federal oversight and regulation of big banks.

A small but significant number of regulatory changes in the first months of Trump's presidency were rule cancellations by Congress – not Trump – under the terms of the Congressional Review Act, a law that had been enacted in 1996 as part of the GOP's Contract with America. The act gives Congress a window of sixty legislative days to block any new regulation via a joint resolution, and it stipulates that if Congress blocks a regulation in that way the rule can only be reinstated by Congress, thus making it more difficult to reinstate in the future. The measure had been used only once prior to 2017. Then it was employed fourteen times in the first three months of Trump's presidency.

Trade

Trump's moves on trade may also prove significant. Early in his presidency, Trump pulled the United States out of the TPP trade deal with Asian countries, launched talks with Canada and Mexico in order to renegotiate NAFTA, and slapped tariffs on foreign steel and aluminum, as well as on a wide range of Chinese goods. Those moves prompted retaliatory measures from China. A trade war had begun.

Conclusion

As this book was being finished, it was not clear how much of Trump's economic agenda would be implemented. Trade negotiations were ongoing, and some regulations were still pending or tied up in court. The same uncertainty accompanied Trump's shake-up of the party system. Indeed, the big question of the early Trump years was whether the "Trump turn" – in both politics and policy – would be fleeting or lasting. Would Trump's GOP be able to maintain its enlarged electoral base? Or would the Democrats reclaim the Rust Belt in the next presidential election? Would Trump fundamentally restructure America's trade policy, or would that agenda by stymied by Congress? Would his regulations stick, or would they be blocked by courts or overturned by successors?

Whereas those questions were not fully answerable, Trump will undoubtedly achieve a good measure of policy success. Many of his regulations will be implemented, and, given the scope and boldness of that agenda, his regulatory policy legacy is likely to rival that of 2009–2010, when a unified Democratic government passed Dodd–Frank and Obamacare. The future was less clear on trade. Trump's preferences regarding a new trade regime were themselves unclear, and Congress was likely to object to anything very dramatic, given that it would hurt many American businesses. However, if Trump were able to radically alter the status quo – by, say, imposing long-lasting tariffs on Chinese goods – then it would be appropriate to mark 2016 as the year the neoliberal era ended. Already, Trump's regulatory agenda had a different thrust than the neoliberalism of prior decades. Indeed, whereas the major reforms of prior decades on, say, telecoms and financial firms, were rooted in arguments about consumer choice, new technologies, and innovation, Trump's agenda seemed ideologically unmoored and focused on either helping particular industries or undoing regulations that Obama had put in place.

A party system shake-up could unfold in multiple ways, or not at all. Trump was highly unpopular with minorities and women, and so his presidency could lead those demographics to swell the Democratic rolls. Yet, Trump's GOP may compensate with other voters who had traditionally voted Democratic – namely, members of the white working class who were attracted to Trump's protectionism and populism. Either change could tilt national elections in a party's favor, which could in turn prompt change in the party system as a whole.

Trump was remaking the GOP in his image, but that image lacked ideological clarity. His policies were very boldly conservative, and yet his domination of the party and brand of politics prompted the resignation of fiscal conservatives like Senator Jeff Flake and House Speaker Paul Ryan, who announced his resignation in the spring of 2018, only two years after he took the job and while Republicans still enjoyed unified government. Furthermore, Trump's conservatism was occasionally tempered by his expressed support for entitlement programs and infrastructure spending. Trump did not move on those campaign statements in his first year in office, but it remained possible that he could find common ground with Democrats on certain issues.

Still, in 2018, a real upsurge in bipartisan collaboration seemed very far away. The polarization and distrust between the parties was just too great. And, Trump seemed to give the Democratic Party more leftward momentum – on top of what was already on display in 2016, when the party almost nominated Bernie Sanders over Hillary Clinton.[15]

So, it is estimable that party politics will remain highly polarized and combative, and the question is whether Trump will make the GOP more conservative, more protectionist, or more willing to go wherever Trump wants it to go. The answer hinges on the remaining years of his presidency. If Trump is able to maintain or improve his support in his party, his influence on the Republican Party will be lasting and large – more than anyone in the past century save perhaps Reagan. If, however, Trump falls from the party's graces, then the Republican Party will pivot away from him and his least popular positions.

Notes

1 See Levitsky and Ziblatt, 2018.
2 Of course, Republican resistance to Trump was not only, or even mostly, about his violations of democratic norms. He was also panned for his temperament, misogyny, anti-immigrant nativism, and flirtations with (anti-minority) white nationalism.
3 See Blake, 2016.
4 *The Economist*, 2018 emphasizes Trump's effect of protectionism in the GOP; and see Gallup News Service, 2017 for data on Republican support for NAFTA. Although the party had been pro-free trade for a long time, that position did not go unchallenged, and there may have been untapped support for protectionism in prior cycles and decades. Most notably, anti-trade sentiments may have played an important role in the 1992 election, in which the anti-NAFTA candidate Ross Perot performed remarkably well for an independent, and the pro-trade Republican incumbent, George H. W. Bush, lost his reelection bid. Also, Pat Buchanan, several times a candidate for the Republican presidential nomination, opposed NAFTA in his campaigns. That position never propelled him to the nomination, but it was not the sole reason for his failures, either. It is also intriguing to recall that two free trade Republicans, George W. Bush and Ronald Reagan, flirted with protectionist policies. Bush imposed steel tariffs in 2002 and Ronald Reagan bowed to the auto sector in the 1980s (see Chapter 5).
5 Some analysts place more emphasis on Trump's race-baiting and xenophobia, which he stoked and exploited to a degree that had not been seen in national politics in many decades. However, the importance of economic factors in the 2016 election is underscored by the fact that many Rust Belt supporters of Trump had voted for Obama, a black man with a foreign-sounding name, in 2008 and 2012.
6 See Figure 4.2.
7 A vacancy on the Court emerged following the unexpected death of Antonin Scalia in February 2016. Obama nominated Merrick Garland to fill the vacancy, but Senate Republicans refused to consider any Obama nominee. The gamble paid off when Trump beat Clinton in the November election.

8 On some of the post-passage blowback, see Tankersley and Rappeport, 2018. See also Rubin and Hughes, 2017.
9 In addition, the TCJA reduced the estate tax by doubling the gift threshold at which the tax would phase in.
10 Still other changes included the elimination of the personal exemption and a doubling of the standard deduction.
11 Deficit projections are from the Congressional Budget Office, 2018. The unemployment rate in 2018 was only 4%.
12 Other aspects of Dodd–Frank had already been weakened. In particular, the rules about proprietary trading were eased in legislation passed in 2014.
13 For more, see Onaran, 2018.
14 See Popovich, Albeck-Ripka and Pierre-Louis, 2018 for a list of other changes to environmental regulations.
15 Among other things, Pew Research Center (2017) shows that Democrats were becoming more strongly in favor of a single-payer health plan.

References

Blake, Aaron. (2016, November 7). 78 Republican politicians, donors and officials who are supporting Hillary Clinton. *The Fix* [Web log comment]. Retrieved from: www.washingtonpost.com/news/the-fix/wp/2016/06/30/he res-the-growing-list-of-big-name-republicans-supporting-hillary-clinton/?no redirect=on&utm_term=.077ffab387d0 (accessed April 19, 2018).
Congressional Budget Office. (2018, April 19). The budget and economic outlook: 2018 to 2028. Retrieved from: www.cbo.gov/publication/53651 (accessed May 7, 2018).
The Economist. (2018, April 19). The president's takeover of his party is near complete.
Gallup News Service. (2017, February 24). Americans split on whether NAFTA is good or bad for US. Retrieved from: http://news.gallup.com/poll/204269/ameri cans-split-whether-nafta-good-bad.aspx (accessed April 19, 2018).
Levitsky, Steven, and Daniel Ziblatt. (2018). *How democracies die.* New York, NY: Crown Publishing Group.
Onaran, Yalman. (2018, May 24). 1,000 cuts to Dodd–Frank: Tracking Trump's wave of deregulation. *Bloomberg News.*
Pew Research Center. (2017, June 23). Public support for "single payer" health coverage grows, driven by Democrats. Retrieved from: www.pewresearch.org/ fact-tank/2017/06/23/public-support-for-single-payer-health-coverage-grows-driven-by-democrats/ (accessed May 9, 2018).
Popovich, Nadja, Livia Albeck-Ripka, and Kendra Pierre-Louis. (2018, January 31). 67 environmental rules on the way out under Trump. *The New York Times.* Retrieved from: www.nytimes.com/interactive/2017/10/05/climate/trump-environ ment-rules-reversed.html (accessed April 19, 2018).
Rubin, Richard, and Siobhan Hughes. (2017, December 16). GOP poised to pass tax overhaul. *The Wall Street Journal.*
Tankersley, Jim, and Alan Rappeport. (2018, March 10). GOP rushed to pass tax overhaul: Now it may need to be altered. *The New York Times.*

9 The Path of America's Democracy

In some ways, the US Congress is not representative of American society. Most notably, women, racial minorities, and the poor are ascriptively underrepresented. In other respects, however, the legislature is the representative body that the Constitution's drafters intended. In Congress, the nation's many interests and values comingle and collide, as each representative seeks to champion the industries and causes of their electoral districts. Similarly, Congress contains a spectrum of both liberals and conservatives, each of whom reflects the ideological leanings of his or her constituency. Elections make members accountable, too. Representatives rarely take actions that are unpopular in their districts, and they know that broken promises and absenteeism will give their future opponents effective lines of attack.

Although elections make the legislative branch representative and accountable, America's democracy would not work in the absence of political parties. Parties enable collective accountability, so voters can punish an entire group of politicians for poor performance. The party system also squeezes diverse interests into two broad, general-purpose coalitions, which allows the nation's elections and legislative activity to center on the provision of public goods and general-interest policies, instead of just particularism and the division of the spoils.

It is healthy and good that party competition has an ideological dimension to it and that partisan debates focus on policies like the income tax and the social safety net. However, high levels of partisanship frustrate governance, because all laws and budgets require the approval of the House, the Senate, and the president. When a party (or faction thereof) shuns compromise, the political system does not function well.

Over the past several decades, partisan conflict escalated and reshaped how Congress behaves. Filibusters, which senators once used sparingly, became the everyday tactic of the Senate minority. Unified governments increasingly used budget reconciliation as a means to advance major legislation without having to accommodate even a few members of the Senate minority. Congress increasingly struggled to avoid government shutdowns, and when it was able to fund the government it often did so only via short-term continuing resolutions. Significantly, no one in Congress preferred short-term budgets as a matter of policy, but the political environment led them to prioritize short-term political goals.

Some members of Congress are willing to tolerate a very high level of government dysfunction to advance their political agendas. Others are more accommodating and willing to bow to the realities of the policymaking system, but they, too, face strong pressures to engage in partisan warfare. Part of that pressure stems from the competitiveness of the party system and the possibility that party control over one or more branches may flip at the next election. The pressure also stems from partisan interest groups and media, which relentlessly push members to prioritize partisan and ideological goals.

Of course, the partisan divide in Congress also reflects the deep partisan–cultural divide in the electorate. As the party system realigned after the 1960s, which was marked by the flight of southern conservatives from the Democratic Party to the Republican Party, the partisan divide became not just about tax rates and regulations on businesses but also about race, religion, and social values. In turn, party politics became somewhat tribal, and debates about guns, abortion, and other cultural values were elevated because disagreements broke along the partisan–cultural divide. The cultural divide also helped widen the partisan divide on economic issues, especially regarding the generosity of welfare programs, although the inspiration and much of the impetus for Republicans' rightward tack on economic issues came from Reagan and movement conservatives. Those party system developments occurred more-or-less simultaneously with the arrival of partisan media outlets on radio, TV, and the Internet. Their programming deepened the chasm between the parties and further sowed distrust, discord, and disrespect between red and blue America.

Some of the party wars on Capitol Hill are just for show, and sometimes the end-result policies are much less remarkable than the political drama that precedes them. However, the party wars are also costly in at least three ways. First, the government shutdowns and ultra-short-term continuing resolutions waste resources, frustrate long-term planning, and reduce the public's trust in government. Second, hyper-partisanship has at times generated or facilitated large pro-cyclical deficits, which compounds the country's long-run fiscal and economic challenges. And, third, some extreme partisans are fraying the nation's democratic institutions by undermining the rule of law, attacking the legitimate and free press, and supplanting free-and-fair election laws with party-biased rules.[1]

Political Reform?

There is no easy fix to the situation. The most promising political reform would be to force the states to adopt neutral, non-partisan redistricting processes. That would eliminate partisan gerrymandering, create more districts that are party-balanced, and increase the number of lawmakers who occasionally break with their party. However, the change in Congress would be more marginal than sweeping. Party polarization, high levels of partisanship, and the geographic divide – with most of the country being firmly red or blue rather than purple – will produce highly partisan and polarized politicians even in the absence of partisan gerrymandering.

Some people argue that polarization could be reduced by reforming party primaries. One idea is to abandon "closed" primaries that are restricted to registered partisans in favor of formats that allow unaffiliated – and presumably less ideological – voters to participate in the primary of one party or the other.[2] A similar idea is to replicate California's "jungle primary" system, which was instituted by referendum in 2010. The system advances the top two vote-getting candidates from an all-party contest to the general election. Thus, a highly liberal district may advance only Democrats to the general election, but in that case the general election might favor the more moderate of the two, because she will be preferred by moderates and conservatives. Although these ideas are sensible, they are no panacea. In fact, studies suggest that they offer no noticeable improvement.[3] Perhaps that is because non-partisans are small portions of the actual voting electorate in congressional races (in primaries or generals). And perhaps it is because virtually all policy debates that touch the public consciousness are highly partisan, and on such issues politicians are disinclined to break with their party – even if their reelection prospects hinge on more than just the party base.

There is even less that can be done about partisan media. In fact, it is neither practical nor desirable to try to police the media, and any such attempt would be prohibited by the First Amendment. Similar issues accompany attempts to regulate political advertisements and campaign finance. Although it is true that big money is spent to help elect extreme candidates to Congress, and it is true that many members of Congress tack to the extremes because they fear attack ads, there are no clear and promising ways to regulate those threats away, especially because the First Amendment's free-speech protections extend to political advertisements and their financing.

In short, there is no magic bullet to deescalate the party wars, and significant de-escalation seems to hinge on a change in the party system. A political or economic crisis could make that happen quickly. Or it could occur gradually, as demographic and political change rearranges the social and ideological makeup of the political coalitions or causes one party to lose its competitiveness at the national level.

In a related vein, note that other reform ideas – such as the abolishment of the Electoral College, a balanced budget requirement, or the adoption of term limits for members of Congress – do nothing to deescalate the party wars or attenuate its effects. In fact, none offers much benefit at all. The Electoral College may be biased in favor of swing states and may occasionally elect the candidate who wins the minority of the popular vote, but those are not major issues that demand reform. A balanced budget requirement would be problematic if it were not flexible enough to allow for deficits in a time of need. More importantly, it would probably do less to deliver budget balance than it would to spur Congress to invent elaborate justifications and accounting tricks to maintain deficits. And term limits for members of Congress would be worse than ineffective. They would reduce expertise in Congress, forbid voters from reelecting effective and popular representatives, diminish the prospects of bipartisan compromise (because long-standing members of Congress tend to be more compromising and respectful of the other party), and further weaken the legislative branch vis-à-vis the president and executive branch.[4]

Democracy and Economic Policy

Some level of partisan-induced gridlock is inevitable in America's separation-of-powers system, and when it is not extreme it is not problematic. A moderate amount of budget brinksmanship is also not problematic. A general recognition that the policymaking system requires inter-branch compromise may be enough to keep those pathologies in check.

Naturally, more compromise is required during periods of divided government. By contrast, a unified government can advance highly partisan legislation if it can manage to get a little bit of support from the Senate minority, and even that is unnecessary when it uses budget reconciliation. But even with minimal or no influence from the minority party the legislation that Congress advances is unlikely to be anyone's idea of policy perfection. Compromises and deals are struck within both the Senate majority and the House majority, and then one or both chambers must make compromises in order to advance legislation to the president, whose preferences must also be considered and who may sign bills even when he dislikes much of their contents. These compromises are required by America's policymaking system, which is designed such that no individual or chamber can unilaterally impose its own idea of policy perfection. The system is not designed to generate economically "efficient" policies. Instead, it is designed to generate outcomes that enjoy sufficient approval from a large number of policymakers, each of whom is electorally accountable to a particular constituency.

The political logic of economic policy varies with the type of policy. For example, pork is rooted in representatives' ties to their districts, whereas broad, general-interest policies can be understood, at least to some degree, by party-building incentives and the median-voter theorem. Meanwhile, Congress's tendency to use debt to defer payment for today's goodies reflects voters' interests and level of attention, and policies that benefit special interests at the expense of the masses can usually be understood from the public choice perspective, which emphasizes voters' rational ignorance, collective action problems, and the uneven political pressures that accompany policies with concentrated benefits and dispersed costs. Of course, these and other political dynamics, including inter-branch negotiations, play out simultaneously, which makes federal policymaking and policies complex and interesting.

Change and Constancy in America's Political Economy

As the economy changes, politics and policy follow suit. The relationship also runs the other way. Politics affects the long-run potential of the economy by maintaining (or not) political stability, financial stability, a well-functioning legal system, a competitive marketplace, and essential infrastructure. Politics also shapes economic behavior and outcomes via tax systems, expenditures, and economic regulations. And politics shapes the distribution of resources between narrow-interest groups and broad-interest groups, between producers and consumers, between employers and employees, and between the rich, the middle, and the poor.

This book surveyed major changes in the nation's politics and economy after the 1970s. The economic developments were profound, and aside from regular churn, evolution, and competition in a market economy, they were driven by leaps in trade and technologies. The benefits to consumers, multinational corporations, and high-skilled workers were large. Unskilled and semi-skilled workers benefited much less, and they faced decades of sluggish wage growth. The effects were also regionally uneven, as the Sun Belt and many urban areas outperformed the old manufacturing centers and many rural areas.

Those economic developments were accompanied by – and, to a notable degree, propelled by – a rightward shift in ideology and economic policy. Both political parties recognized that technology, trade, and innovation would modernize the economy and benefit consumers and America's leading industries. So, trade barriers were lowered, and regulations on banks and telecoms were adjusted. There were benefits to those reforms, but the laissez-faire attitude regarding financial sector regulation also gave rise to the 2008 financial crisis.

The neoliberal turn was also driven by the rise of a larger and more conservative Republican Party, which itself was the result of party system realignment. As southerners moved from the Democratic Party to the Republican Party, the parties became more evenly matched at the national level, and a more distinct cultural divide emerged in party politics. Those two developments heightened partisan conflict. It was not pronounced on issues of trade and deregulation, but it did escalate on issues of taxes, transfers, and welfare programs.

Even so, and despite the sense that the party wars are escalating even further, there remains a good deal of consensus about the main features of the nation's political economy. Neither party really seeks a full-scale retreat from neoliberalism or the welfare state. The latter may be heavily revised, but the government will not stop providing a basic safety net and system of social security. The health care programs may be reformed, consolidated, or expanded, but they will not be eliminated. The individual income tax will face regular tweaks, but it will not be scrapped or turned into a flat tax. The government may increase or decrease the burden of financial regulations, environmental regulations, or labor regulations, but they will neither be wiped out nor expanded to the point that they suffocate American capitalism. And Trump's protectionism will not radically change the nation's trade relationships. In short, the government that was built from the Progressive Era to the present is likely to undergo only piecemeal changes, and America's economy will remain open and integrated with the rest of the world.

Still, economic churn will continue, and perhaps accelerate. Drones, biotechnologies, self-driving vehicles, and other technological advances will upend industries, change behaviors, lengthen lives, and create new sources of fear, stress, and inequality. The rate of economic growth – and the distribution of that growth – will attenuate or, more likely, exacerbate those stresses. The political battles that accompany those developments will center on some novel issues, and there is nothing in the structure of America's constitutional democracy to ensure that the government will respond to them promptly or wisely. However, America's political system does produce public goods. And, because it is democratic, it is responsive to public opinion, and it resolves distributional conflicts in a democratic way.

Notes

1 Levitsky and Ziblatt, 2018.
2 One reason why this idea has limited potential is that, as of 2016, only nine states had fully closed primaries. Thirteen states had systems that allowed certain non-partisans to participate in a party primary, but the act of doing so effectively registered them with that party. Nine states had systems that allowed unaffiliated voters to participate freely – their participation in a party primary did not change their affiliation. And fifteen states employed fully open primaries, in which any registered voter, regardless of affiliation, could participate in any party primary, and their registration would not change as a result. The remaining four states had jungle systems (National Conference of State Legislatures, 2016).
3 See Bullock and Clinton, 2011; Hirano et al., 2010; and McGhee et al., 2014. Another matter is that open or jungle primaries are a little unfair to partisans, who are denied the opportunity to pick their own candidate for the general election ballot.
4 Term limits also cause legislators to shift their attention from voter representation, which helps them retain their legislative jobs, to activities that position them for lucrative careers after their time in the legislature. In fact, that was the lesson from Mexico's experiment with congressional term limits (see Weldon, 2004). Mexico's 1917 constitution banned reelection for members of congress in order to prevent the emergence of entrenched, unaccountable politicians. But the provision backfired, and instead led to unskilled, unaccountable politicians who paid little attention to their constituents and excessive attention to party bosses who could get them their next jobs. In 2017, a century after the term limits were introduced, Mexico passed a constitutional reform to allow reelection.

References

Bullock, Will, and Joshua D. Clinton. (2011). More a molehill than a mountain: The effects of the blanket primary on elected officials' behavior from California. *The Journal of Politics*, 73(3), 915–930.

Hirano, Shigeo, James M. Snyder, Stephen Ansolabehere, and John Mark Hansen. (2010). Primary elections and partisan polarization in the U.S. Congress. *Quarterly Journal of Political Science*, 5(2), 169–191.

Levitsky, Steven, and Daniel Ziblatt. (2018). *How democracies die*. New York, NY: Crown Publishing Group.

McGhee, Eric, Seth Masket, Boris Shor, Steven Rogers, and Nolan McCarty. (2014). A primary cause of partisanship? Nomination systems and legislator ideology. *American Journal of Political Science*, 58(2), 337–351.

National Conference of State Legislatures. (2016). State primary election types. Retrieved from: www.ncsl.org/research/elections-and-campaigns/primary-types. aspx (accessed May 7, 2018).

Weldon, Jeffrey A. (2004). The prohibition on consecutive reelection in the Mexican Congress. *Election Law Journal*, 3(3), 574–579.

Index

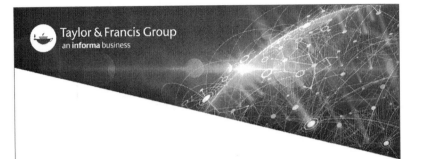